Cesca's Diaries: A Love Story. Volume II

ISBN: 978-1-9161978-6-2

Printed by Gipping Press Ltd, Needham Market.
www.gippingpress.co.uk

1937
Belstead, Cairo, Belstead, Cairo.

1937 is divided between Egypt and Suffolk, and the seaside at Frinton. Servants prove more and more difficult to obtain especially cooks and governesses. Bill is promoted in April. King George VI's Coronation takes place 12 May and Cesca and her Mother watch the procession from Apsley House in the rain. Cesca's parents 'the family' are increasingly difficult, cross and frosty towards her and the search continues unsuccessfully to find their own home. In October Cesca takes all the children and Nannie out to Egypt leaving her parents at Belstead. Cesca and Bill write to each other at least daily when apart but to avoid repetition I have deleted these entries

Friday 1 January
A wretched start to the year. Mum and Dad most frightfully difficult and impossible over our going off to Egypt. They say I am leaving them in a hole, with a new governess and young nurse etc. All most difficult.

Saturday 2 January
Mary and Merlin both better. Heard that the *Neuralia* will sail two days later on 11 January so we will have next weekend at home now. Miss Giordan, the new governess, arrives tomorrow. The 'Family' still exceedingly difficult.

Sunday 3 January
Bad headache and feel so worried about going. Bill went to collect Miss Giordan from the station. She had supper with us and seems a nice woman although the family gaze on her with suspicion. They are more than difficult.

Cesca and Bill had a peaceful day as her parents went to the Circus in London. Fittings in Ipswich, packing, paying accounts and a final day at the shoot at Hemley fill their last few days in Suffolk. Mother seedy, in bed with severe back pain, quite unable to move and Cesca had to help her out of bed and wash her. She is increasingly worried about leaving. On Saturday 10 Rumsey came and took the luggage to the station at 4.15. They said goodbye to their darling children, Mum and Dad and the servants. They both felt worn out and shattered arriving at Southampton at 7.00 and spent the night at South Western Hotel.

Monday 11 January

Had a good night but feel terribly miserable. Rang up to find out how Mother was but no better. Dad too, sounding miserable. Boarded the SS *Neuralia* at 11.00 and were both delighted she is very empty. Only 70 First Class passengers, 17 troops and a few Second Class passengers. Sad to be leaving but really looking forward to a rest.

Very rough for several days and they were both sick and confined to their cabins until they left the Bay of Biscay. A week later they arrived at Malta and were allowed ashore for a few hours. Met Hutch and his wife who drove them around Valletta in their car. The weather is improving and only 35 left on board as so many disembarked at Malta.

Thursday 21 January

Busy packing up as we hope to disembark in Port Said this evening. This was not possible so we went ashore and wandered about. Awful place and no peace on board as they coaled till 11.00 pm.

Friday 22 January

Got up at 5.30 and after breakfast went off in a launch to the station. We got into a dismal train which stopped at every station taking five hours to reach Cairo. Raining, cold and overcast. Met by Wing Commander Openshaw and then went to the Continental Hotel where I found a miserable letter from Mum saying Dad was ill.

Saturday 23 January

The Continental very comfortable but too expensive to stay long. We have a nice room and pay 200Pt a day demi pension. Bill went to RAF HQ and saw the AOC. Poor darling, he was very nervous. Went over to Gezira, now unrecognisable with huge blocks of flats everywhere. Had tea at the Club and looked at the Openshaw's pension and decided to move there on Monday.

Sunday 24 January

It is bitterly cold with a horrid sandy wind. Felt very sad and worried about the situation at home and starting another kind of life abroad away from my babies. Bill and I felt much cheered after looking at flats having found a charming furnished one with an Austrian cook included. We have first refusal of the flat and could move in almost at once.

Monday 25 January

Went to the bank, then paid the hotel bill, £7 for three days, very dear. Went to Cooks to book my passage home, on the *LL Frestino* on 17 April arriving 21 April in London in time for Merlin's birthday. Went by taxi with our luggage to Regent House to this rather wretched pension and found it grim. An awful communal sitting room.

Tuesday 26 January

Bill and I too depressed for words over this miserable pension and wished we had never come. Horrid cold bedroom and vile beds, pillows and creased sheets. Cannot get into the flat for a week and the agreement is rather odd.

Thursday 28 January

Went into Cairo to the Continental and found to my horror two miserable letters from Mum telling me Dad and Merlin both very ill. Merlin had temperature of 104 on 18 January. Most upset and discussed it with Bill and decided to send a wire to see if I should go home.

They move into the flat at the weekend and decide to get rid of the cook, a dirty old thing, which enrages the owner of the flat but Cesca stands firm. She is still receiving miserable letters from her Mother. Bill and Cesca are very upset when he is not promoted in the new list. Polo, squash, Bill's Arabic lessons, evening cocktails and most mornings spent at the Club at Gezira fill their days. Cairo life, Cesca remarks, seems to be "Come in and have a drink and talk gossip and scandal". Cesca has the drawing room decorated.

Friday 12 February

Our 8th Wedding Day. Bill at work as usual but bought me some lovely flowers. A letter from Dad enclosing a cheque for £25 which was very nice of him. A frosty letter from Mum. We went in the afternoon to watch the RAF soccer match v Army which RAF won. Quite enjoyed it.

Saturday 13 January

In the morning walked over to the Club after shopping in Cairo. Went to a sherry party and afterwards Bill and I had a lovely time dining at Shepheards followed by dancing. It was lovely.

Sunday 21 February

We are worried about the cook, Masri, as we are certain he is taking the whisky. Shall keep him until we find another.

Old friends, the Ionides arrive and are staying at Shepheards. Cesca and Bill visit the Mousky [the bazaar] a fascinating place where they buy a lovely and most expensive rug for £10. The Ionides give them an excellent dinner at Shepheard's, six courses, caviar, clear soup, fried sole, lamb, quail and icecream. I am not used to such rich food and big dinners. Mrs Ionides gave Cesca the most lovely Zurcon ring. All the children are now well and Mary's seventh birthday on the 27 February has Cesca wishing she was with her darling little girl. They are taken on a tour with the British Consul of all the mosques followed by a cocktail party at Heliopolis which they both hated. The cook has been sacked and a new one Ismain is engaged, also Aoudh, who looks nice and clean and works well.

Friday 12 March

Went to Cairo for fittings and to say goodbye to the Ionides. Ordered a large bunch of carnations and roses to be delivered on the *Esperia* for the Ionides. Mrs Ionides gave me some nice books and also tickets for the flower show. In evening we went to the Maclean's musical party which was pretty awful.

Saturday 13 March

Went into Cairo to see about my passage home as I think I shall alter it. Had to go with Bill to watch a tiresome and boring soccer match. Wished we could have gone to the Polo instead. Dined with the Flowers. Ismain said he wished to leave on Tuesday so two other cooks came to see me in the evening.

Tuesday 16 March

Went to the Club early to get my hair washed but no hot water so I couldn't. I settled definitely on my passage home on 13 April to Marseilles on the *Patria*. Had tea at Groppies and then home for dinner.

Thursday 18 March

Darling Bill's birthday. Not much fun for him poor dear, as he had such a horrid letter from Mum saying he was no longer to be a Trustee. Dad however sent a nice letter and a cheque. Letters from Dandy and telegram from Mrs Lunn and Pat. I gave him a dressing gown and a pair of pyjamas. Mary and Merlin sent him a book marker they had made.

Cesca is plagued by a series of bad headaches that prevent her from going out to celebrate Bill's birthday at Shepheard's on 20 March. Ali the new cook is excellent. More Polo matches and cocktail parties and Cesca went to the races for the first time but lost 70Pt, a horrid shock and waste of money.

Tuesday 30 March

Went with Mrs Flower to an Auction. This was great fun and amused me a lot as there was an amazing French man who conducted the Sale. Shouting, "Une fois, deux fois, pas de plus. C'est fini!" I did not buy anything as the carpets did not meet their reserves. Bill and I went to the Mousky and bought a set of purple glass for Douglas Packard's wedding present and had it packed up and sent.

Thursday 1 April

Lovely having Bill on leave. Bill had Arabic lesson and then in the evening we went to the Flower's cocktail party. I am getting excited to know result of the promotion list tomorrow.

Friday 2 April

Heard the exciting news that Bill is a Squadron Liaison Officer. Felt most terribly pleased for him. Went off to Mena for the day but so hot and stuffy returned to our nice cool flat for lunch. Bill getting a lot of congratulations and the Squadron Leader seems to be as excited as I am!

Saturday 10 April

Bill back for breakfast and took me out in the touring car. Collected Mer's birthday present, a watch for 85Pt! Pouring with rain and a gale, the most amazing weather for Egypt. Had a fire. Started packing. Rather depressed at leaving. Bill and I busy writing labels etc. Had another bad headache.

Monday 12 April

Bill went off to work as usual. I did the laundry, ironed some clothes and saw Ali about the meals. Wrote my last letter to Mum sending it by airmail. Finished all packing by lunchtime. The RAF tender came at 2.30 to take my luggage then Bill and I left the little flat at 3.00 by taxi to station where Ali attended to the luggage. Very comfortable Pullman to Alexandria where we stayed at the Cecil, depressing place, but everything is depressing today.

Tuesday 13 April

Today a most awful day. Just like that day in September eighteen months ago when Bill left for Malta. He says this is not so bad but it seems to me all partings are equally bloody. Especially as he has to stay and frizzle in the heat in Egypt, and not much chance of any leave. I shan't see him for six months. Left the Cecil at 10.00 and after the formalities at the docks, boarded the *Patria* at 11.00. Nice cabin and spent last hour with Bill. Heartbroken when we said goodbye at noon. Went straight to bed as too upset to face a dining room full of people. Lunched on some soup in my cabin and slept. I have an excellent stewardess.

Wednesday 14 April

Woke feeling very much better. My head is better and my eyes less sore and I feel calmer. The sea is like a mill pond and my excellent stewardess brought me a nice breakfast and I felt even better. Sat on the top deck, read and watched the rather peculiar people. Very few English. At my table there is rather a common Scottish couple from Ayr and a stupid Englishman.

Thursday 15 April

It suddenly got rather rough last night so I stayed in bed all day feeling seasick until after tea, then had a walk on deck whilst we went through the straits of Messina. A concert and dance tonight and much noise and dancing prevented me from sleeping.

Friday 16 April

The sea calm this morning so sat on deck in the sun. Seems ages since I saw Bill, the darling. Still each moment I am getting nearer Moppet (Mary), Mer and the twins. In evening got very rough and stayed in bed but no sleep owing to terrific gale.

Saturday 17 April

Last night was too ghastly with gale and wild seas. Noise all night, people being sick, doors banging, too awful. Stewardess told me I won't catch the 11.00 train as we will be three hours late. Could have cried. Feel very shaky and eventually *Patria* arrived at 12.00. Cooks man met me and secured a sleeper for tonight on the Blue Train. Spent the day at Hotel de Noailles where I had a bedroom, nice bath, rest and tea. It's too bad I shall not now see my babies till Monday morning. After dinner the man from Cooks took me to the station. The Blue Train left at 9.22 for Paris.

Sunday 18 April

Shared my sleeper with a French woman who was already in bed so I undressed and climbed into the top berth and tried to sleep. Very hot. I had breakfast on the train arriving in Paris at 9.00. Went with my luggage to the Gare du Nord and took the 10.40 train to Boulogne. After a calm crossing arrived back in England. At Victoria got my registered luggage and was lucky not to pay any duty. Train arrived in Ipswich at 8.26 met by Mum and Dad on the platform. Lovely to see my babies. Mary and Clare both woke up.

Monday 19 April

This morning they all came along terribly excited and delighted with their presents. Mother, too so pleased with the Mousky glass which is all unbroken.It's heaven to be in England again and a lovely day. An airmail letter from my darling and I wrote to him to tell him all about the children. The garden is lovely and servants have been good but seem rather slack. Unpacking all day.

Wednesday 21 April

Mother in London. It is lovely to be home and with the children again. Went bird nesting with them. Mary has grown so and Merlin taller. He plays the piano so well and can play duets with Mother. Placed advert in *the Times* for 2 Walton Place and another in *East Anglian* for under housemaid. Twins so good and sweet at lunch today. I am so proud of my children.

Thursday 22 April

Still very cold and wet. In the evening Mum, Dad and I, Miss Giordan, Mary and Merlin went to Bertram Mills Circus. Merlin was thrilled especially with the clowns. Mary cried over the trapeze act and did not like the lions, poor darling.

Friday 23 April

Went to London to see about income tax and 2 Walton Place and clothes for the children. On my return found Mother not very well, rheumatism in her legs, poor dear.

Saturday 24 April

Merlin's 6th birthday, so lovely being with him and do wish Bill was here too. Merlin had a tea party and sat at head of table and cut his cake. Grannie gave him a wigwam so he played at Red Indians in the garden.

The parents have gone off to Holnicote in Somerset for ten days and Cesca sets about the spring cleaning and getting the chimneys swept wanting to get it all done before they return. Cesca takes Mary and Merlin over to ride. "Mary is so good at her riding and so much improved. Felt very proud of her". Carpets are taken up and beaten and all the servants are hard at work. Mrs d'Alberque, the cook, returns from her holiday. Jean, the kitchen maid and Gwen both gave notice "which is rather a blow but can't be helped".

Tuesday 4 May

Went to London and shopped all day. Found it very tiring, such crowds about. Went to 2 Walton Place and moved things around there and then to Ivy Hudson's where I ordered two new hats. Bumped into the Duke and Duchess of Kent as I was buying ties for Bill.

Wednesday 5 May

Children all looking so well. Spring cleaning progressing well but no nearer getting servants. Went over in the Lanchester to tea at Rendham with Mrs Lunn. She was very nice and children loved it and were not sick.

Thursday 6 May

Sweep in Mother's room today. Highly delighted to receive two letters from darling Bill and wrote to him and sent it with Sturgeon when he met Mum and Dad, who bought presents of Devon cream for the servants and for us. They are both looking so well.

Tuesday 11 May

Mother and I went to London First Class, May having left yesterday to prepare 2 Walton Place for us, as it has not let, for the Coronation tomorrow. Very cold, crowded and no buses, making it very difficult to get a taxi or to get about at all. London all decorated. Found the caretaker and May all ready for us and big fire in drawing room. Had lunch at Gunters and in evening took taxi, saw the decorations and bought seats at Apsley House. These are very nice and in a lovely covered stand.

Wednesday 12 May

[The Coronation of George VI and Queen Elizabeth. They travelled in the Gold State Coach to Westminster Abbey. The procession back to the palace took an extended route of six and quarter miles and was two miles long taking 40 minutes to pass any given point. 32,500 officers and men either marched or lined the route. It was the first Coronation to be broadcast on radio. The whole service was two and a half hours and broadcast by the BBC's Empire Service.]

Did not sleep well as London seemed to be awake all night and there was the sound of scurrying feet from 1.00 am onwards. We got up at 4.00 and walked in the cold grey dawn to Apsley House and there we remained till 5.00pm. We went down stairs to the buffet and had hot coffee and tea. I had a whisky and soda and some sandwiches. But it was a very long day and the wait so cold. When the procession arrived we were very thrilled and excited. Marvellous view of the Armed Forces, Queen Mary and Princesses and finally King and Queen. Felt quite emotional. Walked home in pouring rain.

Thursday 13 May

Poor Mum and I feeling very tired. She looked worn out yesterday but we both much enjoyed it. Came home and to bed early.

Friday 14 May

John Peel arrived to spend the weekend. After lunch we took Mary, Merlin and Miss G. all to the Regent Cinema to see the film of the Coronation which was very good indeed.

Sunday 16 May

Am very worried about Winnie carrying on with Enefer and have decided to send her over with the twins to stay with Mrs Lunn at Rendham.

Tuesday 18 May

Took twins over to Rendham and Mary and Merlin went riding with Mother. Mrs d'Albuqueque left for good and Miss G. for three nights. Busy packing for the Coronation Naval Review.

Wednesday 19 May

Left Belstead with Mum and Dad, Mary and Merlin and went up to London and from Waterloo by special train down to Southampton for the *Aquitaine.* We embarked about 5.30 and have lovely cabins, both with bathrooms. Most comfortable and a lovely dinner. 500 on board.

Thursday 20 May The Coronation Naval Review.

Mary and Merlin both slept well and we all had breakfast at 8.30 and then put on warm clothes for our trip on the *Kestrel* which took us up and down the lines and we saw all the ships beautifully. Most exciting and the children thrilled. Dad too was most excited and interested in everything. After lunch on the *Aquitaine* we watched the *Victoria and Albert* going up and down the lines with King George and Queen Elizabeth aboard. In evening the fireworks and search-lights were magnificent.

They all went home again by special train and had lunch at Gunters. Mary was sick in the train to Ipswich and ill in bed the next few days with a temperature. Mrs Chalmers the new cook arrives and is a very good cook. Cesca still searching for kitchen maids. She goes to London to see Walton Place as it is being let to a Miss Logan on Friday 28 May. Pat and Ursula Ainslie come for the weekend. She is expecting a baby and taking it very seriously, resting a great deal. Cesca finds she misses Bill even more when friends are staying. Diddles (Cecily) has a horrid stye in her eye which Cesca is bathing regularly. Two maids departed on 1 June to Cesca's relief and new head housemaid arrived. Mary is to have two teeth out with gas.

Wednesday 2 June
Heard that Henry van Straubenzee is very ill with pneumonia in Colchester Nursing home. Went to London with Mother and much enjoyed Paganini at the Lyric. Met Nannie at Harrods and discussed her coming back to me for our proposed trip to Egypt in the Autumn.

Tuesday 8 June
In afternoon took the four children, Mother and Winnie in the car over to Bawdsey. Poured with rain the moment we got there. Hoped it would clear but after getting soaked through came home and had our picnic tea in the dining room. Found a spotted flycatcher's nest with four eggs in it. New cook Mrs Harvey arrived.

Saturday 12 June
Very hot. Took Mary and Merlin over to Holbrook for the King's Naval Birthday Parade. It was very nice and all outdoors in the Bruce Gardynes garden.

Monday 14 June
I went to the dentist and had two fillings. Home for lunch. Dad rather cross and gouty. In afternoon took children over to Capel to

ride and then motored to Stowmarket to see kitchen maid. Did not think much of her but engaged her to come on Thursday.

Cesca is very depressed to get a letter from Bill saying she must on no account come out to Egypt in September. She felt so upset she did not feel she could write to him. However two days later she receives a nice letter from her darling which made the whole world seem different. She misses him so and hates him to be cross with her. Cesca is incubating two deserted moorhen eggs in the airing cupboard. One hatches but does not survive. Aunt Freda borrows YY and collects Henry van Straubenzee from the nursing home. He arrives looking very ill and tired and goes straight to bed. The next day Henry, feeling better is up for lunch. After a few more days convalescing Henry and Aunt Freda depart for York.

Thursday 15 July
Dad's 78th Birthday. He and Mum have gone to off to London to see Victoria Regina. A grilling hot day, but lovely. Mrs Harvey, the cook, left. Thunderstorm in evening. Woke in night, Mary crying so took her into my bed and Dad and I went round the house as she said she heard a crash. All was serene, however.

Friday 16 July
New cook Mrs Allen and new kitchen maid, Grace, arrived in afternoon. Spent morning in Ipswich then made two milk puddings and cooked the raspberries. Mr and Mrs Hewettson came to tea. Deadly dull couple and most refined! Sent invitations to children's party on Wednesday 28.

Saturday 17 July
Another lovely day after last night's rain. Am not at all impressed with the new cook who seems poor and has not much idea of cooking.

Monday 19 July
This new cook absolutely useless. Told her I should no longer require her after Friday. Went to London with May, then went to the house which May proceeded to clean. Rang various agencies about cooks. Dined with Claude and Margaret and saw their new house.

Tuesday 20 July

Up very early and went searching for cooks and children's maid. Very hot and feel very tired. Back to Walton Place at 11.00 and found inventory going full swing. May and I left at 11.45 and had lunch on train arriving home 2.00. Mary and Merlin riding. Found cook was utterly impossible. Hope I can get another but it's terribly difficult.

Wednesday 21 July

Clare and Diddles are entirely with me, sleep with me, I dress them and do everything for them. They are so sweet and good too. Very pleased new cook is able to come tomorrow as Mrs Allen is most trying.

Thursday 22 July

Woken early by the twins. Awful cook Mrs Allen left this afternoon and new cook arrived. Nice girl and quite good-looking. Wrote to Bill.

On Monday 26 July, Cesca, with great relief hands over the twins to Lilian who has returned from her holiday! And two letters from her Bill on her tea tray a great delight. The new cook Mrs Evans is excellent but kitchen maid quite useless and so rude too. The tea party on Wednesday 28 July is a great success, 24 all together and they played grandmother's footsteps, hide and seek, had a treasure hunt, sack and egg and spoon races.

Saturday 21 July

The new children's maid Ursula, who arrived yesterday, seems so far excellent and we all like her. Had a terrific surprise when a letter came from Bill announcing he was asking Lawson for leave arriving in a week's time. Then a wire came to say his leave was granted! Can't believe it and feel quite sick with wild and desperate excitement at the thought I shall see him in a week's time. All too good to be true.

Sunday 1 August

Woke up wondering why I felt so terribly happy, then suddenly remembered Bill is COMING HOME to me. He is flying to Rome and on from there. Busy afternoon tidying up but I can't sit still.

The week flies by. Another tea party for ten children. Cesca goes to London for a fitting for her new evening dress and to interview a new Head housemaid who never turned up. Mother decides to take the Mary and Merlin to stay with the Durhams in Haselmere. Very hot weather. Cesca is frightfully excited and cannot sleep. On Saturday night she is woken by the telephone, Bill arriving tomorrow afternoon at 4.30.

Sunday 8 August

The most marvellous day. So thrilled and so excited! Could not get over the thrill of seeing my darling this afternoon. Went off on 9.27 arriving London 11.00, Waterloo 11.30 and Southampton 1.45 and there I waited till 3.30 at the Southampton Hotel for the *Capella* to arrive at 4.00 and she arrived on time. A few minutes later the sea tender steamed in with my own love. All too exciting for words. We went to London, stayed the night at the Berkeley and dined at Pruniers. Lovely to be with him again.

Monday 9 August

Woke up feeling terribly happy. At Floris this morning, Bill pulled my leg as when the man suggested spraying me and asked what scent I'd like, I said"I feel like Lilac this morning"! We were met by Mother and the children at the station. Bill thrilled beyond measure with them all, especially the twins. A lovely homecoming.

Suzanne [Cesca's old French governess] arrives to stay for a few days. The children like her very much. Bill and Mother both speak to Hempson about the trouble with Enefer and the maid, Winnie. Bill and Cesca go to lunch with Mrs Lunn and George. They are both well and have endless pigs and animals of all sorts. John Peel arrives for the weekend and there is a dinner party. Mrs Evans cooks an excellent dinner. Tennis parties over the weekend and Bill plays awfully well. Cesca feels that this leave is going much too fast already.

Monday 16 August

Mrs Evans having day off in London. Bill and I left in YY and John in his car and we motored along together and had a picnic lunch in a clover field. It was a perfect August day and great fun except I sprained my ankle. We beetled through the country to Bushey where we had tea with Dandy at her horrid little house. Then on to London leaving the car at Shrimptons, had taxi to the Berkeley and had lovely room. Bill interviewed Mrs Dudgeon re furnishing our flat in Cairo. I had a rest, bath and changed into my brown lace. Then had sandwiches before going to see Victoria Regina which is quite marvellous. Returned to Berkeley, had supper and danced.

Tuesday 17 August

Woke up feeling very bright and fresh. Went to Cooks and Harrods. Bill had been to the Air Ministry about my passage out in the autumn. We motored out of London and had a picnic lunch by the side of the Great North Road. Home for tea. Family rather cross.

Thursday 19 August

Bill and I left for Burnham Overy to spend the day with Claude and Margaret Pelly. A perfect day and I drove along the Thetford road. We arrived for lunch and found Jim and Gabriel there too which was fun. We saw the Regatta and the Fair and both Bill and Jim had a go at the coconut shy. We left after tea and had dinner at the Bell in Thetford. I am so happy with my Bill.

The Family continue to be rather difficult and frigid and Cesca imagines it is because she and Bill have talked about going to Egypt in the Autumn. Received a letter from Enefer too saying he would sue Mother for libel about the business of his carrying on with Winnie. All is rather upsetting. Another blow, Mrs Evans gave notice as her husband wants her to join him as a married couple, cook and chauffeur. Annie and Ivy also gave notice! Bill and Cesca go duck flighting at Bucklesham and rabbit shooting with Merlin at Hemley. The last days of Bill's leave go by.

Thursday 26 August

A lovely birthday except for the fact that tomorrow Bill leaves. Mother gave me a dress and a lovely blouse. Mary and Mer a beautiful blue glass doorstop and the twins eau de cologne from Floris. Dad gave me £20 and Bill the zircons. I was so happy to have everyone I love with me. I went to the sale at Hadleigh and bought a tin trunk, some decanters and glass. Felt very sad in the evening. To bed with my love.

Friday 27 August

Up very early feeling miserable. Motored to Colchester and Bill felt wretched leaving everyone. I was full of misery in the carriage. How I do hate and loathe these partings. Taxi to Victoria where I said goodbye to my own darling love. Felt my heart would break. He is so sweet and good to me and I do love him so. However powdered my nose in the ladies and shopped hard, then had a good lunch and felt better. Home to the children who were very sweet to me. Family peculiar and distant.

Cesca is comforted by the fact that Bill has a comfy cabin and that she and the children will soon be joining him. She went over to Harwich with Mary and Merlin to see Mother off to Holland for a week. The children both felt car sick, surprising as they have been so much better lately. Mrs Evans leaves and new cook Mrs Worly arrives who only lasts three days and a Mrs Levington replaces her. She lasts four days and leaves without any warning. Just walks out and sends a telegram to say she had returned to London! Ivy very decently is taking on the cooking for the next few days. Cesca dreads taking all the children over to Martlesham to be inspected by the Medical Officer and probably vaccinated etc. In the event only Mary and Merlin were both inoculated and vaccinated and were very frightened. They were both rather feverish for a couple of days. Mother returns from Harwich met by Dad but she arrives home extremely tired and cross and everything wrong! Enefer has carried out his threat to sue Mother and she is advised to speak to his solicitor.

Wednesday 8 September

Went to London though it's difficult with no cook. Before I went I saw Ivy and arranged meals with her. Really Belstead is getting very hard to run. Went to Air Ministry and saw Mr Russell who was very nice and tells me we shall go by P & O, not by trooper in the middle of October and that Nannie and I will have to pay our own passage. I then saw Nannie and gave her lunch. Then shopped hard all afternoon and returned very tired after 6.00. Told Mum straight away about our passages. She was annoyed and Dad said he would not remain at Belstead. So that's that. I feel I've done my best and am too tired to do more.

Thursday 9 September

May has agreed to be a witness and say what she knows about Enefer and Winnie. Left in the Lanchester at 11.30 and went over to Frinton with Mary and Merlin to the Grand Hotel. Room very comfy and it is such fun to have them with me and to have got away from the worries and miseries of Mum and Dad who spoil all one's pleasure in living there. Went for a walk in the rain and then they both played ping-pong.

Saturday 11 September

Finished packing and paid bill of £3.14.0, quite reasonable, then we all had a huge breakfast and then went down to our hut. They played on the beach until Mother, the twins and Lilian arrived. They took our luggage to Mrs Alton's at Oak Cottage. Then I went back to Belstead in the car, had lunch with Dad. Then returned to Frinton and the car took Mother home again.

The children spend another week at Frinton returning to Belstead on Saturday 18 September looking so well and happy. Cesca is making preparations for Egypt including packing up the dessert service from Walton Place. The family are both cross and frosty. Cesca bought some trunks at a sale at Martlesham for 5/- a good buy. She hears the marvellous news they will sail in the *Orama* on 22 October from Tilbury. Davies' man comes and spends the day packing her glass and china. Cesca is worried to death about servants who seem impossible to obtain. 'New maid arrived and walked off as soon as she looked at us. Olive left and the kitchen maid went for a walk and did not return, little wretch! I went into Ipswich chasing after these infernal servants just when I have so much to do. And the family so difficult too. But Nannie is back looking very well and a lot fatter'!

Thursday 14 October

Went into Ipswich with labels for packing cases. Then to Rendham taking all children and Nannie. Mrs Lunn very pleased to see us all and we all enjoyed ourselves.

Monday 18 October

Mum and Dad more cheerful. All heavy luggage went off from the station by goods train this morning. Only hope it all arrives safely. Spent afternoon paying bills and doing accounts.

Tuesday 19 October

Went to dentist this morning and was upset that my front tooth will probably have to come out. He has put in a temporary filling and must do another on Thursday, if I don't have to have it out before then.

Wednesday 20 October

Went to London for last time for shopping. Met Gabriel and lunched with her. Went to Liverpool Street Hotel to see about rooms for Friday night.

Thursday 21 October

What a morning! Found it was not possible to take the large trunks with us on special train to Tilbury as they must go as passenger luggage in advance to Tilbury. Put it all on the 10.00 train and hoped for the best. My last day at Belstead, feel sad and miserable.

Friday 22 October

Mother from today takes over the shopping and housekeeping. Last lunch at Belstead. Then off with Miss G. and the luggage. Car returned for Mum, Dad, Nannie and the children and we all caught the 3.17 for London. Went first class and the twins first time by train. Found decent rooms for the children and gave them tea. John called for me and took me out to dinner.

Saturday 23 October

Woken early by Mary saying she could not sleep owing to the noise and excitement. All had breakfast and left hotel for St Pancras where we found special train and our reserved seats. We had a worry being unable to find our luggage because a porter had removed it all. Arrived Tilbury and found our cabins, none to clean, and said goodbye to Mum, Dad and John on the platform looking cold, wet and miserable. It got rough and Mary was sick.

Sunday 24 October

We anchored off Torbay to let the pilot off. I had breakfast, then returned to Mary, very sick, poor child. Clare and Merlin also. Got into the Bay of Biscay in evening and a terrific gale and seas and we plunged about all over the place. I sent for the doctor to see Mary. He seemed a fool and thought she had an appendicitis. However he gave her a pill and she slept soundly afterwards. Awful day and I felt completely exhausted.

Monday 25 October

Another nightmare of a day. Still in the Bay, very cold and rough. Everyone sick except Cecily.

Tuesday 26 October

Terrific gale still and the *Orama* rolls like hell. Got Mary up on deck for a while but she still cannot keep anything down. I do hope things improve soon.

They reach Gibraltar on Wednesday 27 and though pouring with rain go ashore in macs and thick things and have chicken sandwiches in the gardens in a shelter. Mary loved the gardens and feels better. The twins are well but very cross. Still cold and rough on Thursday, ship rolling along. Children play games on deck. The twins look pale and tired and are very cross.

They arrive in Toulon the next morning, a very pretty spot surrounded by mountains. They go ashore for the morning. Great thrill in the afternoon as the entire French fleet come into port and they see cruisers, destroyers, and submarines all coming in to anchor. They arrive at Naples on Sunday in beautiful weather. They all go ashore and take the funicular above Naples and the twins are thrilled by the view.

Wednesday 3 November

Woke up at 5.30 and saw very far away the land of Egypt. We got in sooner than expected and before I knew it, Bill was on board and the long wait was over. So lovely to see him, though he looks thin and tired. All children thrilled to see him of course. Bill and I went ashore to the customs then I returned in a launch and took the children to the station. We had a lovely carriage and the children had a picnic lunch. Bill and I had lunch in the Pullman and arrived at Cairo at 4.00. Joan Bruce met us, all hot and weary and motored us out to the flat. Everything is perfect and children thrilled with it all.

Thursday 4 November

It really is so lovely to be here again with Bill. Terribly happy. Mlle Moine came for the day and helped me unpack and get straight. Bill has a few days leave to help me move in. I have a beautiful bedroom. All rooms have balconies and there are two lovely bathrooms and a big hall and nursery.

Friday 5 November

Bill took Nannie to see Everett this morning. He has given her a tonic and stuff to put on her carbuncle. Children and I went to the Grotto gardens to see the fish.

Saturday 6 November

Bill went off to the office this morning. I went into Cairo and booked seats for 'OHMS' an English film at the Regal. Archbishop Johnson came and blessed the flat and the children came and listened. The Bruces and Hicksons came and dined and we all went to the cinema together.

Sunday 7 November

Bill busy trying cars and has now bought a Ford V8, a lovely little car. Took all the children to the Club in the afternoon and let them run around.

Tuesday 9 November

I am very busy in spite of no housekeeping to do as the packing cases arrived and I unpacked them with Nannie and the wogs and it took nearly all day.

Thursday 11 November

Letter from Mother for Bill but just enclosed bank statements etc, but not a word to him, very unkind. When we came in from the Club we kept the two minutes silence. In afternoon went out along the Suez Road and had a lovely desert picnic with Nannie and the children. Sky so lovely coming back.

Friday 12 November

Up early and took Mary and Merlin to the Club for their riding with the Bruces which they enjoy very much. Went to the dentist who said my tooth ought to come out but he would try and save it for the moment. In evening went to the Bruces' Cocktail Party.

Monday 15 November

Merlin woke up not feeling well and found he had a temperature of 104. Bill rang Everett and as he is coming to inoculate the twins this evening he will see Merlin too. Mary and Cecily ill too. Everett came and suspects measles but I do not agree with him.

The children continue to be ill with diarrhoea and sickness, Merlin with a temperature of 104. Cesca has her tooth out and does not like the way things are done in Egypt. Cocaine injections and then a hammer at the tooth eventually extracting it. She felt very peculiar and in a great deal of pain. A dose of the green medicine improved things. And she is fitted with a plate 'with one wretched little tooth on it'. They held a house warming party on Friday 19 November and many friends dined and then danced. It was a great success. Cocktail parties and dinners and dancing most evenings which they both enjoy. Duck shooting and squash for Bill.
A Miss Ray is engaged to give Mary and Merlin lessons. Dancing classes are also arranged for the children.

Sunday 28 November

Bill and I, Robin and Mr and Mrs Feddon went off for a picnic to Madi Metrae in the desert. It was a long way and took one and a half hours to get there. We visited an awful monastery which gave me the creeps and had to drink foul tea. Then had our picnic lunch beside an absolutely purple lake. It was really very pretty. Home at 6.00, in time to be with the babies who had been out with Nannie.

Tuesday 7 December

Went into Cairo, had my hair washed and bought Christmas cards etc. Mlle Moine came for the day and did some sewing and ironing. In the evening Bill and I went to the General's dance at

G.O.C.'s house, Gezira. We both enjoyed it and danced together nearly all evening. I wore my new white dress and Bill his uniform. Excellent supper done by the Turf Club.

Wednesday 8 December

Mum's birthday today. Been thinking a lot about her. Went off to the Mousky with Fiona and tried to get some Christmas presents for Mother, May and Nannie. We are getting a lot of acceptances for our dance on 17 December.

Saturday 11 December

Busy getting house straight and flowers done for our drink party tonight at 6.30. They all came and all stayed and talked and drank and drank. Exhausted when at last they left at 8.30.

Monday 13 December

Wrote all Xmas cards then went the Y.W.C.A. bazaar at Groppies Rotunda where I helped at the cigarette stall and we made £30 which was very good. Bill took children to the Polo and then in evening to the 'Retreat' at the Citadel which they loved.

Tuesday 14 December

Busy sending off parcels and cards. Bill came in with the sickening news that our dance must be postponed as he has to attend a Court Martial on Saturday morning. Quite maddening so will have to ring everyone and put them off.

Nannie out so took the children to the zoo.

Sunday 19 December

Lovely hot sunny day again. Bill and I and the children went to the club in the morning and we gave the twins a donkey ride.

Friday 24 December

Bill left at 6.00 to shoot with the Ambassador and motored down with Major MacCullum. Went early into Cairo to buy final things for our party this afternoon. Finished decorating the tree. Had 35 people including the Seddons, Hicksons, Bruces, Drummonds, Wilsons, and two RAF boys from Heliopolis one of whom played the piano and Robin was Father Christmas. Great fun.

Saturday 25 December

Nannie went off to early service so Bill and I had the children at 6.30 and we started unwrapping Christmas presents. They were all so thrilled with their toys and presents. Clare and Diddles each had a tricycle and Mary a cooking stove and necklace, puzzle and books. Merlin a tool set, aeroplane, books and various mechanical toys. Had breakfast at 9.00 and took all the children to church. Then had lunch altogether with turkey and plum pudding. A large tea. Felt a bit homesick for England.

Tuesday 28 December

Writing letters still. Mother sent us all a lovely box of toys and presents and a box arrived from Dandy too. Took twins in a taxi into Everett who gave them their second inoculations. They were so good we took them into a shop and bought them a present each.

Wednesday 29 December

Bill and I frightfully busy with preparations for our dance tomorrow. Went into Cairo to do final ordering at Groppie's. Bill has arranged for a man from Heliopolis to work the gramophone and play the accordion.

Thursday 30 December

Bill on a few days leave. We were both very busy with preparations for the dance. We dined with the Bruces. We had 70 people, supper in the nursery and danced in the hall and drawing room and sat out on the verandah and the hall. It was a great success and all seemed to enjoy it and stayed till 2.30.

Friday 31 December

Bill and I very pleased with last night. Bill went off early shooting and only had about two hours in bed. I spent the day getting straight. The Bruces came to dinner and we saw 1937 out and 1938 in on the verandah. First time I've seen the New Year in for years. To bed very tired at 1.00.

Riding Egypt 1937

Merlin Mary Egypt 1937

Mary painting Egypt 1937

Twins Belstead

Children with Twig Pardlestone 1940   Mary on Sally 1940

Hurricane and Spitfire, Mary & Newie 1940   Pony & trap shopping Williton 1940

The Cottage Pardlestone   Pardlestone

Belstead

Belstead Loggia

Belstead August 1941

361

St Nicholas Church, Fulbeck

Fulbeck Manor

1938
Cairo, Belstead and Fulbeck Manor

Bill and Cesca are enjoying life in Cairo but finding it rather expensive. The planned departure back to England is threatened by the children's continual illnesses. Cesca feels she must take driving lessons in order to pass her driving test in July. A charming house is rented in Lincolnshire and Bill returns to enjoy his leave there until the threat of war tears him away back to Egypt once again.

Tuesday 4 January

Very cold and dust storm blowing all day. In the evening we went to cocktail party at Wing Commander Mackay's which was very dull and dreary and then onto the Bolsters who gave a large and rather good party in their very attractive flat at Grenville house. The Bruces are worried about going home. Bobby and Fiona Hickson came and dined with us here and stayed till 10.30.

Wednesday 5 January

Another cold and sunless day. Rather worried about Diddle's leg (Cecily's nickname) where she fell over the electric stove, and burnt it. So I rang up Everett who said bathe with Dettol. Did so and bound it up. Heard from South Africa that Premier Mill dividend will be 5 shillings and paid at the end of January. Much cheered up by this news as financial situation is rather serious.

Thursday 6 January

Mary was weighed, 3 stone 6lbs 14 oz.

Friday 7 January

Went shopping in Cairo in morning. In afternoon Bill and I went to RAF v Army Match of Hockey at Abbassia. The Air Force was beaten. Returned home for tea. Went to Cocktail Party at the Aireys and then to dine with Fiona and Bobbie.

Saturday 8 January

Twins went with Nannie out to tea with Mrs Mitchell. Bill and I had Mary and Merlin to tea with us. They read and did drawing and were as good as gold. In evening dined at Groppi's with the Bruces for their farewell party. Quite a good band and we danced, then the others went on, but we went home as it had been quite an expensive enough evening for us.

Thursday 13 January

Worried about Clare who has some small boils under her arm. Decided to call out Dr Pochin, a nice little fat man, who came at once and prescribed antiflogistine and some ointment when pus comes out.

Friday 14 January

Pru Fielding arrived this morning and is staying with us for a fortnight before leaving for Malta. She took me up to the Citadel in Simon Leverson's car and we saw off the Cameron Highlanders from the Citadel Station. Very dusty and windy and felt filthy on our return. In afternoon Bill and I watched RAF v Army rugger match and were delighted that the RAF won. Mlle Moine is making covers for chairs as we now have the Bruce's ones in place of the miserable uncomfortable ones.

Saturday 15 January

In afternoon Bill took children for desert picnic. I went to tea with the Alexanders. Very dull. All sitting around on small gold chairs dangling a teacup in one hand and a plate in the other.

Thursday 20 January

King Farouk's Wedding [King Farouk aged 17 and Queen Farida aged 16 had three daughters and divorced in 1948 due to the absence of a male heir]. Bill and I went up on the roof and saw all the illuminations and fireworks with no trouble, fuss or expense.

The weeks are filled with visits to the Club, Inter Regimental Polo matches, cocktail parties, dinner parties and the Opera where they were lent a box. On Saturday 29 January Bill and Cesca went to the RAF Ball at Heliopolis. It was a very good Ball and Cesca wore her pink. All the Air Force was there from all over Egypt and Palestine etc. She danced mostly with Bill and got to bed at 3.00. On Thursday 3 February Cesca decides to be very economical for the month and takes charge of the housekeeping from Ali. On Saturday 5 February they took the children and nannie for a desert picnic which they enjoyed very much, scrambling over the hills and the children sunbathed with nothing on.

Saturday 12 February

Our Ninth Wedding Day. Can't believe we have been married 9 years. Nine years of happiness with Bill, a perfect and understanding husband. Children each gave me a bottle of Floris bath scent. Bill a large box of chocolates, Mother a book and Dad a cheque for £25. After breakfast a large bouquet of white carnations and narcissus came from Bill. So I have been well remembered. Mary and Merlin stayed up for a special treat for dinner. We had fish soufflé, chicken, meringues and cream, fruit salad and cheese. Afterwards we went to see 'Victoria the Great' at Diana Cinema then to Shepheard's to dance.

Monday 14 February

Clare and Cecily's 4th Birthday. Bill went off early to fly and my darling 4 year-old daughters came in to see me and I gave them their presents. Beatrix Potter books and Granny sent them books and bricks each and a tea-set and Dad money. I shopped for more toys for the party and meringues from Groppi's as the Twins chose roast chicken, baked potatoes, peas and meringues for their birthday lunch. In afternoon six children came to tea with their nurses. Each had a present and a large tea. I decorated their cakes, Cecily's yellow and Clare's pink. The twins have grown up so.

Tuesday 15 February

I am getting much concerned over plans for the summer and have written to Mum accordingly and await a reply. In afternoon went to a tea party at the Embassy where I met Helen Besly whose sister is Nancy Pritchard-Barratt.

Thursday 17 February

In morning took Mary, Mer, Clare and Diddles in a Gari for their Diptheria inoculations. Very cold indeed and raining.

Friday 18 February

In evening we dressed ourselves up. Bill wore his uniform and I my white dress and we went to the Ball given by His Excellency Lord Lampson, the Ambassador and Lady Lampson for HRH Princess Alice and the Earl of Athlone who are here on a short visit before they leave for Saudi Arabia. It was a lovely dance and Bill was thrilled as there were lots of Viennese waltzes. We stayed till the end and were home by 2.00.

Saturday 19 February

Bill went to collect Hutch who arrived by air from Alex from the Continental at 4.00. We took him to a cocktail party then on to dine at the Aireys and enjoyed it very much. Good dinner and played whisky poker afterwards. Then we went on to Shepheard's and danced there for a while.

Sunday 20 February

Lovely day so went to the Gezira Club in the morning. After lunch went to the desert with Hutch and he, Bill and Merlin and Mary went exploring in the dunes. Nannie and I and the twins sat in the sun. Bill took Hutch to the train at 7.00.

Tuesday 22 February

Did not go out as a howling gale and terrific sandstorm got up. The worst in Cairo this winter. Had a small dinner party. I thought it pretty grim but Bill assured me they all enjoyed it and certainly Ali sent in a good dinner. Played whisky poker.

Friday 25 February

Bill returned at 6.30 to collect his gun and go shooting duck. Had a ladies lunch party and Ali gave us a good lunch. Prawn soufflé, roast chicken and sausages and bacon, pancakes, cheese straws and coffee. Rested in afternoon and Bill returned with 21 duck at teatime. Dined with the Lows, I wore my pink. Went on to the Benevolent Ball at the Embassy which we enjoyed very much. Danced mostly with Bill.

Saturday 26 February

In afternoon, Mary's birthday treat was donkey riding in the desert. So we set off after lunch for Mena and rode four donkeys for an hour and a half. It was fun but so very, very cold. We had tea afterwards at Mena which the children enjoyed.

Sunday 27 February

Mary's 8th birthday. She woke so happy and thrilled with all her presents. She had a typewriter, a camel and £1 from Dad, a book, a prayer book and needlework from Grannie, a camera from Bill and me. And powder and scent from Merlin. She chose her lunch, chicken and fruit jelly and a birthday cake at tea.

March is spent hosting dinner parties and and going to friend's cocktail parties and the polo. Cesca is ill for a week with swollen glands and a temperature which curtails a few parties. The children have their last series of inoculations and are fretty and cross.

Friday 18 March

Feeling much better. My darling Bill's 32nd Birthday and it is too bad he is DSO today and Sunday too. I gave him two pairs of pyjamas, the twins, a mapping pen and chocolate. Mary, a tie and Merlin some drawing paper, he had books from Mum and his Mother and a telegram from Dandy. Had chocolate cake and candles in the nursery but halfway through Bill had to dash off back to Head Quarters.

Saturday 19 March

In the evening Bill and I dined at Shepheard's together which we much enjoyed as his birthday treat. Very good cabaret and excellent dinner.

Merlin and Mary both have high temperatures intermittently for the next two weeks. Merlin also has a rash for a time. Dr Pochin is called and is perplexed. Suggests chickenpox, dysentery or sandfly or something of that sort! Advises isolating the children and postponing the departure to England till May. The cocktail parties and dinners continue as do trips to watch the polo. The 8th

Hussars are victorious on two occasions. The brown trunk is packed up to go by trooper by the end of March.

Monday 18 April

Heard our passage is secured on *the Nadera* which sails next Sunday from Port Said. There is no room in the *Strathnaver* only three berths in a four berth cabin, Tourist, which would be hopeless. So decide to take the second class accommodation they have offered us and if it's very foul, shall get off at Marseilles and go overland. I wrote to Mum to tell her our plans.

Thursday 21 April

Very much hotter now, so children resting in afternoons. Getting on well with packing. Went to Farman's cocktail party and met Drummonds there, then after dinner we drove out to Mena to see if there was a dance on but there was nothing at all and the place shut and empty so came home.

Friday 22 April

Letter from Mum and card from Dad arrived for Merlin's birthday. Went to Ferencz and collected dress and coat is nearly finished. Bill and I went to club in evening to post our letters. Dinner, bed and felt very sad.

Saturday 23 April

Up early and continued my packing. Bill and I went into Cairo and got money, paid Ferencz and had an orange juice on Shepheard's terrace whilst waiting for Ferencz to finish off my coat. Later found Clare had a temperature of 100 and Cecily a most dreadful boil on her bottom. Very worried but decided if no worse we should leave in the morning. Felt miserably sad in the evening. Our last evening together.

Saturday 24 April

Mer's 7th Birthday.

Woke twice in the night worrying about Clare. Went along to see her. Coughing a lot. Gave Mer *Grimms Fairy Stories*, 10/- from Mrs Lunn and some books from Dandy. All packed up, Clare's temp. 100. However we left at 6.15 and Ali and Aoud came down to say

368

goodbye. Bill had arranged for RAF tender to take all the luggage to station by 11.00. Comfy journey with picnic lunch for children to Port Said. Met by RAF sergeant and Corporal Bailey. Very much cooler at Port Said. Found our cabins on *the Nadera* and were allowed to put Clare straight to bed whose temperature was 101. Took Mary and Merlin to tea at Castle Palace and had a Gali Gali man for Mer. Then walked back and then came the parting and I cried my eyes out.

Monday 25 April

So upset last night at leaving my darling after six months together. Clare better, temp. 99 but kept her in bed all day. We are travelling second class and I must say it is quite comfortable and the cabins are just as nice as the ones in *the Orama*. We have one four berth cabin where nannie and three children sleep and I have a two berth cabin with two lower beds. Close to bathrooms and lavatories. We had quite nice lunch but tea was poor and the people absolutely frightful. Not a lady or gentleman in all second class. However it does not worry me. Wrote to Bill.

Tuesday 26 April

Poor Mary sick on and off all night and woke up feeling pretty sorry for herself. Clare much better. Fortunately sea is as calm as can be. Am very bored on ship but feel as it is doing the children so much good, decide to go all the way by sea.

Wednesday 27 April

Mary had excellent night. Arrived at Malta at 8.00. We all had an early breakfast and went off in the tender at 8.45 to Customs House Quay where we landed. Took a lift up to the top and walked about Valetta shopping. Bought *the Times* and some plain sponge cakes for the children. Then Mary, Merlin and I went by bus to Guarda Mangra (where Mary left her camera on the bus) and called on Elizabeth, Pat and Mrs Hutch. She has a very nice house and was delighted to see us and took us in her car back to the docks. We sailed at 12.00. A lot more people have boarded.

Friday 29 April

Still calm and arrived at Marseilles at 6.00. Mary very excited and bouncing about at the porthole. After breakfast I went ashore leaving children with nannie and was taken in to Marseille by two nice Frenchmen. Bill would have had a fit! They put me down safely and I did some shopping and changed some money. Bought scent, soap, talc and stockings. After having lunch on board took Mary and Merlin for a drive in a tram all along the Corniche which they both enjoyed. Bought some chocolate and lollipops and stockings for nannie. Coaling which made the ship and all concerned absolutely filthy. Posted another letter to Bill and received one from him and Mother.

The seas become choppier and Cesca anticipates rougher weather as they approach the Bay of Biscay. She feels the trip would have been more enjoyable if she could forget that each day was taking her further and further away from Bill. Cesca with Mary and Merlin disembark for the last time at Gibraltar buying cigarettes, more stockings and a special present from the children for their grandparents. She also buys nice baskets from men in boats off Tangiers for 1/- each. A terrific gale gets up in the night off Tangiers and the following day is as rough as can be. "Lay in agony all day and night, everyone being sick." This continues for the next twenty-four hours.

Thursday 5 May

Arrived at Plymouth three hours late, at 9.00 am owing to the gales. Bitterly cold. Letter from Mum about meeting us tomorrow. Mary still rather sea sick and miserable. Too cold to stay on deck for long so stayed in my cabin and started packing.

Friday 6 May

Woke frightfully early and weather bitterly cold. We steamed up the Thames and arrived at Tilbury at 8.00 after breakfast at 7.00. Mary better. I had to wrestle with the tips and we disembarked at 9.15. Could see no sign of Dad. Went to Customs in a dreadful shed and got it all done. Still no sign of Dad, so rang Belstead and was told Dad had gone to Tilbury but could not find us so had motored straight back! I engaged a taxi and motored home, the children all very good. Arrived 1.15 to a great welcome and much delight from family and we all ate a huge lunch. Miss Giordan there. Lovely to be home but very much miss Bill.

Saturday 7 May

Found lovely letters from Bill yesterday and more arrived today. Went into Ipswich with Mum and Dad, lovely weather but very cold. Sleeping in oak room and busy unpacking and getting straight. Children thrilled with the garden, countryside and flowers etc. Spent afternoon turning out desk drawers.

The first week home is spent unpacking as the brown trunk arrives and moving back into Cesca's own dear bedroom, writing letters and bird nesting with the children who have also been over to see Sally. Cesca goes to London to check on 2 Walton Place. The following day Cesca takes Merlin for a ramble with picnic tea in a string bag, up to Belstead Woods and along Wherstead Road to the railway embankment where they had their tea and watched the trains.

Monday 16 May

We have now been at Belstead four years! It seems incredible and now I am looking for another house. Had a lovely letter from Bill from Palestine. Wrote to him and walked to post with Mum and discussed future plans about another house with her. I have decided I must have driving lessons. [Driving tests were made compulsory from 1 June 1935].

Monday 23 May

Went into Ipswich to British School of Motoring and had my first driving lesson with a Mr Heather. Queer little man but he seems efficient and says if I do as I'm told and concentrate I shall eventually pass my test! Children riding in the afternoon.

Tuesday 24 May

Went to Mr Freeman [dentist] and he looked over my teeth and told me I should not have any for very long. Depressing thought. Decided to start looking at houses, so took Miss Giordan and M. and M with me and looked at Bramford Hall, Bramford House and Wingfield Castle. All hopeless! Tea at Framlingham and Merlin ate a very large tea and rather a stale cake. I was woken in the night by him being sick.

Wednesday and Thursday more driving lesson and Cesca is improving. More houses viewed in Aldeburgh but no good. The following week two more driving lessons and Cesca feels she is really getting the hang of it. Saturday 4 June another driving lesson she feels really much improved and does hope to pass.

Monday 6 June

What a long and dreary Whitsun it has seemed. Do miss Bill so and hate this uncertainty. Family said today I must go by July and they could not have me here much longer as it was too much for Mother. Oh! Dear what shall I do and where shall I go? Do hope I can find somewhere soon that Bill and the children will like. Tomorrow will see if I can find anything near Cambridge.

Tuesday 7 June

Went off on 10.00 train to Newmarket. There I hired a taxi and for 10/- drove to Freckenham only to find the house already let. A completely wasted, bloody journey. Went back to Newmarket where I had lunch at the White Hart and wrote to Bill. Then took 1.30 train to Cambridge and went to Rutters who had nothing and seemed half dead. And to Hockeys to blow them up about Freckenham, and they too have nothing else on their books. Home by 4.00 train arriving 6.30.

Thursday 9 June

Heard from Hockey about a house at Coton near Cambridge which sounds lovely. Very excited and feel must go and see it. Dad went to London and Mother, who seems far from well, went to Shotley for R.N. Review for King's Birthday. Tremendous crowds and very hot day. Boys and people fainting everywhere.

Friday 10 June

Mother went to Cheam for the weekend. Great relief felt all round as she has been so trying lately. Did shopping for Mum in Ipswich and had driving lesson. Children rode in morning. I went to

Cambridge to see the house about which I have been so excited and found it ghastly. Too depressed for words.

Sunday 12 June

Dad and I and the children have really had a most pleasant and peaceful weekend. But feel I'm no further forward than I was a month ago house hunting and am so depressed about it all. Mary, Merlin and I walked to church and home before the sermon. The children have found an injured baby cuckoo.

Monday 13 June

The baby cuckoo was found dead this morning in his box and Diddles cried, poor darling. Had driving lesson, improving but am damn silly over reversing. Children all rode in afternoon. All peaceful till evening when Mother returned.

Driving lessons and more fruitless house hunting in East Bergholt and Aldeburgh but Cesca is cheered by two offers to rent Walton Place and letters from Bill. She drives herself all the way home from Aldeburgh. A trip to London spending two nights at the Rembrandt, lunching with Mary Wilson and tea with Pat Ainslie's wife, "sweet baby but poor little flat" and dinner with Jim and Gabriel one night and John Peel the other. Cesca returns home on Saturday 18 June having much enjoyed her London visit and accepts the offer to rent out Walton Place from July 16 –Oct 31. Family all rather exhausted with the heat and very cross too. However on Monday went in YY for a picnic at Bawdsey which they all enjoyed especially Mother who came too. A letter arrives from Mrs Fane about her house in Lincolnshire.

Wednesday 22 June

A very important day. I set off, after my driving lesson, for Lincolnshire with Sturgeon. We left at 10.45 and went via Stowmarket, Thetford, Kings Lynn, Sutton Bridge to Sleaford where we arrived at 1.45 and had lunch at the Bristol Arms. I thought so much of my darling boy and how we met at Sleaford in the Market Square after the Cranwell Dance thirteen years ago! Posted a letter to him. Then Sturgeon and I set off again to Auborn where I saw Auborn Hall, a most dreary and depressing house. It poured with rain too. Then to Fulbeck Manor which I liked at once, old and shabby but I could see us there. Nice gardener showed me round. Four bathrooms and lots of room for children. Stables etc. Wrote to Bill about it all at Grantham where I had tea at Angel and then motored home via Bourne, Spalding, Kings Lynn, Stoke Ferry and Thetford. Arrived home at 9.00 in torrential downpour, very tired and a headache but feel my task is almost accomplished.

Thursday 23 June

Wrote to Mrs Fane and made an offer of six guineas a week to include their two gardeners wages. Wrote to Bill and told him all about it. Went over to Cambridge to the Copper Kettle to get Mother's cakes for her party tomorrow. Very hot day.

Friday 24 June

We were very lucky to have a lovely day for Mum's party. The garden looked nice too but no roses out yet. A lot of people came, the Milbanks and the Bromfields etc. The cakes from the Copper Kettle were very good.

Wonderful news for Cesca. The Fanes have accepted her offer for their house from July 8 until October 14 for six guineas a week and she is getting very excited about it all. She feels sad in many ways to be leaving dear Belstead but will be so glad to be on her own.

Monday 27 June

Took children in to Freeman and find their teeth need a lot doing to them. Also to inquire about removals to Fulbeck. In the evening a terrific thrill! Bill rang me up from Cairo! Extremely naughty and extravagant of him but it was a joy beyond measure to hear his own dear wonderful voice close to me as if it had been in the next room. Felt so overcome that afterwards burst into tears.

Tuesday 28 June

Wet morning and letters from Billy, also one from the Fanes re Fulbeck. Very busy trying to get servants for Fulbeck now. Took all the children over in YY to Rendham for the afternoon. Grannie Lunn very delighted to have us all and was very nice. George rather coarse and vulgar but feel very sorry for them both. Wrote to Bill in evening. Do miss him so.

Wednesday 29 June

Mary at the dentist. Wrote to a head housemaid and have now engaged an excellent cook, Mrs Fleming.

Thursday 30 June

Went up to London on 10.00 train and had a very long day. Got shoes for self from Rayne and shoes for all the children at Debenhams. Also soap, face tissues etc. Wrote to Bill on the train. Called at agencies as offer for Walton Place has fallen through. Very worried about this. Went to Shapland and bought fish knives and forks. Could do nothing in Harrods till next week due to the Sale. Home at 7.00. How I long for my own darling Billy.

Friday 1 July

Won't it be marvellous when it's August 1. Shall go quite mad. Had driving lesson 3.30 in Ipswich through all the traffic and must say I am much improved. Twins went to dentist in morning.

Saturday 2 July

Letters from Bill. He is pleased about Fulbeck and like me, felt quite bats over the telephone call. I took family in YY to tea with Milbanks at Belstead Brook. A deadly party. Dinner party at Belstead in evening.

Sunday 3 July

Went to Belstead Church for the last time. Sad about this and feel I shall never come back and anyhow if I do never will it be the same.

Monday 4 July

Mary to dentist and he tells me she has to have a tooth out next Wednesday. One more thing to fit in. Diddles had to have a tooth filled. Driving lesson this morning, the last one before Wednesday when I take my test. Oh dear, am so frightened as do not know what I shall do if I fail. The Cartwrights came to tea which was beyond all words boring. Thunderstorm too which delayed their departure. Letter from Bill only bright spot in the day. Glass and china being packed and Nannie and Miss G. both packing.

Tuesday 5 July

Merlin and I went off to London together and we both thoroughly enjoyed our day. Went to Debenhams where we bought an early morning tea set and green tray for Grandad's birthday. Then to Dr Dowling who was very nice and examined Merlin's fingers. Said it was not a fungus but a chronic form of dermatitis and should soon heal up with coal tar ointment and no washing in water. We had lunch at Gunters, chicken, peas and new potatoes and strawberry ice cream and wafers. Then to Harrods and finally bought a guinea pig called Tarzan. Quite black and rather a darling and brought him back with us. Mary is sad she has not got one too.

Wednesday 6 July

Terribly busy day and felt it would never end. Davis man packing all morning. Mary at dentist to have gas and her tooth out. Poor child felt sick afterwards. Then to British Legion Fete in afternoon with Mother and the twins. Left at 3.30 and had final driving lesson and then my TEST. Goodness I was awfully frightened of the man. However I passed it and thrilled I walked home and composed a PC to send to Bill to tell him! Very pleased with myself.

Thursday 7 July

Last day at Belstead. Almost packed up. Have secured cook, parlour maid, and head housemaid for Fulbeck and an under housemaid. Am getting excited about it all. Have at last too got a man to drive me. Son of McNamara the garage proprietor at Ipswich. He is young but hope he will be all right. I took the car to Ipswich station and collected the twin's kittens which Nannie and I are taking with us to Fulbeck tomorrow. Early to bed as I have a long day ahead of me.

Friday 8 July

Woke to find Mother seedy as she always is whenever I go away. This time with giddy attacks. Left Belstead 9.30 with Nannie, the two kittens and a great deal of luggage and McNamara driving. Dad apparently also quite upset and tearful at my going.

Tipped all the servants before leaving. McNamara did not inspire me with much confidence and nearly had a bad accident with a van. However YY went beautifully and we arrived at Fulbeck at 1.30. Found Bevan had unloaded and was ready to go so paid him. Then Nannie and I had a picnic lunch. At 3.00 Grace Willis arrived, then the head housemaid, Johnson, who seems a nice woman and at 5.40 the parlourmaid and cook. The latter is pretty livid to find no kitchen maid and Nannie and I upset to find the house absolutely filthy. I had ordered in all the food. The gardener Hewitt seems helpful and we have secured a good char, Mrs Heuschel. I got to bed at last about 11.00.

Saturday 9 June

Woke to a long and busy day. All the maids seem to be good and hard at work cleaning. I am very pleased with them all. Nannie invaluable and works like a slave. I had lovely letters from Bill to cheer me on my arrival and a huge box of F & M chocs. Sent him a night telegram this evening. Also was delighted to get a definite offer which I accepted from Sir William Fletcher of five guineas per week for Walton Place until Oct. 18 and then six guineas a week till Jan. 18. Shopped in Grantham and got a temporary kitchen maid to come Monday.

Sunday 10 July

Very busy all day getting my bedroom and the drawing room straight. The Fanes came to tea with me and I liked them both but feel they are very unbusiness-like and completely vague. Roared them up over the state the house was in, even sanitary towels in the maid's drawers, he quite agreed and said he was awfully sorry. Roared up young McNamara too as he is a useless young chap. I was furious to find he had gone off with the car this morning. Shall be glad when he is gone but shall be a bit windy of dealing with YY on my own. I feel we are almost straight for children to arrive tomorrow.

Monday 11 July

Went to Lincoln this morning and found the shops there much better than Grantham. Spent £4-10-0 at ironmongers on kitchen utensils and propose to send on the bill to the Fanes. Had my hair washed as it was full of dust after the move. McNamara went to Sleaford to meet the children at 5.40 but lost his way home, so Nannie and I got very anxious and wondered where they were. However they arrived complete with luggage, guinea pig, Brookman and Miss G. All loved the Manor and went off happily to bed with cake and milk. Wrote to family to thank them for having them.

Tuesday 12 July

Letters from my darling and I write to him daily. Children spent the whole day looking at everything and getting used to the Manor and the garden. So glad they like it. The kittens and guinea pig are a great success and I have ordered a guinea pig for Mary. Nannie left and Brookman unpacked while I took the twins for a walk. I signed the lease for 2 Walton Place today.

Wednesday 13 July

Took Miss Giordan and Merlin in the car with me to Sleaford. My first effort solo up here and felt very pleased with myself. In the evening went for walk with Mary and Merlin and slipped and hurt my left ankle badly. Very painful and went straight to bed and had a very bad night.

Thursday 14 July

Ankle very swollen and painful to walk on so wired the agents to cancel going to London today to meet Sir William Fletcher. Wrote to Dad for his 79th birthday and to Mum before she leaves for France on Saturday. Went to meet Sally at Caythorpe but she came on the 6.30 instead and arrived in a horsebox. Great excitement and old Adlett who is now back from helping Mr Fane, came with me and walked her home.

Friday 15 July

Dad's birthday. Children sent him a postcard each they had painted themselves. Children so delighted to have Sally and went for a ride with Adlett. Miss G. and I do not think much of Brookman.

Saturday 16 July

Went over to Sleaford, shopped and collected a parcel from the station. Mrs Fleming is proving an excellent cook. Children all thrilled with Fulbeck Manor and say they like it better than Belstead. The Vicar and his wife called.

Sunday 17 July

Took the four children and Miss G. to church and felt all the village eyes on us. Saw the Fane's rather starchy relatives sitting up in family pew. After service, a Miss Tennant and Mrs Frere seized me and took me into their little house for sherry. Felt I should not get on with those two but have invited them to tea on Wednesday.

Wednesday 20 July

Went into Grantham with Mary, Merlin and Miss G. Shopped and then went to the station in time to see the *Silver Jubilee* go through at 125 miles per hour. Afterwards got to Manthorpe Bridge in time to see the *Flying Scotsman* and *West Riding Ltd* hurtle through. Frighfull thrill for both children. This afternoon we fetched Mary's guinea pig, a dear little brown and black thing, from Caythorpe station. We have been offered a run for the guinea pigs by Miss Tennant.

Thursday 21 July

Oh dear, am getting so frightfully excited about Bill and to think in twelve days he will be here! Oh dear! Oh dear! It makes me so whirly. We had an awful tragedy this morning while Mary and Merlin were having their morning ride. A wretched white terrier got in and killed the two dear little guinea pigs. The children so upset and I was too. Saw policeman about this and wrote a stiff note to Miss T. about stray dogs.

Friday 22 July

Paid wages and then went into Grantham about a children's maid as have given Brookman notice. Twins hate her and so does Merlin. Wrote to Billy in evening telling him how happy I am here. It is so lovely and peaceful on my own away from Belstead's unhappy atmosphere. In evening took children and played mad hide and seek.

Sunday 24 July

Having breakfast after Holy Communion at 8.00, when Wing Commander Barnett was shown in and asked if I would like to go with him to church at Cranwell. Wanted to avoid the RAF but could not get out of it. However the children loved it and it was great fun. Lots of bands and bugles for Mer. In afternoon enquired about trains to Southampton to meet Bill on the Bank Holiday weekend.

Monday 25 July

Told Brookman she can go on Thursday. Have never come across a more useless woman. Set off after lunch with a picnic tea to Lincoln with M. and M. Visited the cathedral and saw the Lincoln Imp. [A grotesque on a wall inside Lincoln Cathedral. A legend tells of it being a creature sent to the cathedral by Satan only to be turned into stone by an angel]. Found several very nice antique shops and bought a decanter, 14 custard glasses and two little jugs. The twins, poor darlings do loathe Brookman so and were very unhappy with her.

Tuesday 26 July

Had the most thrilling news from Bill this morning. He is due home sooner, leaving Egypt Saturday so home on Sunday! I could have screamed for joy and couldn't eat my breakfast with excitement! Children all equally excited. Wrote letters and altered plans.

Wednesday 27 July

Took Mrs Barnett and Merlin to Cranwell and saw the passing out inspection of the Electrical and Wireless School. In afternoon took twins to the Campion's farm to see cows being milked.

Thursday 28 July

Awful gale last night, made me feel this place would be pretty gloomy in the winter. But Bill's return is all that matters. Met the new children's maid in Lincoln. From Whitby and seems a better type. Brookman returned to Chichester. Had hair shampooed by Miss Ruff at village shop. Did flowers and Ian and Isobel Smith arrived to stay the night en route for Scotland. So nice to see them. Mrs Fleming cooked a good dinner of tomato soup, fish soufflé, roast chicken, potatoes and spinach and coffee cream.

Saturday 30 July

Had a wire from Bill from Alex saying he was spending night in Rome. Rang Imperial Airways to know exact time of arrival of flying boat and was told 3.00pm. So shall go down to London tonight. Left house at 6.30 having said goodbye to the children and motored into Grantham, then I caught the 7.30 and got into London at 10.00 and had a room at the Euston Hotel.

Sunday 31 July

Woke up wondering why I felt so happy and remembered I was going to meet Billy. Arrived at Southampton having had a light lunch on the train. Very hot on the train and at Southampton so changed into thin frock. The flying boat was due at 2.45 and arrived on time. Bill the third passenger off! I couldn't believe it was really happening. Too wonderful! Went up to London by Pullman and stayed night at Euston Hotel having dined at Pruniers.

Monday 1 August

So lovely to wake and find Bill beside me. We had breakfast then went to Kings Cross and took the train to Grantham arriving at 12.00. Motored to Fulbeck and Bill thrilled with the house and garden. Children gave him a terrific welcome at the front door. The children showed Daddy everything after lunch. Feel divinely happy to have him back.

Saturday 6 August

Up very early and left at 8.30 for Belstead where we had lunch with Mum and Dad who seemed very fit. On the way we went to see Tostock Place which gave us both the creeps. Went on to tea at Rendham and saw Bill's Mother and George. Home for a nice quiet dinner.

Monday 8 August

Went to London on 9.40 train. Very hot. Went to see the Fletchers at 2 Walton Place and found them both very charming. Met Bill at Harrods where we chose two guinea pigs for the children and brought them up to Grantham with us. Train very crowded and uncomfortable. Hot and exhausted we got back to Fulbeck. Mary and Mer delighted with their guinea pigs.

The lovely sunny days slip past, Cesca and Bill enjoying time together with the children and each other. Friends drop in en route to Scotland.

Wednesday 17 August

Went into Grantham after lunch with Bill, Merlin and Cecily to meet Miss Worsfold who arrived on the 3.30 from London to stay and do my portrait in pastels.

Thursday 18 August

I started sitting for Miss Worsfold, from 10.00-1.00 and 2.15-4.30 and again from 5.30 -7.00. Felt very tired and had headache at end of day. Am sitting in Miss G's room and have bare shoulders and a dressing gown wrapped round me.

Friday 19 August

Another day of sitting until 4.30 when Bobbie and Fiona arrived from York where he has been posted for three years. Bobbie and Bill played L'Attaque after dinner while Fiona and I chatted.

As Miss Giordan was away for the weekend, Cesca and Bill much enjoyed all the children having breakfast in the dining room with them. The sittings continue until the following Wednesday despite the distraction of the cook, Mrs Fleming, giving in her notice at breakfast on Monday after a request from Cesca for some boiled eggs!

Both Bill and Cesca are delighted with the portrait and the charming Miss Worsfold returns to London Wednesday afternoon. A friend, Joan Bruce arrives to stay with her two children and a treasure hunt is arranged on Thursday having been shopping in Woolworths in Sleaford for presents. A success, in spite of rain moving the fun indoors. Friday 26 August is Cesca's 34 birthday and she receives lots of lovely presents. Jim and Gabriel arrive from Burnham and they have grouse for dinner sent down by John and Mary Wilson.

Monday 29 August

Bill and I left at 8.30 to motor down to Suffolk house hunting. First Gawdy Hall, Harleston which was too big. Then lunch at Rendham with Mrs Lunn. Rather unfortunate as we arrived late and the atmosphere was rather strained with Dandy there too. Then went to see Kelsale Manor but told it was no longer for sale. Then feeling depressed we had tea in a field. On to Hasketon Manor, Witnesham House, Bosmere Hall, and the Grove, Walsham-le-Willows all were no good. Feeling we had had a hopeless day we dined at the Angel in Bury and to bed.

Tuesday 30 August

A glorious morning. We continued our house hunt and went to see Bradfield Hall which was in a charming position and beautifully done up but very expensive. Then to Shudy Camps Park, three miles from Haverhill which we both liked and felt it had great possibilities. 15 bedrooms, Queen Anne house and 122 acres for £5,000 or 38 acres for £800 which is cheap. Then to Cavendish Hall, charming but not much of a garden. Lunched at Long Melford and then saw Bentons at Bildeston. Arrived at Belstead at 4.00 and had tea. Then Mum hopped in the car with us and we motored home together arriving at Fulbeck at 9.00 pm.

Wednesday 31 August

Found all children flourishing and fun to have Mum to stay. Took her to Lincoln in the morning which she enjoyed and bought an old pink lustre tea set for 25/-. After lunch I took Mrs Fleming into

Grantham and met Mrs Powell the new cook. Mother thinks the house is charming.

Thursday 1 September

Bill shooting partridges with Captain Reeve. I took him, then came back and took Mother to the station at Sleaford where she left for Ipswich. Wrote to the agents re Shudy Camps as we think it has distinct possibilities.

Monday 12 September

Clare still not well, feeling sick, however we decided to leave for Scotland as arranged but left at 10.30, later than intended. A lovely day, but I had backache so only drove a little between Scotch Corner and Penrith. When we got to Glasgow where we had dinner, we rang Miss G. and found Clare was much better. Eventually got to Carbeth at 10.00. Mary and John were out to dinner and we went to bed as soon as we could.

Four nights at Carbeth, the weather and the staff both poor which made the trip rather disappointing. They then drove to Bridge of Cally, realised they had left behind the attaché case so had to return for it and it poured with rain and very cold having a picnic lunch in the car. But the Wilsons were charming and house and view delightful however Cesca's bad cold spoils her enjoyment. Bill out shooting with Maurice Wilson and shot his one and only grouse.

Sunday 18 September

Felt extremely seedy and cold very bad. Bill and I packed up the car whilst everyone was in church. We left as soon as we could after lunch, thankful not to have to control my sneezing and nose blowing any longer. Awful indigestion on the way down, everything soaked with the pouring rain. On, on, on to Carlisle where Bill had dinner and I, just soup. Rang Miss G. and told her we would be back very late. From Penrith to Fulbeck kept getting into fog and mist, awful drive, arriving at 4.00 am.

Monday 19 September

Slept all morning after our long drive. Mary and Mer better after their sickness, but Mary very thin. Heard Shudy Camps has been sold. Felt depressed about this and wondered what we are going to do in the future. So glad to be back again.

Saturday 24 September

News gets daily more and more worrying over Czechoslovakia. I expect a telegram recalling Bill will come at any moment. In evening Squadron Leader and Mrs Wilson came to dinner, found it very trying though Mrs Powell cooked excellent dinner. To bed after listening to very worrying news.

Sunday 25 September

Bill and I went to Holy Communion early. Later took Mary and Merlin for a lovely walk. Perfect day and went up to the Cherry Tree wood and home across the heath.

Bill and I went to church again in the evening. The news is very bad and we feel very worried. After dinner a telegram came for Bill to report to Air Ministry tomorrow morning. To bed and no sleep after this for me.

Monday 26 September

Up early and off to Grantham with Bill who I saw off. Then to Sleaford to fetch his things from cleaners. I am worried and am afraid there will be war. Bill wired while I was out that he was to return to Egypt. So his leave is over and there is another parting. Children hate it and are upset. Went to collect Bill from Grantham. Rang Mother and told her the news. Packing and getting Bill's things ready. More bad news in evening.

Tuesday 27 September

Feel very miserable. Bill went off shooting driven partridge with Captain Reeve. I packed up and felt wretched. In evening we left for Grantham and on to London. Bill so sad at leaving children. London is in turmoil. Went to Browns Hotel and stayed night there. Our last night together.

Wednesday 28 September

Another ghastly parting to face. News seems very bad and war inevitable. Said goodbye to my darling at 10.00 and he went off with his luggage and I paid the bill and then went to Harrods and had my hair washed and a henna rinse and tried to cheer myself up. Feel so sad and miserable. Met Mother for lunch at her Club. She was very sweet and has arranged to come up here with me. Telegrams from Air Ministry came for Bill cancelling previous arrangements and telling him to embark on the *Aquitaine* tomorrow. Mother and I travelled up to Grantham. The train was crammed with people leaving London. Arrived home at 6.30.

Thursday 29 September

House feels dead without Bill. News is better today as Hitler has invited Chamberlain to go to Munich for another conference. Mother and I decided to get home to Belstead tomorrow. Shopped in Lincoln and gave servants notice. Wired Nannie to return. Miss G. leaves tomorrow for her holiday. Wrote to Bill and had two letters from him and also telephone call from Southampton before he sailed at 10.00 this morning.

Friday 30 September

Very busy packing for the twins. Mother went off with them and Margaret from Sleaford this afternoon. This morning took Miss G to station and luggage and collected Nannie. Feel so tired after all this whirl and rush. However thank God news is better. Went and was fitted with gas mask.

Saturday 1 October

Busy day preparing to leave on Thursday. Great relief news is good as Hitler and Chamberlain have signed Peace for Europe. Bill need not have gone back at all.

The days pass in a rush of packing up and paying bills. Mary is in bed with a very bad cold. The weather is cold too and a fearful gale causes awful damage and trees down. No telephone or telegrams.

Wednesday 5 October

Went off at 9.30 with Merlin to Leadenham to see Sally into her horsebox en route for Bentley Station. On our return found Bevan had arrived and busy packing up his van. He was very quick and all loaded by 10.30 and gone. Cashed some more money in

Grantham with Merlin and saw the *Silver Jubilee* for the last time and came back via Manthorpe Bridge and saw *West Riding Ltd*. After lunch said goodbye to the Fanes and all the other neighbours. Mary feeling better at last. Had car filled up and all ready for journey. Paid servants and all bills and wrote to Bill.

Thursday 6 October

A perfect morning and up early for final packing and cleaning. Then off to station with maids. Then we all packed into the car and drove away from Fulbeck. I gave Adlett 10/- and he seemed very pleased. I did not feel sad leaving Fulbeck as without Bill I feel I want to get away. Car went like a bird and we started with M and M in the back sitting on the blankets and Nannie and I in front. But Mary started to feel sick so we settled her in the front and opened the windscreen. We had lunch in woods near Thetford and the children loved it. Glorious to be back in Suffolk again and arrived at 2.30 after dropping Nannie at station. Miss G. and I hard at work unpacking.

Friday 7 October

It's nice to be back at Belstead again. The garden looks lovely after the wreck of a garden at Fulbeck. Mother has given the twins a rabbit called Peter and they are sleeping with me now as they are waking so early with Margaret. Clare said Peter! Peter! in her sleep last night. Bill is due in Cairo today. Spent most of the day getting my room and desk straight. Everything is going very smoothly and situation seems much improved.

Cesca settles back into her life at Belstead with the parents and her children. She and her Mother spend an afternoon looking round Chelsworth and like the house very much. They go to London together and enjoy seeing a play, Dear Octopus. She received a letter from Bill wanting her to come out and join him as soon as possible. She takes Mary and Merlin to ride at the Andersons and comes home in the dark at the wheel for the first time. She went over to see Orwell Park School but was not at all impressed.

Monday 17 October

Went up to London on 9.00 train. Left the car in the station all day. Went at once to Cox and King to see about a passage and secured one on the old *Orama* departing on October 28 from Toulon. It is slightly more expensive than the *El Nil* but I have a separate cabin to myself which I really think is essential. Shopped for the children and bought all their necessary clothes. Home on 4.54 and drove back to Belstead. Mum had had a tea party and apparently Dad had been very difficult. Wrote to Bill to tell him about the passage. The darling will be pleased.

Cesca makes arrangements for the children to stay in Frinton so they are away when she leaves Belstead for Egypt. Her Mother is being difficult about their return to Belstead without Nannie and says she must find a girl before she goes. Cesca looks at Alresford Hall and Abberton Manor but no good. She is still hoping to acquire Chelsworth. Bills are paid and the twins go to Miss Jeckell for a fitting. All four children are taken over to lunch with Mrs Lunn at Rendham and were given an excellent lunch including a steamed pudding. The children loved seeing all the pigs. The weather is glorious and Mary and Merlin help Cesca choose a Labrador puppy for Bill, a darling called Rob. The twins had to be punished for stealing some pastry from the kitchen and calling the cook an old Bugger!

Monday 24 October

Very busy morning in Ipswich and then loading the car. Nannie was at Frinton when we arrived. Miss G. and twins went with Sturgeon in the Austin and Mary and Merlin with me. Lovely day and took them all for a walk when we arrived while Nannie settled in. I shall miss them so. Drove home via Bentley then Sturgeon came in soon after to say the carburettor on YY was in half so I was lucky to get home. Telegram from Bill to say how pleased he was I was coming out.

Tuesday 25 October

Spent morning packing and got money in Ipswich. Car repaired so decided to go over to Frinton and take the guinea pigs and say goodbye. Found the children had all had a lovely morning on the beach and were quite happy. Unpacked the guinea pigs, then said goodbye and fled. As soon as I got out of the town I had to stop and have a weep. The darlings all looked so sweet but so miserable when I left.

Wednesday 26 October

Final packing. Went to Ipswich to fetch laundry. Then went over to Chelsworth to have final look round. Do like it so and hope we can get it at our price. Left dear Belstead in YY with Mum and went by 3.17 to London. Then by taxi to the Grosvernor Hotel. Then Mr Scarlett from the agents came to see me and the poor little man was sad when I said I could not afford more than £5,000. He said she might accept that for the house and 60 acres but require more for Dower House and other land. Then Mother and I had dinner and saw an amusing play called *When we are Married*. Back to bed at 11.00 but no sleep too tired and sad at leaving the children.

Thursday 27 October

Mother came and saw me on the train. Very comfortable. Felt sad when she left. Weather has changed but crossing was quite fair though a number of passengers were sick which seemed amazing to me. I had lunch on the Blue Train and sat opposite a nice Australian woman. She and I also had dinner together at the Gare du Midi, excellent and all for 22 francs. Then on to Toulon through the night.

Friday 28 October

Woke at 6.00 to find we had nearly arrived at Marseilles. Had an excellent breakfast at the Grand Hotel then got aboard the first tender and found I had a nice cabin near the Pursers Office and same stewardess as last year. Settled in and wrote to Mother and Bill. After lunch went for a good walk in Toulon and shopped. Bought some scent, talc, chocs for Bill and some for myself, some stockings and lace and had tea in Toulon. Thankfully to bed, so tired and took green medicine and slept.

Saturday 29 October

Woke at 7.00 to find we were moving, leaving Toulon. Weather cold and horrid. Fortunately managed to change my table as I was with some perfectly awful people. Succeeded in moving to a table with Mrs Renton, the lady from Australia and a nice old man called Anderson going to Cairo. Slept all day.

Sunday 30 October

Felt quite a different being. Posted my letters and arrived at Naples at 8.00. Went ashore at 10.30 in pouring rain. So Mrs R. and I took a carriage and drove to the glove shop, the only shop open and bought two pairs at 35 lira each, about 7/6.

Came on board and were nearly deafened by sirens and whistles blowing sending off six boats full of Italian Jews who are being sent to Libya to colonise, poor devils.

Monday 31 October

At last the weather is improving. Woke to find blue seas and sun shining and ship steaming towards Port Said. Spent the morning doing some washing and ironing. Rested all afternoon and slept again before dinner. Seem to do nothing but sleep but it does me good and I feel much better.

Wednesday 2 November

So hot and sticky and so excited could not sleep after waking at 5.30. Went on deck early but could not see land. We arrived about 9.30 and soon saw my darling Bill in a launch with Walmsley. Felt terribly excited and he soon came aboard. Lovely to be with him again. After doing passports and customs eventually boarded the train for Cairo which left at 12.15. We talked and talked and before 5.00 we were in our darling little flat which is sweet. Decided to go into Cairo and send wire about Chelsworth. Dinner then bed. So very happy.

Thursday 3 November

Really lovely to be with Bill again, he has taken leave for the day, and I am so pleased with the flat. Small, very comfy and clean and will get the winter sun which will be nice. Unpacked and hung some pictures. Mine has arrived safely.

November is filled with cocktail parties, dinner parties, the polo, the cinema, Bill playing squash, beaten by a man called Turpin at the Squash Championship at Gezira, and the occasional desert picnic. Eventually they decide to withdraw their offer of £5,500 for Chelsworth. Hempson's survey shows that the house has been much neglected and expensive repairs etc. would be required. On Sunday 4 December Cesca and Bill decided they must have all the fearful R.A.F. people in for drinks so invited them to come the following Thursday. It was, as feared, a terrible party and they both felt very exhausted afterwards. The next day they leave early in an ancient Chrysler Bill has hired for the day to go shooting duck. The roads were very muddy and skiddy after the heavy rain overnight. Bill shot 24 duck which they leave at Groppi's for credit. A missing aeroplane causes Bill great concern. Christmas letters and cards are written and posted. A Carol Service at the Cathedral on Sunday 18 December. They held two parties and were glad there would be no need for more. On Monday 19 December Cesca goes to Cooks to see about her passage home on January 4. Cesca enjoys the lovely warm weather noting that in England they are having snow and blizzards and all sorts of horrors. Arrangements are made to transfer the flat to the Southey's on January 15 who are buying all Cesca's lamps, china and kitchen utensils for £20. Cesca feels sad being away from the children for Christmas but cheered up because Bill is now coming back with her on the *Khedive Ismail* having had his fortnight's leave confirmed.

Saturday 31 December

Marian came in and bought my dining room table and six chairs. Very cold and windy. Went into Cairo for fitting and then to library to cancel my subscription. Man came to pack up glass and silver. Went to Robin's New Year's Eve Cocktail party which we both enjoyed. Home for dinner. Feeling most excited about going home together which will be wonderful. Bill has only a fortnight in England but so worth it. Wrote to Mother to tell her. To bed early and did not see the New Year in.

1939
Cairo and Belstead

Cesca and Bill travel home together from Cairo, Bill having a fortnight's leave, having been together in Egypt since last November. Severe flooding devastates parts of Ipswich in January. The interminable servant problems, house hunting, seaside holidays and Bill's leave and absences and the desire to live in their own home continue. Bill's leg injury so alarms Cesca she dashes out to be with him. In June Bill is granted leave and the family enjoy a lovely time together at the seaside. It will be a very long time before they meet again.

On Sunday 3 September at 11.15 Britain, France, Australia and New Zealand declare war on Germany. Petrol rationing, the black-out, a bicycle and a great many chickens take their place in Cesca's day. Merlin goes off to prep school and Mary enjoys riding her pony Sally. Bill and Cesca write daily to each other when apart, noted in the diaries, but to avoid repetition a high proportion deleted by me. Sadly only one letter (1935) survives.

Sunday 1 January

Bill and I went to the Cathedral this morning. Duncan McIntosh collected us in his Ford and motored out to lunch to their new house at Maadi. Back to the flat, changed and went to tea with the Southeys. Then went with them to the Air-Vice-Marshal's cocktail party. All the Cairo Air Force there, of course. Back to dinner alone and to bed. Miss my four darlings very much.

On 19 October 1940 Italian planes roared over Cairo and bombed the suburb of Maadi.

Monday 2 January

Bill is on leave for the day. Went to Cooks to book his passage, went to Ferenez for fittings. Mlle Moine came to finish my packing. Went to the club in the afternoon. Dined with the Cunningham's.

Tuesday 3 January

Our last day at little Amir Fouad. Went into Cairo early to bank and had my hair shampooed. Mrs Dudgeon called to take away her furniture before the Southey's come in tomorrow. Bill back for picnic lunch. Finished packing. Paid final bills, servants, laundry etc. Left the flat at 3.00 for station in a taxi. 3.30 train to Alexandria. Stayed the night at the Cecil Hotel which was most comfortable.

Wednesday 4 January

This flitting together is most exciting and it's marvellous to have Bill with me. Paid our Hotel bill and went by taxi to the docks, customs and quarantine stations and boarded the *Khedive Ismail* by 10.30. A funny little boat only 7,000 tons and painted green. I watched the passengers from Cairo get on board. Sailed at 1.00. We have a very nice cabin on Promenade deck. Sea calm. Read *Times*. Good dinner.

Thursday 5 January

Had a good night. Sea still calm, spent morning walking round the decks with Bill and reading. Quite pleasant people on board, mostly French. Food and service good, so far both enjoying it.

Friday 6 January

Weather not so good, much colder, and sea very rough. In afternoon I retired to bed and stayed there. Bill joined me and we both had a little chicken for our dinner.

Saturday 7 January

After an awful night arrived at Malta at 9.00, three hours late. Had light breakfast, went ashore and had a walk with Bill. Bought some lace for my pillowcases, two work bags one for Miss G. and one for myself. Also presents for Mary. The boat left at 2.00. Weather immediately started to deteriorate. I went to bed. Bill joined me. He had some dinner in the cabin. I did not and felt pretty miserable. Went to sleep

Sunday 8 January

Perfectly awful rough day. Bill and I remained in bed. Went through the Straits of Bonifacio, and when we reached the Gulf of Lyons the weather improved and it grew calmer. Had a bath and went to bed.

Monday 9 January

Marseilles, and of course arrived late. Missed our train and reservations at 9.55. However by much cunning and heavy tips, secured services of a Cooks man who got us seats on the Pullman train from Nice leaving Marseilles at 1.18 and arrived at Paris at 10:45 pm. Bill not feeling awfully well. Had an excellent lunch and dinner on the train. Sat next to a man who was on the boat who talked incessantly. Arrived hotel at 11.30, found a letter from Mum saying all the children were well. We had a lovely room.

Tuesday 10 January

Had breakfast in our bedroom. Paid our bills by cheque as we were short of cash. Off to the Gare du Nord. Train very full and comfy seats but Bill not feeling very well. Worried about him. Very smooth crossing. Then 1st.-class to London, stopped at RAF club for some money. Sturgeon met us at station with the new Armstrong Siddeley, a very super motorcar. Dad to meet us too. Mother at the house. She had not told the children and of course it was a terrific thrill for us all.

Wednesday 11 January

Lovely to see the children and be with them again. All looking so well. The twins seem to have grown up so since I left. Bill charmed with them both, and M and M who of course have not altered. They were all very pleased with their presents. So was Mum with her silk, Dad with his tie and the servants with theirs. Spent day trying to get straight, unpacked etc. Bill took children into Ipswich. They had Miss Death for music in afternoon. It's lovely to be home again.

Thursday 12 January

Bill sent wires to Brambletye [prep school] and to his mother to arrange to see her etc. Getting straight. Lovely weather, cold and frosty. It's lovely to be with the children again. In afternoon Miss Ensor their dancing mistress and the pianist arrived. Children quite good and it's most amusing watching them.

Friday 13 January

Went into Ipswich in morning. Over to tea at Rendham in the afternoon with Bill and Mary, Merlin and the twins. Granny Lunn gave us, as usual, an excellent tea. George showed us the new baby pigs and his recent work. Home at six, children all to bed happily. Miss Giordan away for the weekend.

Saturday 14 January

Very cold. Called to see Hempson about finding us a house in the morning. Helped Dorothy put the children to bed. Twins are sleeping with us.

Sunday 15 January

Went to church at St Mary le Tower at Ipswich with Mother, Twins, Mary and Merlin and Bill. Bill rather cross. Bill took M and M and the twins for long walk. I put them all to bed as Dorothy was out. And they were all so good. It is lovely being with them.

Monday 16 January

No reply from Brambletye. Bill and I went with Merlin to Frinton to try to find an unfurnished house there. Had tea at Annie's Tea rooms then home. Bill fetched Miss Giordan from station at 6.00.

Tuesday 17 January

Mary and Merlin went riding at Mrs Anderson's. Bill and I took them over there. Wrote to Miss Webber about a caretaker for 2 Walton Place.

Wednesday 18 January

Bill and I went up to London. I went straight to Pitman about the insurance. Bill to Air Ministry. Then I went to Walton Place. Installed Mrs Jeffries as caretaker and was annoyed to find the Fletcher's had left the house very dirty and untidy. Depressed as there seems no demand for houses at present. Lunched at Cordon Bleu. Back to Belstead on 6.19. Mother on same train.

Thursday 19 January

It is peculiar how difficult Mother is after first few days of our return and how she always seems to get a bead on poor Bill. He got so upset and depressed about it. Bill wired Elizabeth to find out about the position at Brambletye. Arranged to go down on Saturday and spend the night at Boxley.

Friday 20 January

Went for a walk with children in the morning. In afternoon went over to Woodbridge to look at a house at Sutton and to see a children's maid. Merlin ill all night, violently sick. Slept with us and we had a very disturbed night.

Saturday 21 January

Merlin not well enough to come with us, poor boy. Very disappointing, but Moppet came and we had a lovely day. Set off at nine and drove down past Colchester, Chelmsford etc. Through Blackwall Tunnel arriving at Tunbridge Wells at 12.30. Saw Hogben and Mrs. They were delighted to see us, then lunched at Wellington. Met Mrs Bawtree there. Good lunch, Mary no trouble and enjoying herself. On to Brambletye at East Grinstead. Bill and I went over the school, liked it and the Blencowes very much. Then on to see Harrison at Eridge and Mary and Bill both thrilled with Rob [labrador]. Tea at Tunbridge Wells, then motored out to Boxley arrived about 6.00.

Sunday 22 January

Enjoying our visit very much as it is nice to see the Styles again. Betty has such a nice husband, John Hatfield. Went to church with Mr and Mrs Style. We left after lunch, Mary thoroughly enjoying her visit and so good. Motored home by Ferry. Back for tea, Merlin up, but not looking very well yet.

Monday 23 January

Bill has decided to send Merlin to Brambletye if they have a vacancy. Wrote and told Blencowe this. Mother had a tea and sherry party.

Tuesday 24 January

Took Merlin into Mr Freemans about his tooth. Mary went riding at the Anderson's. She enjoyed her ride but fell off and had bad arm. Mrs Anderson brought her home after lunch. Merlin has temperature of 104.

Wednesday 25 January

Mary and the twins had their music. Merlin in bed with temperature. I think it must be flu caught perhaps from Dad. Bill and I looking after him have separated children from him. Heard that Blencowes will have Merlin so that is settled and he will now go to Brambletye.

Thursday 26 January

Bill's last day. Feel sad. Merlin not much better, so decided not to go up to London for the night and see 'Quiet Wedding' as we had intended. Mother ill with sick attack and diarrhoea. Bitterly cold and poured with rain. Dancing class just for Mary and the twins.

Friday 27 January

Felt absolutely miserable in the night and when I woke realising Bill was going back. Could not go to London as do not like to leave Merlin. Dorothy is useless and Miss G flaps so if anyone is ill. Floods terrible everywhere in Ipswich after heavy rain yesterday. [The River Gipping burst its banks and a combination of heavy rain and melting snow saw hundreds of homes abandoned and one person killed]. Took Bill to the station, Mary came with me to see him off on the platform. We both felt terribly sad and cried. Waved and waved, then Mops and I drove home. Later I took Mum and Dad into Ipswich. Had to go over Stoke Bridge, got cut off and had to return by Claydon.

Saturday 28 January

Felt better today. Had letter from Bill from Dover and one from London. Floods in Ipswich a disaster. Impossible to estimate the thousands of pounds of damage caused everywhere. Very cold. Looked after Merlin who is now in my room in a cot.

Sunday 29 January

Did not go to church but looked after Merlin. Clare seedy too with temperature of 100. Have her too in another cot in my room. Mary and Cecily both all right so far. Dorothy has a terribly bad infectious cold but will insist on going out.

Monday 30 January

Went off at 9.30 with Mary to Corder's sale. Bought her and the twins some socks, gloves, ribbons etc. Also some household rubbers, swabs, floor cloths etc. went to laundry. Merlin better but still in bed. Clare better but now Cecily has a temperature of 100 and is in my room which we call the hospital.

Tuesday 31 January

Mary went riding. I took her over to Mrs Anderson's. She had a lovely ride while I went to see a nursery housemaid at Brantham. Found her useless. Collected Mary. Merlin and the twins better, though Cecily very weepy, poor darling.

Wednesday I February

Went to London for a flying visit to Walton Place. Left on 10 o'clock train and went to Walton Place with cleaning materials. Mrs Jeffries is there. I had Mrs Webb to come in daily to clean up the house. Do hope by so doing shall let it quickly. Shopped at Harrods, and ordered 'Countryman's Creed' to be sent to Bill for his 10th wedding day. Went to Shaplands for repairs to silver then home on the 3.40 arriving for late tea.

Thursday 2 February

Mother and I went over to Wetherden to see an under parlourmaid but no good. I enjoyed my afternoon as I drove the Armstrong Siddeley. Lovely on return to find a letter from Bill posted at Brindisi saying he had had an excellent journey, sea calm and a cabin to himself.

Friday 3 February

I went off at 9.30 to Kelsale in YY to the sale. Bought a very nice cut glass water jug for 10 shillings and a very nice old Famille Rose bowl, some oddments in china for 2/6, some sheets and eiderdowns. I left at 11.00 and went to Framlingham to interview a children's maid. It was lovely in the country and I thoroughly enjoyed my day.

Saturday 4 February

Delighted this morning to find a letter from Bill from Alexandria. Lovely to hear from him. I have a bad throat, worse this evening and I'm afraid I am now in for it. Miss G out at a cinema afternoon and evening. Dorothy and Mother helped me to put children to bed. Then I had a hot bath and put myself to bed.

Cesca ill in bed for the next two days.

Tuesday 7 February
Went to Ipswich after taking children over to their riding lesson in morning. After lunch went to Ixworth to see a nursery housemaid. Mother came with me. Quite a nice girl but am waiting to see if I can do better.

Wednesday 8 February
Not feeling very well, Mother went to London to Walton Place on my behalf, to pay Mrs Jeffrey and Mrs Webb. Went for a walk with twins after lunch. Miss Death came. Miss G looking very seedy.

Thursday 9 February
Went off after breakfast to Ipswich to do some shopping. Took in two chairs to be re-rushed at Blind shop; then went to Harlesdon to see maid who answered my advertisement. Had to drive awful long way round owing to the floods. Eventually interviewed her but felt she was no use. Too late to get back for lunch so stopped at Scole and had lunch at the Old Sun and on my way home saw another girl at Gislingham.

Friday 10 February
Miss G collapsed last night with flu so put her to bed and she is in bed today. Mary and Merlin rode in afternoon. Dorothy took out the twins. Heard from Bill.

Saturday 11 February
Miss G a bit better but still slight temperature. I have breakfast in schoolroom with children and Dorothy and find it's great fun, but a longish day with all the other things to do. In afternoon took Merlin and Mother and went over to Harwich to see another children's maid whom I engaged. Elsie Osborne is only 14 and probably useless, coming on Monday morning. Mary and twins

out with Dorothy. Lovely spring like day. Bill sent me magnificent box of lilies of the valley and white carnations for tomorrow.

Sunday 12 February

A lovely day. I have been married 10 years. Can't believe it and feel rather sad I am away from my darling. Send him a NTL yesterday and I had one from him, also three lovely books. The children were so sweet, came in at 7.00 with a bunch of violets and Bill's books. Really felt quite overcome. Bill sent me a letter too I was not to open until today. Do love him so and miss him very much. Wrote him a long letter and went to church in morning. Pepper was run over by under keeper and is very ill.

Monday 13 February

Miss G much better, but decided she would be pretty useless at teaching so persuaded Dorothy to stay on another week and packed Giordy girl off on a train at 10.00. She seemed rather cross and difficult. Shall love having children to myself for a week. Took Mer to have his hair cut. Collected new children's maid from station. Had a letter from Bill. Twins sleeping with me which is fun.

Tuesday 14 February

Merlin woke up shrieking last night and is having bad dreams again. My darling Twinnies 5th birthday. Lovely to see how happy they are with their presents. I gave them each a Dobbin and a book. Mother gave them books, also Dandy. Bill some things for their dolls house. They had a special lunch. Sausages and mashed potato, treacle pudding! Dorothy out so put them to bed after a birthday tea party with cake etc.

Wednesday 15 February

Left children today in Mother's charge and dashed up to London to see Gilkes about an offer for 2 Walton Place, from two Swiss men who want it till August. Saw Aunt Edie whom I have not seen since my return to England. Found her in bed and very much altered and aged. Took her a tablecloth and some flowers. Shopped and came home on 3.50 so as to put children to bed.

Thursday 16 February

Heard offer is off which is sickening.

Friday 17 February

Took children riding and then went to see Lawford Place, Manningtree as shall not have time on Monday. We all went for a ramble in afternoon. Pepper almost well again.

Saturday 18 February

Miss Death came 9.00 am. In afternoon took Mother in Armstrong over to Walsham-le-Willows to see some maids. Much prefer driving YY.

Monday 20 February

Mrs G returned and Dorothy Clover left. I took twins over to lunch at Rendham to Grannie Lunn's, left them there and went to lunch with Ian Smith's at Aldeburgh which I enjoyed. Most lovely warm sunny day, sat on verandah after lunch. Went down to the village bought some sweets and returned to fetch twins at Rendham at 4.00. Home at six, Miss G looking very well and most brisk.

Wednesday 22 February

Horrible pouring wet day. Dad in London. Mother and I went over to the Lawford sale after lunch. She bought a set of china for wash stand, some toilet runners, bedspreads and eiderdowns etc. I bought two pairs of linen sheets for £2. Dad back at 7.00.

Thursday 23 February

Went over to Lawford again and took Mother. I thought I would buy a dining room table. Unfortunately it fetched £8.15.0. Dancing class and children are really getting on well.

Sunday 26 February

Went over to Cambridge with Mother, Mary and Merlin in the Armstrong Siddeley. Left at 9.30, arrived at 11. 00. Left the car in the garage then walked up to Leckhampton House and Herschel to show children and through Kings backs. Lunched enormously at Varsity Arms which was very full. Children thrilled with the hotel and food. Then to Kings Chapel for Evensong which I do not think children appreciated. Tea at Copper Kettle where we bought cakes and home at 7.00.

Monday 27 February

Mary's ninth birthday, many presents and much excitement. Lovely day. Her special lunch was chicken, fruit jelly and meringues. Tea party in library and a birthday cake. Can't believe she is nine.

Wednesday 1 March

Mother in London. Went over to Newmarket and ordered children's riding kit. In afternoon had fitting at Smith and Harvey.

Thursday 2 March

Went to London and saw Hughes who, poor chap, has had an operation to his jaw after the dentist broke it. Went to Ivy Hudson, the house and brought home some blankets, ordered some soap for Bill and a book for his birthday and a manicure set from Finnigans. Home on 4.54. Sturgeon met me.

Friday 3 March

I took Mary, Merlin, Claire and Cecily over to Goldings in Newmarket for M and M's fittings. Lovely day and lovely drive. Had picnic tea on the Heath on the way home. Enjoyed it very much. The children are such fun.

Saturday 4 March

Miss Death came at 9.00 and I have decided to let the twins start with her after Easter. Mother wanted to see a girl at Stowmarket. Took her there. Interviewed Ethel Hooper in morning to take Elsie's place. Engaged her.

Sunday 5 March

Went to church at St Mary le Tower and decided not to go there any more. We always seem to get behind a pillar.

Wednesday 8 March

Heard this morning from Bill that he has phlebitis due to an injury playing hockey. Rang up Mr Todd to see if he can get me a passage on this week's *Adriatica* on Friday. I am determined to get out to him as soon as possible as it is a dangerous thing. Letters from Bill in afternoon saying he is in bed but better and lower temperature. Mother agrees I should go and so do the children. Hate to leave them but feel I must be with him. Todd rang to say no 2nd-class, so going 1st and as soon as possible to my darling.

Thursday 9 March

Letters from Bill saying he was better but feel very anxious about him. At teatime had a signal from him saying no need for me to come. Replied 'Coming Cesca'. Heard from Mr Todd he has fixed my cabin, 1st class on the Marco Polo and all my other reservations. Went into Ipswich in the morning. Lovely warm spring day. Miss Ensor came in the afternoon for dancing class. They are getting on so well, love to see them. Poor Diddles [Cecily] cried so about my going away, poor darling. Worried to death about Bill.

Friday 10 March

Busy doing final packing, had bad night with Merlin and the twins. Then left the house, a lovely sunny morning, at 9.30. Dad took me to the station and saw me off for London. My luggage is two suitcases, hat box, attaché case, and case for rugs. Went to Cooks and met Mr Todd who was delightful and gave me my tickets, money and all I needed. Then to Walton Place where I paid Mrs J., rang Hughes, Bank, King and agents and Mr Evershed. Bought books at Harrods and took taxi to Victoria. Bought some papers and got on the train. Felt very tired. Channel very smooth and found my compartment all most comfy. Dinner on the train and then to bed, my compartment companion is a Guy's Hospital nurse.

Saturday 11 March

Woke up at 6.00 when my travelling companion got out at Montreux. From there I had the carriage to myself, saw a bit of Switzerland which looked very pretty with snow. Had breakfast which made me feel much better. Then on to Milan and then to Venice. The people in the next-door compartment introduced themselves, called Lloyd whom Mr Todd told me of. They are very nice, live in Chester Square and have four children. Arrived in Venice in a snowstorm. Boarded the *Adriatica* which is comfy and spotlessly clean. Lloyds are at the same table. Took a cachet as feared it might be rough and went to early to bed.

Sunday 12 March

Last night felt so terribly tired, fell asleep at once and did not wake up till eight. So had 10 hours. This ship is extremely comfortable, but the people are really most peculiar. If it wasn't for the Lloyds I should spend entire time in my cabin. Got up 11.30. Found Lloyds had got a deckchair for me on deck. Food is good and we arrived at Brindisi at 3.30. It looks a miserable place. Sent off a letter there to Mum. Worried about Bill and wished boat would go faster. Talked to the Lloyds who I like very much.

Monday 13 March

Lovely calm day and warmer. Did not get up until 11.30. Read papers and my book. Then went up on deck and sat with the Lloyds. After lunch sat up on the top deck. Bill sent me a cable to say he was much better but in the Citadel [the British garrison was housed in the Citadel]. This worried me a lot. I am apparently staying at the Aireys.

Tuesday 14 March

Woke up to find weather much hotter. Lovely day. Sat on deck with Lloyds all the morning. Then packed after lunch, felt quite exhausted and had a lie down afterwards. We got into Alexandria soon after 4.00. A man from *Adriatica* supposed to meet me but no sign of him. Lloyds took me with them to station and Cook's man did my luggage. Arrived at station 5.30 and train left at 7.00. Arrived Cairo 10.30 at station. I got to Aireys at 11.00. Rang up Citadel and found Bill was better after having his leg cut open last week. He comes out tomorrow.

Wednesday 15 March

Had bath and breakfast. Bill rang up, suggested I should collect him from the Citadel. However after much telephoning found it was impossible owing to the crush in the streets on account of the

Royal wedding. [King Farouk of Egypt hosted a glittering banquet in honour of Crown Prince Mohammand Reza Pahlavi, H.I.M. Shah of Iran and H.R.H.Princess Fawzia of Egypt at the Abdeen Palace after their wedding]. Bill arrived after lunch looking very white and ill and on crutches. After tea we went off round to Marian's flat which she has lent us. I unpacked and got straight.

Thursday 16 March

Bill already seems better after getting out of the Citadel, but looks very seedy still. Apparently the MO made a wrong diagnosis and it was a poisoned leg, not phlebitis at all. However after opening it up it has given him no more pain. The Lloyds came into tea and were charming. I went into Cairo after the doctor had been, to shop and get things for Bill and then to Cooks.

Friday 17 March

It is lovely being with Bill again although he can only hobble about on crutches. It is lovely just being together. Had a letter from Mother saying all well at Belstead. Wrote to her and Grannie Lunn. Went round to Grenville House to collect letters and the *Times* .

Saturday 18 March

Bill's 33rd birthday. Lovely to spend it with him. We both think this flat is depressing and return to Grenville House on Tuesday.

Monday 20 March

Bill seems much better and leg is beginning to heal up. Busy packing to leave tomorrow. Went into Cairo to Cooks as we are very worried over the International situation. [German occupation of Czechoslovakia and Hitler's demands for Poland to give up Danzig.] It looks as if I might have to return in a hurry.

Tuesday 21 March

All packed up. Did tipping, paid bills and servants and after Dr came, left M's depressing flat and returned to Grenville house. It certainly is a lovely bright flat. Bernard seems nice too. Went to bed early in the old Amir Hussein's white bed. Slept well, and happy Bill is better.

Wednesday 22 March

[Germany and Italy sign Pact of Steel].

Doctor came to see Bill. I feel very worried over this situation generally. Rang up the Lloyds to find out if they had made arrangements to leave sooner. Heard from Mum. Horrid day of Khamsin [a hot wind from the south, of high velocity carrying quantities of sand and dust].

Friday 24 March

Bill better. Dr says he may go out. Lloyds, Chapmans, Andrews (from Embassy), and Mrs Adair lunched today. B's Major Domo is marvellous and produced the finest lunch. Afterwards took Lloyds to the Polo. Met Cunningham's and asked them into dine on Saturday. Lloyds came back to tea. Weather and situation much better. Feeling happier.

Saturday 25 March

Bernard went off to the Desert for weekend so we have the flat to ourselves. Went for a walk to club with Bill, met the Grants. Cunninghams dined in evening. They were both so charming.

Monday 27 March

Situation still seems to be very uncertain and tricky after a speech made by Mussolini yesterday. Lovely day. Went to watch the 2nd round of the Open Polo Cup at club this morning, afterwards went on to Continental Hotel where we picked up the Mena bus and went to lunch with the Lloyds. Enjoyed it so much and stayed to tea with them there. Bill going into work tomorrow.

Tuesday 28 March

We seem suddenly to have summer. Very hot indeed today. Bill went into M.E. and I went with him in a taxi. Went to La Petite Reine and bought two pairs corsets, a white belt and two pairs stockings. To Cooks to fix up my passage on *Gerusalemme* on Saturday. Mlle Moine here packing and tidying up for me. Bill and I went to club in evening.

Wednesday 29 March

Another grilling day. Had bad night and felt very tired, also most irritated with letters from Mother who has apparently lost a good let for Walton Place. Bill went to work as usual. Wrote to Miss Giordan, Bank manager and Mother from Club. Major and Mrs Evans Lombe, Marian and Bernard came to lunch. Hassan produced an excellent lunch. Went to see final of Open Cup which was won by the 8th. Sad it is our last evening in this nice flat. Very hot, 94F.

Thursday 30 March

Bill and I decided to go up to Alexandria. Packed and went with Bill into Cairo. Went to La Petite Reine and collected my belt and stockings. Bank for more money, and then to the flat. Left on 3 o'clock train for Alexandria. Got out at Sidi Gaber and went to Beau Rivage Hotel which appeared very depressing on arrival but has a nice garden. Had dinner and went for walk afterwards.

Friday 31 March

It is lovely and much cooler up here than in Cairo. Bill and I had breakfast in our bedroom, then wandered along the seashore looking for shells for Mary. Sat in the garden, and then had lunch. Then decided to go into Alexandria and see the Great Waltz after tea. Went to the Cecil first, where we read most alarming news which thoroughly frightened us both, that Chamberlain was lending all support in his power to Poland should she be invaded. Bill felt I ought to return by air. I feel it would be a great waste of money. To bed after dinner, both sad.

Saturday 1 April

As always felt more than miserable, and can't bear leaving my darling. Each time it gets worse. Packed and left Beau Rivage for the docks. Boarded *Gerusalemme* at 10.00 and found I had a nice cabin, on top deck. Watch the people coming on board then at 11.30 my love left to catch 12 o'clock train back to Cairo. Felt bitterly sad. Faced lunch, three men at my table, two English and one Pole or Russian. Rested all afternoon. Had dinner and went

straight to bed. Very, tired sad and done. Took green medicine.
[The green medicine was produced in times of physical and
emotional distress. No one living can recall what was in it. Cesca's
father a physician, supplied it.]

Sunday 2 April
Woke up with splitting head, pains inside and feeling all to pieces.
Could not get up so remained in bed all day. In afternoon was very
sick. Thought the day would never end. Thought of Bill and how
much I love him and miss him.

Monday 3 April
Better, headache gone but still pains and diarrhoea, no more
sickness. Starved till dinner time and then had a little cold chicken.

Tuesday 4 April
Was woken at 2.00 am by people getting off boat at Brindisi. This is
a poor old boat, very smelly and shocking food, but we are having
the most marvellously calm and sunny trip. Feeling much better.
Sat in lovely sunshine on deck. Wrote to my love which will go
from Venice.

Wednesday 5 April
Woken up frightfully early by the usual tiresome and excitable
people. Actually no sign of Venice till 9.30 and did not arrive till
later. Packed, tipped, and eventually disembarked at 11.00. Met a
very nice woman in the customs called Miss Maxwell and we had
lunch at the Luna restaurant. We took a gondola up the Grand
Canal to the station. The train there was late. I found I was in a
sleeper with a Bulgarian woman.

Thursday 6 April
Could not sleep last night, the sleeper was just over the wheels and
rattled and jolted along terribly. It was very hot too. I got up after
the Bulgarian girl, and had breakfast as we were nearing Paris.
Arrived Paris 8.20 and then on with a sleeper to myself to
Boulogne. Met a nice man on the boat who came and sat next to
me but I suddenly felt so sick that I had to go below and lie down.
It was very rough. I joined him again later and he and I travelled

up to Victoria together. Found he was at Eton. The train was late so I missed my train to Ipswich, not arriving till 11.00. Mum and Dad met me and gave me a great welcome. Children all flourishing. I went to bed and to sleep at 1.00.

Friday 7 April

In the morning my four darlings were with me and it was simply lovely to see them. Went out all afternoon with them. All talking hard. Lovely too, to get letters from my darling whose leg is better and he seems quite happy. Lovely to be home again. Country looking beautiful too, daffs out and lambs and nests everywhere.

Saturday 8 April

Mother distracted with most unsatisfactory servants. Miss Giordan off for Easter holiday. In afternoon took Merlin out to ride at Anderson's and have tea there. Wrote a long letter to Bill. News is very bad as Italians have now invaded Albania.

Monday 10 April

Letters from Bill. Wrote to him and posted it on our way to Woodbridge Horse show. The great day for Mary has arrived. We started off at 10.30. Mum, Mer, Mary, twins and I with picnic lunch. A gorgeous day. Mary rode awfully well and though she did not get a prize, the judge tried out Sally and Mary would probably have got one had she been in a smaller class. Anyhow she thoroughly enjoyed it and it was great fun.

Wednesday 12 April

Another really beautiful day and warmer than ever. Mary and Mer came to see me and then got dressed early and went out in the garden. Picked some flowers for Mother. Wrote letters, changed before lunch for Wordsworth wedding to which we went with Mary and Merlin. Their first wedding which they both thoroughly enjoyed. Very pretty country wedding, met Bromfield's, Packards etc. there.

Thursday 13 April

Took Mary and Merlin to the pony club rally at Kesgrave this morning. We got there at 11.30 and Miss Giordan instructed them in saddling and unsaddling their ponies and riding each other's ponies. All very good for them. We then had lunch. Then there was a paperchase. Mary begged to be allowed to go in for it, so I said reluctantly that she could as Virginia was going. It was terrific and how she stayed on I don't know. Went hell for leather for three quarters of an hour. Brought them home exhausted.

Friday 14 April

After two days of no letters, got two from Bill this morning. Went off on the early train to London. First to Metier about income tax for this year. Then to Walton Place where I saw man re carpets and made arrangements to close it from next week. Had lunch at Searcy's, ordered new hats for the twins at Harrods. Came home after interviewing Harrods man re sale of some furniture. Brought back presents for Mer's birthday.

Sunday 16 April: Summer Time begins

All had an hour's less sleep last night. Mother and Dad were very cross with me at breakfast and I felt sad. Later Mother came up and said she was sorry. Went for walk in morning and got some daffodils. Servant problems getting more and more difficult.

Monday 17 April

Poor Mother distracted over servants. Went over to Hadleigh after interviewing some at Copdock and saw two temporary cooks. Home for late tea. Mother dismissed Iris, the cook, and she left on the spot. I gave Ethel notice this morning as she is bone idle.

Tuesday 18 April

Had two letters from Bill. Wrote to him. Had a very busy day. Dashed off in morning to see if I could get Mrs Wright to help clean. Went to Pony Rally at Tendring. Mary had a nasty fall and hurt herself.

Wednesday 19 April

A simply terrific day! Up at 7.00 but missed 8.07 as Sturgeon was late with the car so set off and caught it at Colchester! Had breakfast on the train. In London went to 2 Walton Place. Found pandemonium. Bevan there and 2 men taking up the carpets, men cutting off telephone, and gas, electric light and water! Eventually Bevan left with 1st load at 4.00 and I took 4.57 down to Colchester. Home at 6.30. Bevan came on with things at 8.00, unloaded and I went to bed early very tired. New cook arrived.

Thursday 20 April

A lovely day. Quite like summer. Spend morning sorting blankets and curtains from 2 Walton Place. In afternoon went shopping for Merlin's birthday. Mother is servant hunting at Thetford and Yaxley. Servants are awful and Cook hopeless.

Friday 21 April

Another lovely day. What weather we are having! Took Mary and Merlin over to tea at the Masons at Felixstowe. Mother came with us and sat on shelter in the sun on the front. Posted letters to Bill on the way. Mrs Mason very pleasant and we had a very nice tea Twins had an animal's tea party with Giordy and Dad in schoolroom.

Saturday 22 April

Took children, Miss G and Mum to Felixstowe again in afternoon. Lovely in afternoon. Children played on sands. Mum and I went to a view of furniture sale at Monks Barns.

Monday 24 April

Merlin's 8th birthday. He was very cheerful and happy and had lots of presents. Accumulator for train set and buffers from me, signals and a book from Bill. Meccano set from Mum. £1 and an aeroplane from Dad, 10 shillings from Grannie Lunn, 5 shillings from Dandy. Coal mine from Miss G. He had special food and a lovely birthday cake from Copper Kettle.

Tuesday 25 April

Wet and cold. Went into Ipswich in morning. In afternoon I brought Mary home as she had a nasty tumble and hurt her head. I put her to bed as she had a headache. Went to fetch new head housemaid for Mum. Four servants left, thank heavens and five new ones came and they really do seem to be a better class.

Sunday 30 April

Very cold. Mother has had central heating put on again. Wrote to my love and walked to the post with it.

Monday 1 May

Ethel Hooper left and a new girl Anne Welton arrived. Such a lot to straighten out after the move from Walton Place. Paid Miss G £33.6.8d.

Tuesday 2 May

New girl seems quite good so far. Do wish international situation would settle down and we could plan ahead a bit. Have sold two high chairs, cot and one eiderdown as a result of my advertisement in N.W. [Nursery World] but no guinea pigs yet. Letters from Bill. Do so pray he gets leave soon. The children are getting on well with their music.

Wednesday 3 May

Do miss Bill so. Still it's not long now ABW. [I am unable to clarify these initials.] And the children are a great comfort to me. Went over to Rendham and arrived with all the children for lunch there. Mrs L and G in good form and delighted to see us all. Gave us excellent lunch and tea.

Thursday 4 May

Wrote to Frinton about houses, and also to London agents as so far there seems no sign of the house selling and it's a great drain.

Saturday 6 May

Weather much improved, lovely day. In afternoon took Dad and Merlin up to Copdock to see cricket match and we saw Sturgeon and Morphew play. Ralph Millais arrived after tea in an old 30-98 Vauxhall!

Sunday 7 May

All walked up to church at Belstead this morning. Such a really glorious morning too. Ralph helped Merlin with his aeroplane which pleased him a lot and he is most popular with the girls. Lunch, then I took Ralph over to Rendham to see Grannie Lunn and George and had tea there. They did not expect us but were very pleased to see Ralph. Motored home through Suffolk, such a lovely hot summer's day and I did so wish Bill had been with me.

Monday 8 May

Another simply glorious day. Ralph and I started off together. He and Merlin in his 30-98 and me and Mary in YY. We went via Claydon where he went right for Eye and we went on to Bury where we stopped and saw Rutter re. furnished house for the summer. Then to Newmarket for fitting and some sausages. Then to Cambridge where we went to Copper Kettle and then to lunch at Varsity Arms. Children had an enormous lunch and thoroughly enjoyed it and were such fun. Then onto Debden, to see the aeroplanes and David Atcherley, returning by Clare and Long Melford. Twins with Mum.

Tuesday 9 May

Letters from Bill, such a joy. Wrote to him. Shopped in morning and in afternoon took Mary over to Capel for her ride. Then to Frinton taking Merlin and Anne and twins. Enjoyed it as it was such a really lovely day and glorious at the sea. I inspected houses with Mrs Thomas while the children played on the beach and then joined them for tea at Mrs Thomas's hut. Came home at 6.15.

Wednesday 10 May

Lovely day again and very warm. Went off to London with Mother for 10 o'clock train. Straight to Margaret's where I left my luggage. Then to lunch with Ursula Ainslie. Saw her sweet baby Virginia and then onto Academy where I joined Mother and much enjoyed it though it was very tiring. Then to tea at Margaret's. In the evening Jim and Gabriel came to dinner.

Thursday 11 May

Am enjoying my stay in London but as Margaret's room is on the ground floor it is really extremely noisy! However it's great fun and she and Claude are very sweet to me. I went to Harrods and Peter Jones where I got a new petticoat and nightie. Called at all the agents and then on to see Aunt Edie. Found her very feeble, poor dear. Lunched with Fay and Richard Peck at their very super and sumptuously appointed service flat at Queen Anne's Mansion's. Dinner and cinema with C and M.

Friday 12 May

It was lovely last night when I got in to find a letter from my darling Billy. Felt so happy to have his letter and I dreamt of him. Shopped and went to the National Gallery to see British schools which I enjoyed. Then to Gunters where I was very greedy and had a cup of hot chocolate. Felt quite sick afterwards! Back to lunch with Margaret. She went to Wincanton for weekend and I home to Belstead.

Saturday 13 May

Family rather grumpy, but glorious to have two letters from Bill this morning. YY back from Locks and going like a bomb. Took Mother and Merlin over to Woodbridge this afternoon to see a butler. Lovely day again and warmer.

Sunday 14 May

In afternoon took children and Mum to Bailly Woods to gather bluebells. Found a French partridge nest in the wood and took one egg which I blew.

Monday 15 May

Wrote to Bill having had three letters from him. Mother's head housemaid and the under housemaid both gave notice this morning. Can't understand it.

Tuesday 16 May

Went to Miss Jeckell in the morning for fitting of my new coat. Went to interview Helen Rain, nursery housemaid who seemed a much nicer type of girl than Joan Johnson.

Wednesday 17 May

Dad went to London, Mother went to Mrs Milbank's Fork Lunch and so I was left with Miss G and the children. Had scene with Mary who refused to eat any junket and would have plain rhubarb. So annoying when I had hoped for a nice quiet peaceful lunch. Merlin too had to be punished this morning. He suddenly seized Mary by the throat when she played a wrong note in duets and I had to whip him.

Friday 19 May

Merlin awake a lot in the night with toothache. Eventually slept with me. I gave him an aspirin and he settled down. Took him to Freemans and eventually at 12.15 Freeman decided only to stop two teeth. Drove over to Frinton in YY, first saw Landemere Hall at Thorpe which I did not care for and then on to Frinton. The nice house Wyndways has been let but the last one I saw called '29' I liked very much.

Saturday 20 May

Went off at 9.50 with Mother, Merlin and Mops [Mary] and on arriving in London posted letter to Bill. Then Mer and I went to Harrods to get his aircraft book, an RAF tractor and a book on Robin Hood. Inspected menagerie and 2 Walton Place and then met Mum and Mary for lunch at the Club. Mother and Mary had been to South Kensington Museum to see the stuffed whales and fishes. Had a very good lunch. Then to Olympia by taxi for the Royal Tournament. Had very good seats and it was an excellent show. Lifeguards, musical ride and the drive by the battery of Royal Horse Artillery were excellent. Merlin preferred the motorbikes! Home on 4.54.

May 21 Sunday

After lunch motored over through country lanes to tea with Jane and Isabel at Aldeburgh. It was a simply glorious afternoon and I enjoyed myself so much. I thought so much of Bill and wished he had been with me. Wrote to Mrs Thomas and made an offer of £50 for "29", the house at Frinton for 15th of June to end of July.

Tuesday 23 May

No news of Bill's leave or the house at Frinton. Heard from Rainsford (agent at Aldeburgh), that he has nothing at the price at all. Mary and Mer both have to have two teeth out so arranged for this to be done next week. Took Mother over to Aldeburgh to see two maids, home by Campsea Ashe where she saw another. The car not going at all well.

Wednesday 24 May

Great day for the twins and Giordy who went off at 9.30 to London where Mother took them to the Zoo, ending with lunch and mixed ices at Gunters! Mary and Merlin and I had a lovely ramble over the fields, birds nesting. A really lovely day, went to the train bridge and saw twins in the train dash past at 4.30, much hanky waving. A picnic tea and home 5.30.

Thursday 25 May

Heard my offer for '29' has been refused and that they won't take less than 60 guineas for the period. Rang up Mrs T from Ipswich and offered 50 guineas for the house from June 20 to July 26. Wrote to Bill and had letter from him but no news about leave yet.

Friday 26 May

Having now unpacked all glass, china and silver from Egypt find all silver is ruined by salt water. Sea must have got in. Sally brought over this afternoon to Capel.

Saturday 27 May

Miss C rang up to say Sally had cleared off in the night, so the children couldn't ride. My offer for '29' accepted! And then oh! Joy! Cable from Bill at breakfast time to say "Hasken laid on and Dunn approves, mid June, end July. Very much love Darling, Bill". Overjoyed went to look for Sally. Heard too May is coming. Everything seems marvellous. Davies's man came and repacked glass and china. Wrote to my love. Took Mother, M and M to Hadleigh Show in afternoon.

Monday 29 May

Another lovely day. Had cable from Bill at 12.00 which sent my spirits soaring to tell me he is coming on leave on 7th arrives by air 8th and will be here till July 19th! Nearly had a fit with excitement and delight. Wrote to him. Told children and Mother and read papers in afternoon but could not take them in and felt quite bats with excitement.

Tuesday 30 May

Another lovely day. Took M and M to dentist. Banks gave gas and they both had two out. Mer did not take it very well. In afternoon went over to Frinton, took Mother in YY. Went over "29" and hope I have succeeded in getting it for a week sooner which will be lovely. Oh dear, am so excited. Then looked at the huts and then met Mother for tea at Anne's.

Wednesday 31 May

Another gorgeous day. Had letter from Bill full of his leave and coming by air on 7th getting here 8th. Am so excited. Shall go to Southampton to meet him. Went into Ipswich and met May and settled with her. Heard cook can't come which is a bore.

Thursday 1 June

Very busy day. Merlin to dentist in morning and Mary riding. While she rode, sat on train bridge and read. Mother very cross at lunchtime.

Friday 2 June

Had lovely letters from Bill and am overjoyed at his coming. It really is marvellous. Went off to London on 9.00 train. Left YY at station. Went to Shapland and then to Lloyds bank, then to Imperial Airways to find out that Bill will arrival at 12.40. Then to lunch at Gunters had some nice salmon and an ice. Then to bank for balance, Peter Jones for bathing suits then home on 5.16. Mother in better temper on my return.

Saturday 3 June

Yesterday I wrote my last letter to my darling. Heard this morning that he may not get away by the 7th as D has to go to Palestine for conference. Busy morning. Mr Collyer, Pitman's assessor arrived and I spend all morning with him going through damaged silver.

Sunday 4 June

A gloriously hot day! Went to church in car. Walked up to see Sally in evening with Mary. No more letter writing to Bill which seems most peculiar. In four days time my darling will be home again.

Monday 5 June

Another glorious day. In afternoon took Mer over to Frinton and went to house, which he liked, to agents, to huts to decide. Had tea. Merlin had chocolate cakes! Home via Copdock to pick up Mary after her riding. It really is lovely to feel Bill will be leaving Cairo and the heat tomorrow.

Tuesday 6 June

Telegram from Bill to say he leaves today and is arriving tomorrow. Can't believe it! Had a hectic day! In afternoon the children's party. We had a Treasure Hunt in the garden. Very, very hot. Each minute Bill is coming closer! Oh dear oh dear it is so exciting. This time tomorrow he will be home.

Wednesday 7 June

A marvellous day. Up early and caught 8.07 to Colchester. Changed there for London arrived at 10.00. Taxi to Waterloo and just caught Bournemouth Belle at 10.30 for Southampton where my darling arrived in *Centaurius* flying boat at 12.30. Went quite mad with delight. Marvellous to see him and be with him again. He had had a lovely trip. Very hot 89F today. Went up to London and stayed at Connaught which is very comfy but expensive. Unpacked and then later went to tea at Gunters. Then dined at Pruniers, cold salmon and strawberries, then on to "Grouse in June" an excellent show at Criterion.

Thursday 8 June

Woke at 8.30 and had our breakfast brought up. Then packed and left at 10.00. Bill went to Bank and Air Ministry. I went to Harrods and Harvey Nichols returning to collect luggage and so to Liverpool Street where I met Bill again. Alas they cannot manage to absorb him. This seems too sad for words, more partings. Oh dear! Oh dear! Home by 12.25 and had a terrific welcome from the children. Bill out with them all afternoon in garden. Tea and more games after tea. Took Mary up to ride and Merlin too.

Friday 9 June

It seems as if it will never rain again. Glorious weather but cooler today. In afternoon went to Lady Belstead's cocktail party. It is marvellous to have Bill here and I can hardly believe it when I wake up each morning. Mum and Dad are both very pleasant too.

Saturday 10 June

Footmans came to collect all the furniture from Walton Place to store it, so was busy most of morning. Bill writing letters. Went to Ipswich and later in the afternoon Miss Death's Concert at which Mary and Merlin played 2 duets, 'Valsette' and the 'Boat Song". All went off very well, Merlin only making a slight mistake. It was a very hot afternoon and rather boring listening to a lot of children in a stuffy hall for over an hour. Home for tea.

Sunday 11 June

Much cooler after pouring wet night and morning. Bill and I went to church with Merlin at East Bergholt. In afternoon went over to Rendham to see Grannie Lunn and George. We stayed till 6.00 and then came home. Country looking so very lovely after the rain. Glorious evening. It is so lovely to have Bill home and I am so utterly happy.

Monday 12 June

Bill went in to Chiropodist in the morning and I had my hair washed. Then after lunch over to Frinton in the car taking with us the linen, silver, and children's clothes and some suitcases. Wrote letters when I got in and did final packing up. Mother and Dad are both very difficult in the evening.

Tuesday 13 June

Up early, went off to fetch May taking her and Helen to station to go to Frinton. Then Bill and I went over arriving in time to get the key from Tomkins, unload the car and meet May and Helen off train. We lunched at Anne's and met Mrs Hecketh, then Bill went over to fetch Miss G and the children who all arrived at teatime. Tea and a run in the garden and then to bed while we unpacked. Lovely to be together and alone.

Wednesday 14 June

Went down to the beach to our nice hut on the front, 242, Bratton. It is very comfortable and near to the house at the end of 4th Avenue. On the beach with Miss G and the children all the morning. In afternoon took Miss G to station and saw her off for her holiday. Returned to the beach and back for tea in the playroom at 5.00. The children seem to love their time and look the picture of health already.

Thursday 15 June

Mrs Hecketh is turning out quite a good cook and May seems very happy here with us again. Poured with rain all afternoon, so stayed in the house and played with the children.

Friday 16 June

The weather seems to have broken. Went down to our hut and Bill and children all bathed and enjoyed it. It is so lovely to be altogether. Helen out and Bill and I put all children to bed.

Saturday 17 June

Went to beach in morning. The household seems to go very well. May quite settled down and Mrs H an excellent cook. Mother, Dad and Barbara arrived at 3.30. Very chilly and damp. Children, Bill and Barbara bathed. Had tea at the house and a fire and they all left at 6.00. Alone and together which is perfect.

Sunday 18 June

Lovely day. Spent morning on beach lazing in sun. Bill and children bathed. Lunch and slept and to the sea in afternoon and evening.

Monday 19 June

I am much enjoying myself. Children are really no trouble and so good and sweet. Spent the day on beach in lovely weather. Children very happy and well, except Merlin who is having a bout of bad dreams.

Tuesday 20 June

Bill and Merlin off at 9.00 for East Grinstead to lunch with Elizabeth, see Brambletye and stay at Wellington. Rather cold so we went to Anne's Tea Shop and had a raspberry milk whip and some cakes as a treat. Bill rang up from Tunbridge Wells to say that Merlin liked his school and all was well.

Wednesday 21 June

Spent day with Mary and twinnies. All very good and better without Merlin. Feel rather worried as to what we are to do when we leave here. Bill heard from Richard that there is no chance of his being absorbed. Bill and Merlin returned, very full of their time and how they had seen Hogben, also Harrison and Rob. All went very happily to bed.

Thursday 22 June

Had a lovely day all together on the beach. All bathed. Mer went with Bill to see Dr Ewing who has prescribed glucose, Minadex, quieter evenings and less rich food. We hope this will cure Master Mer.

Tuesday 27 June

John came to stay in the morning. Children delighted to see him. Bathed before lunch, all slept in afternoon and played games in evening before bed. All are very happy. Mrs H gave us an excellent dinner.

Wednesday 28 June

Cold and wet and windy. Bill, John and children bathed. In afternoon the Alexanders all came over, and though none bathed all enjoyed the seaside and built castles and ate an enormous tea. John left after dinner at 9.00. Sad he has been with us such a short time but so nice to see him and he never alters a bit.

Thursday 29 June

Wrote letters, shopped, paid bills and spent day on beach with Bill and children having a truly lovely lazy time. Bill and Merlin went sailing at Walton in afternoon.

Friday 30 June

In afternoon went over to Ipswich with Mary who rode and I shopped and took laundry. Had tea with Mum and Dad at Belstead. Mother very frigid and offhand and does not seem to want to have the twins to stay with Miss G and so I feel very depressed on my return especially as I left my bag behind. Bill had to fetch it for me in the morning.

Saturday 1 July

Paid Helen who seems to be very happy and settled. Fay and Richard arrived in an enormous Packard at lunchtime for weekend. They are both just the same and Richard especially delightful. He and Bill getting on like a house on fire. He spent most of afternoon on the beach picking up shells with Mary and doing the aquarium and taking photos of the children.

Sunday 2 July

We all spent a morning on the beach. In the evening took them for a walk along the front. After tea I put the children to bed. Fay seems to love the twins and very interested in Diddles (Cecily) her godchild. They left after dinner to return to London in their Packard.

Monday 3 July

Bill, M and M and I went off to London on 8.40 from Colchester and spent a most enjoyable day there. Took Mer and Mops to Harrods and there ordered all his clothes for Brambletye. Mary had her hair washed and set and looked very nice. To lunch with Fay and Richard at their flat at Queen Anne's Mansions. In afternoon went to Walton Place and interviewed a Mr Guy Church, architect and his surveyor about doing up the house.

Tuesday 4 July

Paid 2nd instalment of rent today and called at Tomkins office to inquire unsuccessfully if they had any other houses for letting during August and September. Bill and I are rather worried as time is getting short and I don't want to go back to Belstead. London is impossible until the autumn and everything seems very difficult.

Wednesday 5 July

Ian and Isabel Smith came to lunch. They left at 3.00 and we all spent afternoon by the sea. Bill and children all bathed, Merlin ever so much better re his dreams.

Thursday 6 July

Feel very worried as to what we are to do when we leave here. Bill and I dashed off to Hollesley to where we had heard of a house this morning, but find it hopeless. Very disappointing. Called at Pope's office in Ipswich and went to fish shop and laundry. Patricia arrived in the evening to stay.

Friday 7 July

Took Pat for a drive and showed her Frinton. In the morning children bathed. Isabel Durham and Jane came to lunch and then more bathing afterwards. Then Margaret Pelly and Jane arrived and more bathing! Tea and then dinner. Pat left and we all went to bed.

Saturday 8 July

Jane and Merlin seem to get on marvellously together and are very happy. The trolley swing and see-saw in the garden are a joy to the children when not on the beach. Went down to the hut and enjoyed a pleasant morning there. Claude arrived and bathed with Bill, Margaret and the children. He looks very tired. Mrs Hackett gave us a very good dinner of melon, chicken, ice and strawberries. Margaret brought us a box of sweets.

Sunday 9 July

A lovely day spent bathing and castle making. In afternoon Claude and Margaret and B. and I all slept. In evening had supper and to bed early as Claude has to catch an early train up to London.

Monday 10 July

Margaret and Jane bathed early with Bill and the children. Then they left and motored up to London. Miss G returned in the evening for which I was thankful as I am really feeling very tired of looking after children. She looks well and it was nice to see her again.

Tuesday 11 July

Bill and I left after breakfast to have a days house-hunting. Went to Ipswich and shopped and took laundry. Then went to see Dock Farm, Boyton which Bill immediately fell in love with and longed to buy. Then on to have a picnic lunch at Snape and so to Glebe Farm, Sternfield, a horrid dirty little place. Back to tea at Belstead and find family most awfully nice and very anxious that I should return there with the children in August.

Wednesday 12 July

After yesterday did not feel so depressed about plans for the future although it does seem pretty grim to have to go back to Belstead. Busy packing to go to London after lunch in YY. Bill and I took it in turns to drive. Went to Hyde Park Corner where Bill went to see Hughes. I went to Harrods to buy Dad's birthday present. Then to Jim and Gabriel's and changed there, then we all went in YY to the Berkeley where we had an excellent dinner and danced and very much enjoyed ourselves. Motored back to Frinton arriving 3:40 am.

Thursday 13 July

We woke and had breakfast with the children. Bill bathed before lunch and then we both rested. Mum and Dad came over after lunch and spent afternoon bringing with them boxes of fruit and vegetables. Children all bathed.

Friday 14 July

How sad it is we have only a few more days together. Felt full of misery at thought of my darling going away.

Saturday 15 July

Dad's 80th birthday. Bill and I busy getting packed up and ready to leave. Bathed as usual and spent afternoon together. Took children out for walk and M and M sat up with Miss G for dinner. Feel terribly sad.

Sunday 16 July

Very sad. This afternoon Bill left on 4.54 and it was awful. Mary, twins and I all cried. I tried to keep cheerful all morning and pray God it will be the last parting we shall have. I do hope it won't be long before he is home. Bill went to Holy Communion, then to beach and bathed. In afternoon packed and we sat together on the seat in the garden utterly sad and miserable. Tea and then the awful goodbyes. I took twins and M and M for a little drive to cheer them up, poor darlings. I rang him up at S. Western this evening at 11.00. He leaves Monday 3:45 am.

Monday 17 July
The house seems so awful without Bill. Had two letters from him. After lunch motored over to Belstead. Took Mary, Mrs H and May with me. Took laundry and a good many things too. Poured with rain and thunderstorm. Mother very nice.

Tuesday 18 July
Marian came to stay arriving after lunch. Took her for a walk along front and put YY in the garage for repairs to brakes. It is nice to have Marian here. Telegram from Bill to say he had arrived safely in evening.

Wednesday 19 July
Spent morning on the beach. In afternoon Marian and I went to watch tennis at Frinton Tennis Week and enjoyed it.

Thursday 20 July
Letter from Bill from Rome, apparently the wireless of the flying boat went wrong but after repairs all was well and they stayed in Rome instead of going on to Athens. Marian left early to motor home. Mother came and spent the day and Dad arrived in afternoon bringing fruit and vegetables.

Saturday 22 July
Mother rang up to say Ralph and Irene wanted to come to see me and the children. They came and sat on the beach. After tea I took Miss G, May and the children over to Clacton for the evening. Went on the pier and bought some things for weekend.

Monday 24 July
Had my first letters from Bill from Cairo this morning. Lovely to get them. He says it is very hot and dry there. Mer is getting on with his swimming splendidly. Took Helen over to Belstead with

me in the afternoon and was very busy getting straight. Made beds. Had tea with Mum and Dad, and returned in pouring rain at 7.30.

Tuesday 25 July

A lovely day. Our last at Frinton. Have been so happy here and enjoyed myself so hate to go. Very busy all morning paying bills. Heard from Elizabeth who wants Bill to be a godfather. Went down to the beach.

Wednesday 26 July

Had bad night waking several times with a horrid headache and so felt very tired in the morning. Off early after breakfast with the children and Miss G and Helen, three suitcases, aquarium and oddments. Arrived Belstead 9.30 and left them all, then back to Frinton for May, Mrs Hacketh to station. Goodbye to Frinton and back at Belstead for lunch.

Saturday 29 July

Mary, Merlin and I went off by train to London for a day out and to get away from Belstead. Went to Shapland for repairs to silver. Then to Piccadilly Grill for lunch which was excellent. Went then to Open Air Theatre in Regent's Park and saw Midsummer Nights Dream which M and M enjoyed very much. Mum and Dad both very cross when we came in late. To bed, livid and wish my Bill was here.

Monday 31 July

Took Mother shopping as Sturgeon on holiday. Wrote to Bill and had three letters from him which was lovely. Wrote to Collyer about trunk which has come without a key.

Thursday 3 August

Took Mother and children to Lord Woodbridge's Garden Party where they had a very good entertainment and an excellent conjuror which the children loved. Merlin went up on the platform.

Saturday 5 August

Went into Ipswich first with Mum and Dad and had my hair washed, secondly with twins to get Mer's trunk and laundry. Then as key of trunk lock had been found unpacked silver.

Monday 7 August

Packed before breakfast and hoped to leave at 9.00. However when I arrived at the garage found the car wouldn't start again. Fortunately Gosling sent his man up at once and put it right so I left with Mary and Merlin by 9.50 for Burnham. We made very good time. Went via Stowmarket, Woolpit, Thetford, Swaffham, Fakenham to Burnham arriving 12.30. Claude, Margaret, Jane made up the party. In afternoon children played on the shore and Merlin hit his head badly on a wooden bridge.

Tuesday 8 August

Claude left early to return to London. Merlin's head better today. Then we went bathing over at the Sands, which the children enjoyed very much. Merlin and Jane get on very well indeed together and are great friends. Margaret and I chatted and I suggested they should all come here in the event of War.

Wednesday 9 August

Another lovely day and the children bathed again. We left after lunch to return to Belstead. I was worried about the flywheel and self-starter but it started without a murmur and I kept old YY going until we got to Belstead. On the way ran into a partridge, killed it and brought it home for lunch with us.

Thursday 10 August

Busy day making preparations for Somerset. Took YY in and she is to be ready first thing on Saturday morning for our trip. Bill is most anxious I should keep filled up whilst we are away in case of an emergency.

Friday 11 August

Have my AA Routes and all necessary maps. Wrote to Bill and had 2 letters from him. Things seem to be settling down so hope to be able to get on with Walton Place on my return.

Saturday 12 August

Left at 10.00. Mother in front. Luggage on back, M and M and suitcases etc, macs and gumboots etc all in the back. The traffic being a Saturday and a lovely day, very heavy as far as Braintree, then eased off. We lunched at St Albans. Went via Tring, Aylesbury and Thame to Abingdon where we arrived at 5.00 at 'Crown and Thistle'. Had tea and then walked down to the river. Put M and M to bed, then had dinner with Mother. A very comfy Inn and well run.

Sunday 13 August

Could not sleep well for the very great noise last night and worrying about a new route for today. Left at 10.00 and went via Faringdon, Swindon, Devizes, and Trowbridge, we had lunch at a miserable place called Portway Arms. And then to Glastonbury where we arrived at 3.00. Found we had been given very nice rooms at The George. All settled and comfy so we went for a walk up the Tor to the top and got a lovely view.

Monday 14 August

Started at 9.30 and retraced our steps to see Wookey Hole Caves near Wells which thrilled the children. We had a long trip to get to Holnicote in time for lunch especially as the roads were very twisty all through Porlock and Minehead. Arrived 1.30 and thought the hotel charming and most comfortable. Mr Lamb the manager is quite delightful and runs it with his sister.

Tuesday 15August

Children are very thrilled as they sit up for dinner, the food is excellent and so they thoroughly enjoy it all. I took the car to Porlock and left it there to be greased up and shall fetch it tomorrow. Had letters from my darling; miss him so and how he would enjoy being here. The weather too is perfect, lovely sunny days and warm nights. Mary and I share downstairs bedroom; Merlin has one to himself and so has Mother.

Wednesday 16 August

Went to fetch YY but found she was not ready as the man had had to mend a ballrace in the back axle, so M and M were not able to go to Minehead for their bathe in the open air swimming pool. The weather is too hot for much walking.

Thursday 17 August

Another lovely day. YY was brought round at 11.00 so we went to Minehead and sent the Twins cream, bought some sweets, papers etc.

Friday 18 August

Went to Minehead for children's bathe which they enjoy. In afternoon went to Dunster to the Polo which was extremely poor. Mother seems to be enjoying herself but has unfortunately started a bad cold. Wrote to Dad and Giordy and told them we shall be home on Tuesday evening. Another lovely day but very hot. Had tea in the garden.

Saturday 19August

Went to Minehead and took the children for their last bathe. Holnicote is a perfect country hotel.

Sunday 20 August

Our last day here and went into Porlock to take in YY for final grease-up etc. Telegram came from my darling to say he thought we should get home **as soon as possible** and the news seems bad today. Packed as soon as we got in from church. YY came over looking clean, polished and already for the road tomorrow. Wrote to my love.

Monday 21 August

Had bad night after prodigious thunderstorms. We set off homeward bound by same route but got further, to Devizes for lunch at 1.00. Rotten lunch and Mother walked out without paying. Arrived Oxford at 4.00 and had tea and stayed at Randolph. Felt very tired indeed. So hot and thundery. Had car filled up.

Tuesday 22 August

Read in the papers that the news is very serious. The Germans having signed a non aggression pact with Russia behind our backs. Car went well, but we ran into rain at Tring and arrived for lunch at Saracens Head, Dunmow at 1.30. Very good lunch. Everywhere met troops and busy roads. Home for tea to find my darling twins and three lovely letters from my Billy.

Wednesday 23 August

Getting straight all day. News is bad and it looks like war and another terrific crisis. Wrote to Bill and feel very worried. Had a letter from May, also two from my darling.

Thursday 24 August

Miss G in a fever to see her sister in law, which is very tiresome at this particular time. However she must go tomorrow. Went to Ipswich and had hair washed and a fitting. In afternoon took Mother to Diss and Helmingham to see servants.

Friday 25 August

Took twins into Ipswich shopping. Laying in stores of food which we may need in case of emergency and evacuation. Feel very worried but refuse to believe the worst will happen. Oh dear how I wish my darling was safe and here with me. Can't sleep at night for worrying about him.

Saturday 26 August

My 35th birthday. Feel very middle aged and look it. Feel sad too and wish my darling was here and there was no war or threats of war. Went to Ipswich and bought more supplies with twins. My darlings have showered presents on me. Mary, an address book, Mer a pair of folding scissors and twins a puff. Bill has sent me a lovely powder case and a nightie and pair of knickers. Mother gave me £5, Dad £20 and Aunt Edie £1. Had a lovely birthday cake and feel everyone is trying to make me happy.

Sunday 27 August

Send a wire to Bill last night to thank him for all his presents. News seems to be no better and things are very critical. Added to which I feel extremely distressed as Margaret rang up to say might she come tomorrow and settle in and Mother immediately said she could not have Louise. Have not spoken to Mother since this, as I really felt too livid for words. Do miss my darling Billy so much.

Monday 28 August

I felt so annoyed with Mother over the whole thing I decided to go to Ipswich and see if Pope has any other houses to let. He says Sproughton Hall is available. Went to see it but could not get in. Was then told Sproughton Hall had been let.

Tuesday 29 August

Went to London for the day. Had letters from Bill before I left and wrote to him in the train. Busy shopping and getting final things settled in case there is a war. News looks very bad and situation seems to be very tense. However I have a feeling all will be well. Went and saw poor Aunt Edie who is very frail. I feel she ought to come here if war starts. Told Mother so who rang her up and suggested she should but it was hard to make her hear. Family much more pleasant.

Wednesday 30 August

Went to Ipswich for fitting. Bought more supplies and food in case of emergency.

Thursday 31 August

Went over to Aldeburgh after lunch with all the children, Helen and Mother with a picnic tea. Mrs Bowyer found us. We have arranged I am to fetch her as one of our refugees in the event of War and she is anyhow coming on Saturday. Heard on wireless evacuation from London starts tomorrow for the refugees. News is very bad. Had letters from Bill. Feel very worried and wonder whether they will stop the Air Mail to Egypt.

Friday 1 September

[The Germans unleashed their attack on Poland. The Polish Army was no match for them, with largely obsolete weapons, and surrendered 27 September].

Had another fitting at Smith and Harveys. Heard that Germany have attacked and bombed Poland and can see now no hope for it and that we shall be for it. Felt very worried. No good though. Tried to write a cheerful letter to Bill. God knows when I shall see him again if war does start, if ever.

Saturday 2 September

Awful day. Germans bombing the Poles and an ultimatum has been sent to the effect that unless they stop we shall fight them. How awful it is. Hectically busy all afternoon sticking black paper over windows and putting up thick curtains. The refugees arrived and I rushed backwards and forwards collecting them from Belstead School. Installed them in men's rooms, and cottages. No time for writing or anything. Very, tired but am unable to sleep.

Sunday 3 September.

[Britain, France, Australia and New Zealand declare war on Germany]. War declared at 11.15 this morning. How awful it is. But anyhow I feel it's right and the only to do. Thank heaven Italy is to be neutral so Bill should be all right as long as he is in Egypt. Spent day hectically trying to darken windows and help generally get the house ready. Feel very miserable and worried and wonder when I shall hear from him and also if we shall have air raids. Listened to the news. To bed early but could not sleep.

Monday 4 September

[The first victim, the *Athenia* sunk in the Atlantic].

Woke up wondering what on earth was the matter. Realised that we are at war with Germany. Listen to the news and heard that the Germans have sunk British ship *Athenia*. Took twins and Mary into Ipswich for a fitting at Miss Jeckell's. Busy morning. Lottie Bowyer busy blacking out windows with her maid Kate. Found Mother very trying and difficult. Feel if there is to be war I must move from here and get established somewhere if possible at once before petrol rationing starts.

Tuesday 5 September

Woken up at 6.45 to hear Air Raid Siren going. Got children together and took them down stairs. Then went up to my bedroom to see if I could see anything. Heard aeroplanes and eventually saw bombers being attacked by fighters and the machine guns going off like mad! Heard one of ours was down at Hintlesham and one at Tattingstone. Awful and such glorious peaceful and quiet September weather.

Wednesday 6 September

[This Air Raid was a false alarm. A tragic shambles resulted in the first British pilot fatality of the War, Pilot Officer Montague Hulton-Harrop. Hurricanes from North Weald and Spitfires from Hornchurch Airfield were scrambled. There was no identifying procedure for pilots and poor communication between planes and command centres. The Court Martial exonerated both Spitfire pilots ruling the case an unfortunate accident].

Another really lovely day. Wrote to Bill by airmail as I find there is one again. Mer and I set off after lunch to look at houses. Looked at Westerfield and Nether Hall, Ottery. Then to Winston Grange, Debenham, a terrible place. Home at 7.00. So warm too, and sunny. Perfect for partridge shooting.

Thursday 7 September

Ordered Merlin's tuck box and bought some tuck too. Wrote to Bill and posted it air-mail. Mother very difficult but hoping to move soon or shall not be able to stand being here.

Friday 8 September

Went to bed tired and very depressed. War news serious. The Germans seem to have practically finished off Poland already. Went to see Fiona who arrived at Blanche's, injured having driven into a telegraph post and smashed her car completely.

Saturday 9 September

The refugees in the cottage all left today for which we are thankful. Wrote to Mrs Blencowe about Mer. Went off at 11.00 with M and M for picnic lunch, which we had in a field and enjoyed. Then to see Grannie Lunn at Rendham and on to Southwold to see Mary and John Wilson and the boys. Found them all very fit except John who is really not strong yet. Merlin and Johnny took to each other and got on very well.

Sunday 10 September

Went to church at Belstead with the children. Went to see Fiona. Mother better and not so difficult. Margaret rang up to know whether I would care to share a house with her near Wincanton as Claude goes to France next week so she is shutting up London house.

Tuesday 12 September

Still lovely weather. No letters from Bill so don't know when I shall hear now. Feel at times extremely depressed and hate the thought of Merlin going off to school soon. Got his tuck box, his suitcase and everything. Wrote to Bill and am posting them on Mondays and Thursdays to catch Tuesday and Friday airmails. Had a talk to Mother and do not feel can remain here indefinitely. House is so difficult. I do not know what to do at all.

Wednesday 13 September

Went to see Fiona and say goodbye as she goes back to York tomorrow. Picked up my new bike that I have just bought and which goes like a bomb. I did not fall off either.

Friday 15 September

No letters from Bill yet. Do miss them so much and him too. Poor darling I feel so very sorry for him all alone out in Egypt with no hope of coming home. Have discussed with Mother the prospects of keeping poultry again and as she agreed I went to see Wilson about hiring his field. He also has agreed so went off in the car to Copdock Poultry Farm Sale; and bought a nice field house and two water hoppers and 24 Light Sussex 1939 pullets. Paid £11.9.0 for the lot, and got man to bring them all down. Spent afternoon and evening settling them down.

Saturday 16 September.

[Petrol was rationed and coupons were made available from Post Offices].

Am keeping my hens shut in for few days. They are quite a nice lot and the house is very nice indeed. Got food from the miller. Wrote to Blencowes and sent cheque. Went to Ipswich taking Merlin and Mary with me and bought several things for the poultry. Mother and Dad's 48th wedding anniversary today.

Sunday 17 September

My pullets keep me very busy. Let them all out today. Mary is very interested in them and is a great help. Am giving her one shilling a day for help she gives me with them. NTL from Bill came at lunchtime. Marvellous to hear from him. Wrote to him and also a NTL in reply. Mary cleaned out hen house with me. Lady Ailwyn called to know whether I would allow twins to have a Pekinese puppy, 9 months old as a present.

Monday 18 September

We seem to be getting inundated with animals. This morning I called to see Lady A. and thanked her for giving twins 'Baby,' I collected 'Baby'. She really is a perfectly sweet tiny sable Peke and no trouble so far. What was marvellous was two letters from Bill this afternoon. Oh dear such a joy! Sat down at once and wrote and sent a NTL telegram to him. My hens are all very well; now I want to try and get another two dozen.

Tuesday 19 September

Another letter from Bill. Wrote to him. It's beastly for him, poor darling, out in Egypt like this. War news not very good but I try and forget its horrors and bury myself in the country and with the children. Advertised for a pony and trap today. Last few days of Merlin being at home makes me feel sad.

Went with Mary to see some Light Sussex pullets today at Capel, also on to Boxted but we were warned by a policeman not to go as the man was a cheat. So we returned to Mr Birkett at Capel and bought a dozen L.S pullets, two prize winners. After tea went over to Barham to see pony advertised for sale. I thought it quite a good pony and a bargain so decided to buy it for £13.10.0. Home 7.30.

Thursday 21 September

Went over to Capel this afternoon to collect the pullets, paid 9/- each for them. In evening Mr Pratt arrived with the pony. Not impressed with my purchase but perhaps she will turn out better than she looks. Sad tonight to think my little boy will not be here tomorrow.

Friday 22 September

Off to London on 9.58 with dear Mer dressed in his school kit. Mother took his photo. Bought him a Rainbow and travelled up in a very full train arriving in London 12. 30. Victoria where we booked the luggage and then to meet Mary Wilson at Peter Jones restaurant. Found Beale there with the news that Johnny had had to have his tonsils out that morning. Poor Mer very disappointed not going with him but he cheered up when he was given the Wonder Book of Ships. I saw him off and felt utterly miserable. Hurried away and home as soon as I could.

Saturday 23 September

Felt a bit better but very sad without dear Merlin. Do miss him so. It was joy though to get a postcard from Mrs B to tell me he had arrived safe and was very cheerful, also to have two letters from my darling Bill written 14th and 16th. I lunched with Lady Ailwyn at Stone Lodge. Spent a good deal of day with the hens. Went to bed very early feeling utterly worn out after yesterday.

Monday 25 September

Felt very much better. Feel worried about Jenny [pony] who appears to have mange and a very sore back. Wrote to Bill and was thrilled to get five letters from him written between September 3rd. and 8th this afternoon.

Tuesday 26 September

Col. Castle came to see Jenny and pronounced mange. Rang the bank and stopped cheque to Mr Pratt. Mother and I went over to see him in the evening. He said he could not take Jenny back. However called at police station at Claydon on our way home. Called at the Alexanders, who said the war will be over in six months. An air mail letter from Bill this evening also one from Merlin and one from Blencowe saying he is getting on very well.

Wednesday 27 September

Took my bicycle and went for a ramble in Bentley Woods. Chickens seem well. Pratt came over this evening and collected the poor pony. She was as wild as a hawk and charged off up the hill. Very pleased she has gone.

Thursday 28 September

Lovely letters from Bill. They seem to be coming more regularly now. Wrote to him and posted in Ipswich. Took Mary out for a ride with me this afternoon. I walked beside her while she rode Sally round Sandy Lane and home.

Friday 29 September

Miss Giordan away for weekend and found when we arrived at the station she had left her gas mask behind. I sailed back here to get it and took her in again. Do miss Bill so dreadfully. It seems ages since we have been together.

Monday 2 October

Miss G returned at lunchtime and told me she would have to leave in a month's time as her sister in law has tuberculosis and she must look after her children. I expected this. It will be hard to replace her with anyone as adaptable. Mary and I cleaned out the hen house then she went for a ride on Sally.

Tuesday 3 October

Colder today. Mum very grumpy over children's food. Seems to think they eat too much. Took Mary up to Belstead to ride after lunch. Wish the pullets would start to lay.

Wednesday 4 October

Very cold today. Went to Ipswich in the car with Mum and Dad who are more pleasant. Miss Ensor, dancing mistress, came in afternoon and the children simply loved it, especially Mary, who really dances very nicely.

Thursday 5 October

Pouring wet morning. Up early, fed and watered the chickens and then got the car out and hurried off to Sale at Bredfield. Got there about 11.00. Bought Mary a curry comb and a grooming brush.

Then after lunch came the poultry. I bought six L. Sussex pullets for 7/9 and 8 pullets for 5/3. Disappointed with second lot who I did not think much of as are too young to be much good. Home for tea. Let the pullets out and they soon settled down. I fear one is a cockerel.

Friday 6 October

[Fighting in Poland comes to an end].

No letters from Bill. Went into Ipswich in the car and had 4 gallons of petrol put in. Miss Death came to give Mary her music lesson. Wrote to Bill and Merlin.

Saturday 7 October

Lovely as I have two letters from my darling and some photos. I feel quite different now. Found one of my best Birkett pullets seedy lying huddled in the grass. Took her and put her in the coop on a bed of hay and gave her a dose of castor oil. Feel she will not live. Mrs Murdoch had a heart attack after dinner.

Sunday 8 October

A lovely day but cold. Bicycled up to church at Belstead before breakfast. Pullet better which is surprising.

Monday 9 October

Tried unsuccessfully to get Mary's dancing slippers. Pullet much better. Do not feel others will fatten successfully so shall have both killed tomorrow.

Tuesday 10 October

Morphew killed the pullet and cockerel. The other pullet is back with the others, quite recovered. Wrote letters to governesses etc. And shall go to London on Tuesday to see Miss Shephard, Miss Button, Miss Welsh and Miss Riley. Went for bike ride round Chattisham and Washbrook as it was such a lovely afternoon.

Wednesday 11 October

Wrote to Bill and had 2 letters from him enclosing one for M and C and C and a book for them. Went for bike ride up to Copdock in afternoon. Mrs Murdoch still ill and Mother, poor dear is doing the cooking. Helen gave notice yesterday.

Thursday 12 October

Another lovely day, after very heavy rain all night. Up early as usual to feed chickens. Advertisement in *East Anglian* today for children's maid. Went up with Mary to Miss Cubitts. I went on my bike and Mary rode and like that we got along very well. Mrs Murdoch left this morning. Made out expenses list for Hughes when I see him on Tuesday.

Friday 13 October

Such a glorious day after a very misty morning. Mary and I set off at 11. 30 for an expedition which was great fun. Went to Chattisham to Church Farm. She on Sally and I on my bike. Went by Mrs Wise's and on through the country lanes. It was lovely. We tied Sally up to a post, sat and had our lunch at the foot of a hayrick. Mr Hempson was the auctioneer. We did not buy anything though we bid for some ducks, Khaki Campbells up to 3/9 each, and some hen coops. Pepper bit a pullet and I have had to put her in a coop. Doubt if she will live, poor thing.

Saturday 14 October

Very wet day after yesterday's glorious one. Sally quite tired after her outing. My pullet seems better but was bitten through the leg so can't walk, poor thing.

Sunday 15 October

Gave Baby a worm capsule. Fed chickens. Went with Mum and Dad and Mary to St Mary le Tower. Pouring wet all day long and east wind. Pullet improving.

Tuesday 17 October

Went off to London on 7. 45 train, up at 6.30 and out to chickens, feeding, watering etc. Then had some tea, bread and butter before leaving at 7.30 for station. Caught train, changed at Colchester. Saw Hughes and was with him until 12.15. Discussed my will, guardianship of children, and the surrender of Walton Place which he is hopeful about. Interviewed six governesses after a quick lunch at Fortnum's. Ordered felt hat and home on 4 o'clock train. Three letters from my darling, to cheer me up.

Wednesday 18 October

Wrote a long letter to Bill and posted to Wing Commander Paynter as he is flying out by Imperial Airways on Friday. Enclosed Hughes letter. Heard from F/O Gauvain at Martlesham that he wants to know about accommodation there. Don't know in the least who he is. Wrote to Miss Stephenson and engaged her as governess to come instead of Miss G. Very annoyed to find that Lady Ailwyn wants to have Baby back when Miss G leaves. Wrote her a stiff letter and sent Miss G. up with it.

Thursday 19 October

Had letter from Lady A. who is keeping Baby. Vile woman. Took Mother over to Stowmarket in YY to see a cook as Mrs Robins is leaving tomorrow. Pouring rain all day long and cold. Miserable for the hens.

Friday 20 October

Worried about governess problem, as seemed to be no further forward. Heard from Mr Gauvain that he is coming to lunch on Sunday. Expect he will be an awful bounder.

Sunday 22 October

Walked up to church with Mary and Mother, such a lovely morning. An appeal made by old Usherwood for widows and dependants touched me and I sent him one guinea this afternoon. Mr Gauvain came to lunch and is very nice. Tall and big and very good looking. Mum and Dad both liked him too. He is to be married on Saturday.

Tuesday 24 October

Mother went away to Newbury to stay with Harold and Ursula for a few days. Wrote letters and did mending all afternoon. Very, very dull.

Wednesday 25 October

Marvellous to have two letters from my love this morning. Makes life seem quite different. I do miss him so. Very cold day.

Thursday 26. October

Posted long letter to Bill. Mother returned from Newbury at 6.00. I spent nice day in the house as it was so bitterly cold but Dad had heating put on which helped matters a lot. Mother very full of talk of Cheam. [Fanny's first cousin, Rev. Harold Taylor, bought Cheam School in 1921 and is Headmaster].

Friday 27 October

Went over to Hintlesham to Poultry sale in the car. Pouring with rain and a poor lot of L. Sussex, other hens and odd scrap lot of poultry appliances. Bought large linen basket in very good condition. Spent afternoon cleaning it and the hen house out. Postman bought me a letter from my darling that will be a joy to have and read again and again over the weekend.

Saturday 28 October

Miserable wet morning for our trip to Brambletye but we started at 9.20. Our suitcases packed and off we went in YY leaving Helen and Mother to deal with the hens. All went well till we got to Brentwood where I lost my way, however we got to Tunbridge Wells at 1.15 and had lunch at Calverley. Good but dear, 4/- each. Then on to Brambletye. Saw Mr and Mrs B. and then my darling Merlin. Lovely to see him, and he seems a complete schoolboy with schoolboy language and quite different somehow. Went to tea at Felbridge Hotel which was poor but I was so afraid of using too much petrol. Mary and I went to Roebuck on Ashdown Forest which is lovely and a nice bedroom. Bitterly cold.

Sunday 29 October

Still very cold and wet. Mary and I had an excellent breakfast. Then went for a walk till it was time to fetch Merlin in the car. Collected him and then went to Elizabeth's house which is quite nice. She and Gordon were very kind and it was lovely to see nannie again and my nephew Richard, a dear little baby. We left after lunch then collected Johnnie Wilson and took him and Mer out to tea at the Roebuck. They ate a huge tea. Took the boys back at 5.30. Felt sad to say goodbye to my darling boy. [Elizabeth, Bill's sister, married Gordon Hubback, a Naval Officer].

Monday 30 October

Mary and I got up early, paid bill, £2.18.0. very reasonable. Then to see Peggy. Great fun to see her and Vernon again. Mary and I stayed till 11.30 then on to Tunbridge Wells. M. and I had lunch at the Weavers and then to Gravesend where we just missed the ferry and I posted a letter to Bill. We got home only putting in two gallons of petrol, so have six left for month of November.

Tuesday 31 October

Very busy getting straight after being away in every way. Letters, clothes to tidy, hens to clean out and all their utensils etc. Twins remaining in Mary's room together, so I have Mary to sleep with me and have had one oak bed moved into spare room.

Thursday 2 November

Miss G went off at 9.30 with her cheque for £17.10.0. The children did not seem to mind though. Lovely to get a letter from my love. And one from the governess in Cumberland who sounds quite hopeful.

Friday 3 November

A lovely day and quite warm, hens all well but I do wish they would start to lay. They are jolly lazy! Heard from governesses and wrote to them. Children and I all had breakfast in dining room. They are no trouble. Took twins into Ipswich and left Mary with Sally riding. Tea and then to the hens. Wrote to my love. Do miss him more and more as days go by.

Saturday 4 November

Very wet morning. Up early to get twins dressed and out as usual to deal with the chickens before breakfast.

Monday 6 November

A lovely day, spent with the children. Took them into Ipswich with me in the morning and shopped. Have very little petrol left. No letter from Bill. Mary went to Freeman who said she must have a tooth out so we arranged for Dr Banks to give her gas on Friday.

Tuesday 7 November

Went to London on the 9 o'clock train. Left YY at the station. Had a long day interviewing governesses. In morning saw a Miss Dixon who was doubtful. In afternoon saw a Miss Morgan-Davies who I liked the best and decided to engage. A terrible Miss Hall and a Miss Curtis, also a Miss Stapleford. Did not like any very much.

Friday 10 November

A lovely day. Took Mary to Freeman at 10.30 and Dr B gave her gas and she had her tooth out, poor child. Then to Mrs Wise's for tea in afternoon with Mary which we both enjoyed very much.

Saturday 11 November Remembrance Day

Heard from Miss Morgan-Davies that she is coming on Monday. Out with children for a long walk over to Belstead.

Sunday 12 November

Such a lovely day went off for a walk all the way up to the train bridge and collected wildflowers etc. on the way. My last day with the children [without a governess]. Took them out again in afternoon.

Monday 13 November

Letters from my darling and sent him one today. Hens all better, except one who shows no sign of improvement. After lunch went to meet Miss Morgan-Davies at 3.00. Have sold six pullets for 6/6 to Miss Jowers so making a good profit.

Tuesday 14 November

Lovely warm day. Another letter from Bill. Felt very sad and depressed all day. So miserable, cried and cried tonight and do long so for my Bill and a home of my own.

Wednesday 15 November

Felt better today, and determined to cheer myself up, so went off to a Sale at Alderman Rand's house, 20, Fonnerau Road and bought two lots of glass for 4 shillings. Very nice glass too, jugs, butter dishes, etc. stayed all the morning. Miss M-D seems to be settling down. Lovely day, but colder.

Thursday 16 November

Had a lovely letter from Bill. Mary is busily preparing Sally for the expedition to Hintlesham Meet tomorrow. Unfortunately, found she had lost a shoe. Morphew had to take her to the Blacksmith at Copdock and get her shod. Do not much care for Miss M-D.

Friday 17 November

Up very early. Fed the pullets and then took Mary on my bike up to Belstead to join Miss Cubitt. From there she went to Hintlesham to the Meet. Very few people there but Mary simply loved it and followed before getting home at 1.00. I took Mother in YY into Ipswich and took the six L.S. pullets to Mrs Jowers.

Saturday 18 November

No letters from Bill. Feel so tired of it and dried up, this beastly war and do miss my sweet darling so. Went for bike ride after lunch up to Copdock and round to Belstead and from there home. Turned all clocks back one hour, end of Summer Time.

Tuesday 21 November

Went to Ipswich in YY almost on last drop of petrol! Went to the market. I had never been before, heaps of hens, ducks, cocks, pigeons and rabbits all herded together in small pens. Mother came too. In afternoon took Mary for a ride.

Wednesday 22 November

A lovely letter from Bill, wrote to him. Miss M-D quite hopeless, children don't like her so have decided to give her notice.

Thursday 23 November

Went into Ipswich and had car filled up with petrol. Posted my letter to Bill, do miss him so.

Friday 24 November

Mary and I went for ride in afternoon. Had two hens killed by Morphew which have had colds. The Southgates here all day finishing my coops and duck house.

Saturday 25 November

Had a letter from Bill that made the whole day lovely. Went off to a sale at Stowmarket. The poultry all fetched good prices and the ducks that I was after, 8/6 each. I did not get anything, but I do want to get some Khaki Campbell ducks.

Monday 27 November

Letter from my darling, how I wish I was with him. Went to Ipswich in the morning and cleaned out hen house after lunch. Eileen Taylor [cousin] came to stay arriving at teatime. [Eileen Taylor's father was Ralph Taylor, the Bishop of Sodor and Man].

Tuesday 28 November

Had a letter from Merlin saying he was top of his form last week. Awfully pleased about this. Went to the market and took Eileen, M and M and the twins. Twins enjoyed the market. I took Mary for a bike ride up to Wherstead. She on Sally, and me on my bike. Eileen, a nice girl, but exceedingly dull.

Wednesday 29 November

Had a letter from my darling. Hens not laying yet. Had a pullet killed so now have 37. Saw 12 balloons up over Harwich way this afternoon when out feeding the pullets.

Thursday 30 November

[Soviet troops invade Finland].

Helen had day off today so busy with the children. Posted my Christmas parcel to Bill and wrote to him as I believe convoy goes on 2nd.

Friday 1 December

Letter from Bill. News seems to be better too and it was a nice day so I felt very happy. No eggs yet. I am getting very fed up with the pullets. Food going up in price, scarcer and difficult to obtain. Went for bike ride with Eileen and Mary up to Copdock, Mary on Sally and Eileen on Helen's bike.

Tuesday 5 December

Decided to wire Miss Phillips to come temporarily to me over Christmas. Miss M-D pretty useless and gets on my nerves. I dislike her very much and shall be pleased when she is gone.

Wednesday 6 December

Went into Ipswich in YY and shopped with Mother. In afternoon Mr Garvain came to tea and brought his wife with him. She is a nice girl and very nice looking. Feel I am starting a cold. Went to bed early and took an aspirin.

Thursday 7 December

[Denmark, Norway and Sweden declare their neutrality].

Felt very seedy, with a streaming cold! However started writing Christmas cards and letters all morning and most of the afternoon. Went off to bed as soon as I had fed the chickens.

Friday 8 December

Mother's birthday. I gave her a vase and Bill six soup cups and covers. Dad a prayer book etc. I stayed in bed as my cold was so bad. I had temperature of 100 last night. Letters from my darling which was lovely and made me so happy.

Saturday 9 December

A lovely day though, so the twins and I set to work to clean out the hen house in the sun. Had lovely time reading my darling's letters over and over again. Do miss him so very much.

Sunday 10 December

Lovely day. Hutch wired that he was arriving by air at Ipswich airport for lunch so took YY to meet him there. John Peel arrived for lunch by car and to stay. John does not seem to think that is much hope of Bill coming home. This is very sad. We all went to see Hutch off in his aeroplane. Weather glorious. I wish the hens would lay and do miss my Bill so utterly.

Monday 11 December

A lovely day. Mary went for a ride with John. John left after lunch to motor up to Cranwell where he is to stay for a few days hunting. Wrote and posted long letter to my own darling love. Dad went off to Tunbridge Wells.

Tuesday 12 December

Dad returned in evening. Posted all Xmas cards and letters. Busy in Ipswich buying Xmas presents. How I wish this bloody war would end.

Wednesday 13 December

MY FIRST EGG! So thrilled nearly died of delight when I went out first thing and found it. A lovely long pointed brown egg. Miss Morgan-Davies left which was another joy. Took her to station. Thankful she has gone.

Thursday 14 December

Lovely day, spent with children. We all went to Ipswich and shopped for Christmas. In evening met Miss Phillips whose train was very late, and she brought a frightful lot of luggage. She is a lady but do not care for her very much. No eggs today.

Friday 15 December

[5th British Regular Division arrives in France].

Miss P out with the children. Went to Ipswich in YY to see about Miss P's luggage being sent out. Shopped for final Christmas calendars and presents and posted them off.

Monday 18 December

Had two letters from Bill. Went off up to London on 11.35 train after doing laundry, seeing hens (two eggs today). Lunched on train and arrived 1.40. Met Miss Newling, new governess at The Grosvenor. Like her and engaged her. Unpacked and then walked to Queen Anne's Mansions to tea with Fay. Stayed with her till 6.00 then had a bath and wrote to Bill. Then John came and took me out to dinner at Pruniers. I did not enjoy it as I could only think of Bill.

Tuesday 19 December

Had breakfast in bed, then paid my bill and wrote to my darling before meeting my little son at 9.40 at Victoria. Met Mary and John Wilson on the platform. Then saw Mer. Lovely to see him again looking well but very dirty. Went to Harrods and ordered a bike and bought some toys for him. Home arrived late at 3.40 where

Sturgeon met us with YY. The twins, Mary and grandparents all were thrilled to have him home.

Wednesday 20 December

Mer's report which was in his trunk is wonderfully good. He is top in exams and 2nd in term work. Feel awfully pleased and proud of him. Went into Ipswich with Mer and Mary to do their Christmas shopping. Pullets laying and more eggs today. One lays daily under the dining room window, called May by the twins.

Thursday 21 December

Letters from Bill. Parcels are arriving daily in shoals for the children. Wrote to Bill's Mother arranging to go there on 29th. Wrote for Miss Newling's reference as have decided to have her after Christmas. Do not care for Miss Phillips. Mrs Gauvain came to lunch after riding on Lucy with Mary. Mary much enjoyed it.

Friday 22 December

Very busy doing final Christmas preparations. Decorated the tree. Mother has given M and M a ping-pong table which is a great thrill. Pullets laying quite well and I'm getting three or four eggs a day now. Wrote to my darling and had a letter from him. How sad it is to think of Christmas without him here with the children.

Saturday 23 December

Cleaned out hen-house. Got very little petrol left. Did up last of Christmas presents. Children very busy doing theirs. Wrote my diary and poultry accounts book up-to-date.

Sunday 24 December

Christmas Eve. We all went to Belstead Church. Mrs Milbank gave the three girls each a pearl necklace which they were delighted with. In the evening had the Christmas tree and all the servants got their presents. Dad gave me £10, Mother a dressing jacket, Mary and Merlin and twins each had some of their presents. Very cold and really quite like Christmas with the frosty crisp weather.

Monday 25 December: Christmas Day.

Oh how I have missed my own darling love today. Simply can't bear it and being away for so long is so awful….. Awful! Went up in YY to Holy Communion and took Mother. Breakfast and opening of parcels and clearing of paper, cardboard and string! What a day. Sir C.S., Miss Davies and Mrs Gauvain came to lunch. I hated it and wished we had been alone. All children very happy, and all got something from the pudding. To bed at 9.30, so very tired. Do love and miss Bill so.

Wednesday 27 December

Bitterly cold. Children busy writing letters of thanks with Miss P who I really much dislike. Helen arrived back very late after her day off which made me very cross. I roared her up, she gave notice and was very rude indeed.

Thursday 28 December

Went off at 10.15 by train to Saxmundham where we arrived at 1.00 and were met by taxi sent from Mrs Lunn. It was a bitterly cold day and we felt frozen. Mrs L and George very pleased to see us and gave us a very good lunch. Roast chicken and beef, jellies and treacle pudding, cheese, coffee and sweets. Came home on 3.50 train. Snowing hard. Mother had taken C and C to lunch at Felixstowe. We picked them up at station and I drove them all home to tea in YY.

Friday 29 December

Mary not feeling very well. Took YY into Ipswich for last time. Hardly any petrol left. Great difficulty in getting poultry food and hay for Sally. Helen most idle and trying.

Saturday 30 December

[Finns inflict humiliating defeat on Russians**]**.

Mary sick all night and temperature of 102 and very seedy. Had a very busy day looking after her. Miss P. is giving Merlin arithmetic for half an hour daily which he loathes. Mary better in evening.

Sunday 31 December

Merlin has a temperature of 102 and feels sick and dizzy. I am isolating the twins. Fire in my room all day and put Merlin into my bed for night and slept in dressing room with Smigly [Siamese cat}. Hens laying very well and am getting 5 to 7 eggs daily now. Am selling a dozen to Miss Davies weekly now. Felt very sad and depressed at being away from my darling. Do hope and pray this miserable war will soon be over and my darling will soon be home again.

'Parting. The parting of people who love each other and are separated, whether endured oneself or witnessed in others — mothers and sons, husbands and wives, lovers and friends — without news or only with uncertain news, with alternating fears and hopes, this belongs to the category of pain that is never wiped out, that leaves a permanent scar. "Ayez pitié de ceux qui s'aimaient et ont été séparés".'

Taken from *Images and Shadows* by Iris Origo.

The children & Sally 1938

Mary and Sally Woodbridge Show 1939

Mary Frinton 1939

Frinton '29' 4th Avenue 1939

Merlin Frinton

Merlin leaves for Brambletye
with tuck box & gas mask Sept. 1939

Lee Abbey Lynton Brambletye evacuated here 1940

Mary, Twins and hens 1939   Cesca and Light Sussex hens 1939

Tostock Mary's 12 Birthday 1942

Parham House 1931

Parham after being rebuilt on Forest Road, Tunbridge Wells

1940
Belstead and Pardlestone.

The winter of 1939/1940 was the coldest since 1881. The River Thames froze. On 20 January -18C degrees of frost were recorded in London followed by floods. Cesca's flock of chickens prove to be a good investment, but take up much of her time. In March Bill is promoted. The escalation of the War- invasion of the Low Countries and France followed by the retreat of the Allied forces culminating in the evacuation from Dunkirk- forced Cesca to leave Belstead (and her parents). On 27 May Merlin's prep school decides to decamp to Lynton Somerset. In June Cesca succeeds, with great difficulty, in evacuating her four children, Miss Newland, some chickens, the pony Sally, Smig the Siamese cat and furniture to a cottage near Kilve, away from the bombing. But the bombs follow her. And the months apart from Bill increase with no end in sight. I have deleted many of the entries of 'wrote to Bill' to avoid repetition. They both write daily. Shopping in Ipswich is a daily occurrence but has mostly been deleted.

Monday 1 January
Felt very sad all day. So sad without my Bill & no prospect of seeing him & no letters at the moment. Miss Philipps, the temporary governess, is a tiresome old bird.

Thursday 4 January
Miss Philipps left at noon. Children and I extremely delighted to see the back of her! 'The Philippine Islands' as Mer calls her. Two letters from my darling which cheered me up a lot.

Friday 5 January
Mer, Clare & I went into Ipswich by bus. Took two doz. eggs in for Miss Davies & left them at Freemans [the dentist]. Lovely, cold and frosty day, glorious for a walk.

Saturday 6 January
Terribly foggy and cold day. Miss Newling should have arrived this afternoon. At 5.00 the telephone rang to say she was at station. But Osborne refused to come out owing to fog so she had to spend the night at Station Hotel, poor thing. Made hot buttered toast for tea and had egg sandwiches.

Sunday 7 January

Miss Newling arrived at 9.15 in Osborne's taxi. I liked her and so do the children who she immediately took for a walk. Dad went off to bed with bad cough and looks very seedy. Weather still cold and thick fog.

Monday 8 January [Ration books for sugar, butter, ham and bacon are introduced. Followed in due course by meat, jam, biscuits, breakfast cereals, cheese, eggs (1 per person per week), lard, milk and canned and dried fruit]. Did the laundry and went into Ipswich. Cecily not very well, found she had temperature of 102. Wrote to Bill and wonderful to get a letter from him at teatime.

Tuesday 9 January

Cecily still temperature of 102, and very seedy, poor child. Gave her cod-liver oil. Mr Packard came to tea.

Wednesday 10 January

Cecily better. Two letters from Bill which was glorious. Had hair washed, went to Ipswich by bus.

Friday 12 January

Dad up for first time since Sunday. Looks very seedy, poor dear and cough is bad.

Saturday 13 January

Very cold indeed. Miss N. a great success with children who like her and call her 'Newie'.

Monday 15 January

Helen is beyond measure impossible. However dealt with her and am writing to the new girl Bernice, asking her to come as soon as possible. Letter from Marjorie suggesting that I should go out to Egypt with her. It seems too wonderful to be true: if only I could! Went to fetch Mary and Sally at the blacksmith's who was being shod. In the cold evening twilight walking home, Egypt felt so utterly delicious and desirable that I feel like throwing all caution, care of the children, to the four winds and going with Marjorie to be with my darling.

Tuesday 16 January

A letter from Bill saying I should not come out unless I was quite happy if unable to return. I suppose he is right, but oh such a chance missed. Oh dear! Wrote to Marjorie and said I could not come with her. Decided to send Helen off on Thursday and get new girl Bernice Marsh to come that day. Thick snow everywhere and all pipes freezing up. 16°of frost.

Wednesday 17 January

More snow and frost. Wrote to Bill a long letter, miss him so. Poor hens still laying very well and have had six eggs most days.

Thursday 18 January

Helen left, squabbled over her wages and generally behaved shockingly. Wrote and posted letter to my darling love. New girl Bernice came. Six eggs from hens. Still a lot of snow and ice everywhere.

Friday 19 January

New girl seems to be getting on very well so far. A treat, after Helen's rudeness. Lady Hope came to lunch. She has aged a great deal and looks ill, poor dear. Very good lunch of eggs au gratin, Roast chicken, sausages, cold beef, vegetables and raspberry cream and plum pudding. Merlin went skating with Mother in afternoon. More snow and weather icy. Snow fell again, do hate this cold. Out tobogganing in afternoon. Mother has two new housemaids.

Sunday 21 January

Snowed all day. Poor hens and animals, it's awful for them. Mum and Dad very grumpy. Feel very cold and depressed.

Monday 22 January

Snow 10 inches deep and drifts in places of three and four feet. Terrific weather, snowed nearly all day and freezing all the time. Five eggs which considering weather is a marvel.

Tuesday 23 January

A sunnier day and no more snow. Letter from Bill enclosing cheque for £1 for Mer. Had letter from Kensington Rates at Kensington Town Hall saying the government have commandeered 2 Walton Place for an Air Raid shelter for 75 people. What happens now about rent to Cluttons? Will it help or not? Writing to Hughes about it.

Wednesday 24 January

Miss Ensor came for second lesson. Children all love their dancing classes. Busy packing Mer's things. Had six letters from Bill yesterday.

Thursday 25 January

Mer's last day at home. A much better day and warmer. Busy packing Merlin's things in the morning. Then to Ipswich, with him and Mum in the car. Shopped and bought presents for twins and Mary's birthday for Mer to leave for them. Then we went to Limmers and had some hot chocolate and coffee. In afternoon I cleaned out the hen house and gave it a thorough spring clean. Disinfected it all and the utensils. Had seven eggs. In evening played games, then a man called Mr Oxburrow was announced. He was a detective inquiring about Helen and the kitchen maid Elsie who have been associating with two soldiers who have committed a serious robbery.

Friday 26 January

Had a bad night and woke up feeling tired and depressed. No letters from Bill. Up early and bitterly cold. Went out early to do the chickens and then up to London on the 9 o'clock train with Mer. Dear little boy is so good and sweet. We left his luggage at Victoria station. Then up to see Hughes at 11.30. Found he had made various enquiries about 2, Walton Place. I decided to go and look at Walton Place but Harrods had not got the key. Then went to the house found it in the most ghastly state, four men tearing down the basement walls and pulling the whole place to pieces. The bath was in the area full of rubble and the men sitting by a fire made of my bathroom wood fittings. To think of Walton Place like that is awful! Took Mer off to lunch with Mary, Johnny and Andrew Wilson at Queens restaurant, Sloane Square. Mary gave us a very good lunch. Afterwards M. and I went to Peter Jones.

Then to station and goodbye to my little son on 3.18 train. Came home sad and very cold. Heavy fall of snow again. Arrived home in a snow drift.

Saturday 27 January.

Another heavy fall of snow and snowed all day.

Sunday 28 January

Frightfully cold freezing all day and icy east wind. Pullets exceeded themselves and laid nine eggs today.

Monday 29 January

Still bitter. Miss N. out in afternoon so I had the children, we made hot buttered toast and had egg sandwiches for tea. Pullets marvellous, 10 eggs today.

Tuesday 30 January

A letter from Mer saying he had been moved up to 4 B. Very pleased about this. Went to Ipswich with Dad by bus. Snow in drifts 5 foot high down the lane! Morphew cleaned out the hen house for me. A joy! Had a nice hot cup of coffee in Limmers before coming home by bus.

Wednesday 31 January

No letters from Bill yet. Oh dear! When will they come? Do miss him so utterly. Snow thawing slightly but everything terribly slippery. Had a dozen eggs today, very good.

Thursday 1 February

No letters from Bill or news of Merlin. The Garvains came to tea and Betty Bromfield. The twins adore the former and were quite ridiculous over them. Very cold still and freezing.

Friday 2 February.

Heard from my darling posted by a flying boat pilot returned from Egypt, that he had heard from John that instead of returning home as he had hoped they are increasing the period in Egypt from three to five years. Possibly Bill may exchange with someone in Iraq and go there for the two years. I can't bear it and feel more miserable than words can say. Mrs Garvain came over to help exercise Sally.

She was very nice and kind but I felt desperately upset all day long.

Saturday 3 February

Felt a bit better, but still utterly depressed. Heard too that Merlin's school has German measles. More misery. Also Cluttons still consider me their tenant at 2 Walton Place. How I hate Cluttons. Hens laying well. Mary and twins flourishing. These are my two bright spots, oh dear! In afternoon Mother and I went over to the Sale View at Horkesley Park. Caught 1.45 bus to Colchester and from there taxi to the dreary and primitive house. Not a bathroom! Not very much we liked and the few things we want I shall get Stamford's clerk to bid for. Home by bus after tea in Colchester. Ten eggs. Felt better and more cheerful.

Monday 5 February

Four letters from Bill this morning and three more this afternoon. Feel very worried as in the last ones he is not well. Also heard Merlin has Flu again. Worried about my two darlings and feel helpless and miserable. Went to Corder's sale in the morning and got some things for the children.

Tuesday 6 February

Off to London on 9.00 train. Very late getting up to town owing to fog. Arrived 11.45 and went straight to see Metier about the Income tax that seems very satisfactory. Then to see the surveys for 2 Walton Place and then to lunch at Searcy's which I enjoyed. Telephoned Miss Webb for Mother and Hughes, to whom I went later. Home by 5.12 and back at 7.45 very late, owing to fog. Mary awake, she got ten eggs today. Enquired at Cooks about prospects of going out to Egypt which seem good.

Thursday 8 February

Heard from Mrs Blencowe that Merlin's temperature was still up. Feel worried and shall ring up later today to enquire. Took Cecily into Ipswich to dentist by bus and returned same way. Letters from Bill in afternoon.

Friday 9 February

A pc this evening saying Mer was still in bed with temperature. Mary and I had the day off and went on 9.50 bus to Colchester to collect Mother's cut glass water jugs which she got at Horkesley Park. Found the things had not been brought out. This meant we had to go and fetch them by bus to Nayland and then walk. Got the things and by bus back to Colchester by 1.30. Had lunch at Neale and Roberts and ordered cakes for twins' birthday. Back to Belstead at 3.30. Fed chickens and got Sally in. Such a cold day and icy wind.

Saturday 10 February

A very worrying letter from Mrs B about Mer, referring to his bronchitis, first I had heard of it. I rang up but line out of order. Then rang up Elizabeth and she confirmed that he had bronchitis. Decided to go down tomorrow first train.

Sunday 11 February

Had a sleepless night of worry and dreams of Mer. Packed my suitcase and caught 9.30 to London. Then 12.42 Three Bridges and taxi from there to Elizabeth's. Thank God, the child had not got pneumonia as I feared. She and G took me up to Brambletye. I saw Mrs B and then up to see Mer who I thought looked very ill and drawn. He was in a small room with another boy. Temperature normal but up at night and had been 104 yesterday, don't like him being in sheets and having a gas stove and no kettle but, what can I do? Went to tea with Elizabeth and saw my nephews. And then rang up Dr Somerville who seem satisfied with Merlin. Wired Bill. Rang Mother. Stayed night at Telbridge.

Monday 12 February

What a queer wedding anniversary day. However thank heavens Merlin is much better. Poor dear little chap. I took him some grapes, saw the doctor about getting him home, he doesn't approve. Then I lunched with Elizabeth at Letherby & Christopher. Then went back, saw Merlin and took him some toys and then came back to hotel. Felt utterly tired and sad. Wrote to Bill and rang Mother and Elizabeth.

Tuesday 13 February

Up early. Bitterly cold still, and snowing hard. Hate this awful weather that seems unending. Had breakfast, paid bill and telephoned Mrs Blencowe and was delighted to hear Merlin was really better. Elizabeth called for me at the hotel and took me to the station. Then I went up to London arriving at 11.00. Left my luggage at Liverpool Street and spent the day shopping. Went to Plunketts to see about a toilet table set for Mary and then to Raynes, Fortnum & Mason and Harrods where I ordered some more pyjamas for Merlin. I went to the bank and had lunch at Searcy's, then to Peter Jones and Harvey Nichols. Came home on the 3.40 and had tea on the train. Felt terribly tired and done. Mother had a lovely fire in my room and after dinner I simply tumbled into bed and slept and slept.

Wednesday 14 February

My darling, twinnie girls' 6th birthday. If only Bill had been here. I had a telegram from him yesterday. Twins inundated with lovely presents and so happy and sweet. In afternoon Mrs Gardyne brought Patrick and Simon and Mrs Jeffcock, David and two nurses so we had quite a party. A lovely cake for the twins, red and white with six candles each side. Isobel D and Marian sent presents. Aunt Edie and Bill gave them toys so did Mother. Painting books, a paintbox and Nannie a huge parcel of things. Also things from Newie.

Thursday 15 February

Trying to get a bit straight and then off to the Sale in Westerfield Road where I took sandwiches and spent the day thoroughly enjoying myself. I bought a brass stew pan for 10 guineas, a set of coffee cups and saucers, pot and cream jug for 6/-,a Delft tea service of 39 pieces for 8/- and ten egg poachers and eighteen scallops in French fine china for 2/- and for Mother a wicker chair 11/-. Came home by bus.

Friday 16 February

Two letters from my own darling, best beloved sweetheart which made the whole day rosy! Read them in bed. Off to the sale at 10.00 in the car, Mother collected her chair and my things. I stayed till lunchtime and bought some lovely linen that pleased me very much. Had a lovely day. Home in Osborne's taxi for lunch. In afternoon out with Mary twelve eggs. Very cold.

Saturday 17 February

Snowing hard again, miserable weather. Went to Ipswich with Mother. Sorted my new linen and marked same in afternoon. A lovely letter from Bill arrived posted last Monday.

Sunday 18 February

Bernice been here a month today. So far she is quite a nice girl. Took children out in morning as Miss N went to church. Snowing again and very cold indeed.

Monday 19 February

Miss Davies rang up wanting two dozen eggs. Went to Ipswich shopped and came home by bus. Hens laying well, thirteen today. Sally troublesome about coming in and Morphew had to help me. Mother very tired, cross and savage in the evening.

Tuesday 20 February

Had a NTL from Bill that rather worried me, saying he was making plans for me and children which he was sending by letter. Wet day. Wrote letters in morning and saw to hens. Got Miss Ensor's present ready.

Thursday 22 February

Went to Miss Jeckell for fitting at 11.00. I had the children and Miss Ensor came for dancing class. Gave her present of silver sauceboats which she was very pleased with. Sixteen eggs today. Much warmer.

Friday 23 February

Scarborough [butler] and Mrs S arrived yesterday and Pepper bit him this morning. This at long last made Mother buy him a muzzle. Wrote to Merlin. Smigly [Siamese cat] to Col. Castle. I went to the Sale and bought some tablecloths and left Liffen with commisions to buy some plates, dishes and croquet set.

Saturday 24 February

Had very bad night, headache and poor Smig sick after being doctored poor little beast.

Sunday 25 February

Much colder. Very dull and still feeling depressed and not able to write to Bill cheerfully, so did not write at all.

Monday 26 February

Send six eggs up to Mr Packard. Sixteen eggs today.

Tuesday 27 February

Mary's 10th birthday. Can't believe the child really is 10! In another 10 years she will be 20. Seems incredible! Heard from Cooks. Am thinking of making a dash out to Bill.

Wednesday 28 February

Mother and I went to London on 9 o'clock train. Mother went to see Aunt Edie taking with her 1 dozen eggs. Went to Coles where I got Bill a very nice silk dressing gown for 5 guineas. Then Harvey Nichols for material. Then Cooks to enquire about my passage out to Egypt and to my darling. Lunched with Mother at her club and then she took me to 'Shepherd's Pie' which was very good revue. We both thoroughly enjoyed it and laughed a lot. Home on 5.12. Felt very sad as Cooks couldn't let me get a passage and dash out to Bill, and I must wait till April before going.

Friday 1 March

Lovely day, pullets laying splendidly. Had nineteen eggs yesterday and today.

Saturday 2 March

Gave Morphew a dozen eggs this morning. Sturgeon has asked for a rise in wages which infuriated Mother and me at this time. The butler and Mrs Scarborough continue to be a success. Went to Ipswich for fitting at Miss Jeckell's. Am having new duck egg blue dress and coat, also new black dress and coat. Mary rode for half an hour before lunch. Miss Stoney came to see me and Smig this afternoon. Mother went to Ipswich to fetch the new head housemaid. Lovely to have two glorious letters from Bill.

Monday 4 March

Had 'Red Rose' a chicken, killed this morning. Last one for some time. Went to Ipswich and shopped, a lovely day. Ordered my day old chicks and felt seedy in evening.

Tuesday 5 March

Found I had a rash on my chest and on my face. Fear it is German measles. Went to Ipswich by bus and shopped, felt very cold. When I came in felt so very tired. Told Dad after lunch who confirmed it.

Wednesday 6 March

Spent the day in bed reading. Face still irritable and my ears ache and glands are a bit tender. Otherwise feeling all right with this peculiar complaint. Mary looking after the hens for me.

Thursday 7 March

Paid Newie and finished letter to Bill. Bernice went to Ipswich for me with letters etc. on her bike. Found Dad down the lane on her return, having fallen and cut his nose and hands. Didn't know how he had done it. Mother very worried.

Friday 8 March

Much better, got up for lunch feeling a little shaky but rash and pain at the back of my head all gone. Mary very busy looking after the hens for me. Dad in bed all day but seems better.

Saturday 9 March

Had two letters from Bill, do miss him so very much. Went out to hens, am having a worrying time with broodie's, but hope for the best and that the two new ones will settle by Tuesday when I have two lots of baby chicks coming.

Monday 11 March

Went to Ipswich on 10.09 bus. Went for fitting to Miss Jeckell and had my hair washed. Enquired at station about baby chicks arrival time etc. Worried over broody hen problems, 19 and 15 no good in spite of trying them out on boxes. 19 seems wild and useless.

Tuesday 12 March

Expect one lot of chicks tonight or possibly early in afternoon. Went to Ipswich getting chick food etc. Home by bus and wrote to Bill. Heard from Mrs Blencowe and Merlin that Merlin has German measles. Took Mother to Ipswich in car in afternoon and called station, no sign of chicks. At 6.00 man rang up to say they had arrived, dashed off on my bike, after much preparation of hot bottles, coops and baskets etc. collected them and found on opening box, 12 lovely little yellow balls of fluff. Put one carefully under no. 3 who has been sitting nearly 3 weeks and all was well. Later took out remainder and fixed them up safely for the night.

Wednesday 13 March

Head housemaid on waking me, announced another a lot of chicks and eggs had come! Mother said I could have car but couldn't get it to start! So went on my bike and bought chicks home. Sent Bernice later for eggs, 15 beauties, and on unpacking chicks found 13 darlings all splendid very strong and well. Decided to try them under number 27 in spite of fact she has only been sitting for three days. She pecked first chick but gradually took to it and settle down with the rest. All well and move both lots to orchard. After lunch read frightfully thrilling and exciting news that my own darling has been promoted. Felt so thrilled and happy about this, it is lovely. Sent him a wire at once. Went to bed feeling exceedingly happy and proud of my love.

Thursday 14 March

Can't believe Bill is really a Wing Commander. Mary very pleased, sweet child! Twinnies of course don't understand! Busy day and woke to find snow again! Really too sickening, out early to chicks, all well in spite of bitter cold. Covered runs with old mac and settled number 39 on eggs from N Graham.

Friday 15 March

Mary's eggs from Eastman's arrived safely this morning, one dozen W. Wyandotes. Helped her put them down this afternoon under Tulip! Great thrill.

Sunday 17 March

Twelve years ago I sent all my heart to my Darling so today on the eve of his birthday, I again sent him all my heart in my NTL. I do love him and miss him so, wrote to him and Merlin. Little families flourishing, but only seven eggs from others. Dad in bed all day.

Thursday 21 March

Went to Ipswich by bus and took Mrs Freeman one dozen eggs and Miss Catchpole six eggs. Busy buying Easter Eggs. Heard of very successful RAF raid on Egypt.

Friday 22 March Good Friday

Had a depressed letter from my darling telling me Drummond had said the only two vacancies with East Command were Aden or Khartoum. Poor darling, so miserable and depressed at the idea of going to either. Felt so worried I forgot the broody hen 39 and shut her off the nest leaving her off for 40 minutes so I should think all the eggs would be addled.

Saturday 23 March

Busy shopping and arranging about Mary's bridle and shopping for Mother. Afternoon searching for Sally, who had got out. Busy doing up Easter eggs and parcels. Heard from Bill in afternoon a very cheerful letter to say he had seen James the SPSD, who had said that Drummond had been leg pulling and that there was no plan to go Khartoum or Aden. So felt much cheered

Sunday 24 March Easter Day.

Miss my two darling boys so very much today. First Easter I have been away from Merlin. Miss N and Mother went to Holy Communion at eight and I had breakfast with the children who were inundated with Easter eggs.

Monday 25 March

The Great Day arrived for Mary and she was properly in a twitter. We went over to Woodbridge in YY, it was lovely to have her out again and the dear old car went like a bird. Arrived there after picking up Barbara Gauvain at Bealings at 11.15. and found Jean Campbell and Sally there. Mary's class came on about 12.30 she did not have long to wait and she got Reserve. I thought she ought to have had Third as she rode beautifully and looked so nice. We all had lunch. John Gauvain joined us and has been posted to Codrington where he goes to morrow. Such a lovely day.

Thursday 28 March

Snow again. Dad had central heating put on. Went off to sale at East Bergholt in YY and spent the day there thoroughly enjoying myself. Bought 2 entrée dishes 15/- some linen, stick stand and 30 sticks, umbrellas, hunting crops etc. for 30/- Letter from Bill which was the crowning point of a very nice day.

Friday 29 March

Still very cold, cleaned out hen houses, coops etc. Have seats Royal Circle for the White Horse Inn and Mary Wilson, John and Andrew are lunching first at Piccadilly. Paynter rang up to tell me he had just flown from Cairo and Bill was very well.

Monday 1 April

Lots of April Fools Day leg pulling! Caught Mary three times and the twins twice! Bill's Easter book for the children arrived.

Tuesday 2 April

A letter from John Peel came last evening telling me he thought Bill would be home within three months. This is too marvellous for words. So, so happy that I couldn't sleep! Up very early and off in YY with Mother and Mary after doing hens. Went with Mary to Beale's house, 22 Woodfall Street and there found Merlin happily playing chess with David, John and Andrew. Collected him and went to Harrods to get Mary a pair of jodhpurs and boots then to Piccadilly Grill where I booked a table for nine. Rang up John Peel and asked him to lunch too. He came and so we were 10, lunch was poor. Mary and Mother, Beale and the five children. We then went to the White Horse Inn and saw this musical show which I enjoyed very much. So did the children, but owing to the shortage of trains, had to leave before the last act. Had tea on the train and home in YY at 7.15. Merlin very tired and all to bed by eight. I fed chickens, eighteen eggs today and all well.

Wednesday 3 April

Lovely to have Merlin home, but above all the joy to know Bill is coming home to me is more blessed than anything in the world.

Thursday 4 April

Went to Ipswich in afternoon with Merlin and Dad. My chicks chipping their shells this afternoon, so excited about this.

Friday 5 April

Very cold. Miss Newling went off to London. I had children all the morning and we went to Ipswich where Merlin had his hair cut and I shopped. We all had hot chocolate at Limmers. Mary and I very busy with hatching eggs and chicks.

Saturday 6 April

I had thirteen chicks out of my sitting of light Sussex eggs. Put them all out in the coop. Busy morning dealing with Mary's, so far she has five hatched. Went off 11.30 to lunch at Rendham with Granny Lunn. Children thoroughly enjoyed their day. Had an excellent lunch of roast chicken and cold tongue, vegetables, sponge pudding and cream and meringues.

Sunday 7 April

Find the early morning is a bit of a strain these days while Miss N is away. To be at breakfast by eight having first to get dressed, see they are dressed and the three chick outfits are fed takes some doing. Mary has eight chicks out of her twelve eggs. Today we transferred her brood to tennis court with number 30 and mine with number 39.

Monday 8 April

Busy morning cleaning out and moving the henhouse to fresh ground. Mary is most helpful but I find Mer and the twins take very little interest. Went to post at Copdock with Merlin on bikes but he fell off so had to return to see to his knee and remove a large flint.

Tuesday 9 April

Heard news that we have had Allied minefields in Norwegian waters to stop Germans getting iron ore. Good show but expect

Germans will be livid and do something. Busy with chicks, also went to Ipswich for fitting. Mary fetched Sally from the new field over the other side of brook.

Wednesday 10 April

Chicks all well and egg production first rate. Taking six dozen to Miss Davies this afternoon. Went to lunch with Lady Hope at her sister's house, Weston Mill, Nayland. A nice house with lovely things but I should not care to live over a mill. Excellent lunch. Found it was 20 miles so shall not have much petrol left this month. Busy with chicks in evening. Much warmer. Twenty eggs.

Friday 12 April

In afternoon car went to fetch Isobel and Jane Durham, who arrived at three. Very nice to see Isobel again and took her for walk to see chickens and garden etc. All children seem to be quite happy.

Saturday 13 April

Busy with Mary cleaning out chickens etc. In the evening played games with children. Bitterly cold.

Monday 15 April

Isabel and Jane staying till tomorrow. Miss Newling finds children quarrel a great deal. I don't care for Jane.

Tuesday 16 April

No letters oh dear! Miss them so and feel so lonely without them. With all this Norwegian business and threats in the Balkans, keep on feeling something will stop my darling from coming home to me. Jane and Mary had fight just before the Durham's left. Poor Mary with a torn ear and kicked shins, I felt furious with Jane, and Isobel for spoiling her so.

Thursday 18 April

Sally escaped from her field and kept the children busy trying to catch her. Eventually Morphew and S and S had to go down and get her back. Very cold and pouring wet.

Friday 19 April

Two more letters from Bill which was lovely. Feel quite different and so thrilled with the news that he may soon be home.

Saturday 20 April

Johnny Wilson arrived Mary having rung up yesterday. Miss Newling very cross as she was very late in last evening and Mum was furious about it. Feeling very well and happy. Miss Catchpole rang up and asked for eggs for herself and Mrs Freeman today.

Sunday 21 April

A lovely day, warm and sunny. Mary and John get on splendidly, apparently having much the same tastes.

Monday 22 April

Had a lovely letter from Bill. Off to London on 9.00 train by car to station, had to be up early to do all chickens before I went. Went to Bill's bank, Liberty's, Plucknett where I got Merlin's ninth birthday gift of two engine turned silver brushes. Twinings for tea, Justerini for port, whisky and gin, as we expect these to be taxed in the budget tomorrow. Also to see Hughes about 2 Walton Place, to Harrods for Merlin's clothes. I had lunch at Gunters, and tea at Searcy's. Home on 5.12 train very tired.

Wednesday 24 April

Merlin's ninth birthday. Woke up to help him open his presents. He had two silver brushes from me, bow and arrows and a cricket ball and a screeching device for his bike from Bill, £1 from Mum and a prayer book, a cricket bat (a beauty), and a book on cricket and £1 from Dad. 10 shillings and a book from his Granny Lunn and a telegram, also a lovely knife from Newie and a book from Nannie. Took John to the station in YY this afternoon and Mer came with me. Then we had a large tea in drawing room with two cakes, Mrs Scarborough's and Mother's bought from Sally Lunn. The four children sat up for dinner which was great fun, Merlin choosing all his favourites. We had vegetable soup, chicken and meringues.

Thursday 25 April

A lovely day. Went off with Merlin on our bikes at 10.00 to the train bridge and thoroughly enjoyed a morning outside. Watched trains and went through the Belstead woods and heard the nightingale. Lunch and afterwards went to Ipswich driving the car for Mum. Merlin came with us. Mary and the twins went with Miss N. for a long walk. Letter from my darling.

Friday 26 April

Busy morning cleaning out all hen houses and coops, bike shed and utensils. Have really done all thoroughly. Decided to have early lunch and go to Felixstowe so took car to Ipswich and then bus from Barrack Corner arriving at Felixstowe at 2.30. Stayed till 4.50 and home by 6.30. A lovely day all children loved it.

Saturday 27 April

Another lovely day. Went to Miss Jeckell's and took eggs for Miss Davies etc. Hens laying better but not so good as usual this week.

Monday 29 April

Letter from my darling. Posted letter to him today on my return from Aldeburgh where I went to lunch with Ian Smith's. Enjoyed my day. Heard on wireless eggs are to be rationed in the autumn.

Tuesday 30 April

Very worried in evening, heard that the Mediterranean is to be closed to British shipping. I do so wonder what that means and whether my darling won't come home after all. Heard frightful explosion about 11.00 after going to bed and wondered what ever it could be. [HMS Dunoon, a Hunt Class minesweeper based at Great Yarmouth during a sweep detonated a mine at Smith's Knoll. This resulted in a further explosion of the 4th magazine. She sank after 20 minutes. Twenty-six men lost their lives, 47 were rescued.]

Thursday 2 May

Another windy day. Went to Ipswich in afternoon with the children and Newie and shopped. Harold and Ursula arrived after tea and Mrs Anderson and Virginia later in afternoon.

Friday 3 May

Mer's holidays are over. No letter from Bill today. Went up to London on 11.35 train and had lunch on the train. Took luggage to Victoria and then went to Sloane Street for shopping and ordered winter vests and some shoes. Took M for walk in Park and then had tea at Searcy's which he much enjoyed ending with a vanilla ice. Very hot, to Victoria Street and then after seeing the dear chap off had a hectic rush for my 5.12. Luckily it had been altered to 5.16 so I just caught it and got home at seven. Fed chicks and put them all to bed.

Saturday 4 May

Mrs A. and Virginia left after lunch and so did Harold and Ursula. Find the latter very trying, so talkative. Busy afternoon with chickens and evening.

Wednesday 8 May

Mum very cross and gone to London which is a blessing. Wrote to Bill and went to Ipswich in YY. Shopped and got some chocolate before going to the sale at Belstead Road. Enjoyed the sale though did not buy much. Dad came about 12.30 to tell me there were some chicks for me at the station. Went to fetch them and found they were all White Sussex. Put them under 42 and later transferred them to the field. Went for picnic tea with M and C & C and Newie to Belstead woods and picked bluebells and listened to the nightingale. Had three letters from him, so terribly in love with him and do miss him so. Bought sheets and pillowcases, small knives, a mincer and a biscuit jar at the sale. Mum home cross and tired in evening.

Friday 10 May [Germany launches invasion of Belgium and Netherlands. Chamberlain resigns as British prime minister and Churchill forms Coalition government.]

Went out early and Morphew told me the Germans had invaded Luxembourg, Holland and Belgium at 3am so now the War really starts, I suppose. Went to Ipswich with Mother in afternoon and took in last lot of Mrs Freeman's eggs for preserving.

Saturday 11 May

Seem to spend most of the day listening to the wireless hearing the news and reading papers. Also attending to the chicks. Such glorious weather one really cannot believe there is a War on and it's not far from here now. German parachute troops dropped about would be most unpleasant. Cleaned out coops and hen houses.

Sunday 12 May Whit Sunday [Leading Panzer troops begin advance into France.]

Twins were very scared of aeroplanes during the night and came along to me at 1.00. Poor Clare walked into the wall and hurt her nose. Listened to the news this morning after getting up early to Holy Communion at Belstead Church. Listened to news about fighting in Belgium and Holland. How awful it all is. Feel so worried about my darling. Dread his coming into danger. Do long for him so and the comfort of his presence. Hens laying well, have now preserved over 400 eggs and hope to put down 500.

Monday 13 May

No holiday today owing to political situation. Read and listened to news.

Tuesday 14 May [Recruitment of Home Guard begins.]

No hope of his return yet I'm afraid. Wrote to him. Went to Ipswich in YY to Freemans and to Miss Jeckell. Sold six eggs to Miss Catchpole. The Quilter brothers came into tea.

Wednesday 15 May [The Netherlands surrendered.]

Another simply lovely day. Busy all morning cleaning out coops, preparing for the Khaki Campbell ducklings who are coming to morrow, and scrubbing sides of henhouse etc.

Thursday 16 May

Man rang up at 9.00 from station to say that ducklings had arrived. Went in at once to fetch them. The ducklings are too sweet and seem all to be very strong and healthy. No 41 wouldn't take them and pecked them. No 39 all right but obviously thinks they are not her cup of tea. They are very strong and were out on tennis court in evening. Feel I must have something to distract me from the misery of this War and now Italy seems to mean to come in, and my darling won't come home. Feel incredibly sad and frustrated over it all.

Friday 17 May [Germans take Brussels**.]**

Had very bad night. Do worry so about Bill being still out there in all this heat. The misery and disappointment after expecting him to come home is awful. Fell asleep at dawn and then of course couldn't wake up! Out early to ducklings and chicks, all flourishing.

Saturday 18 May [Germans take Antwerp.]

No news of Bill. War news is bad. Feel very depressed, have lost weight only seven stone 11lb. but this is a good thing.

Sunday 19 May

Had a better night but wake and worry so about my poor darling. Chicks all well and ducklings except one, Charlie Chaplin, who seems half dead so I gave him to Southgate to finish off.

Monday 20 May

Letter from Bill, still hopeful about his return and one from John very doubtful about it, so don't know what to think. Read papers. Southgate came up to see me about repairs to henhouse. Sturgeon had an ARP parade, and gas mask party in evening, Bernice refused to appear. Gave her notice as a result of this cheek. Officer in charge of troops came down to see us to arrange for men to have baths in men's quarters. News not very good from France.

Tuesday 21 May

Bad news all day and felt depressed. Rested and slept in afternoon. Very hot.

Wednesday 22 May [British break Luftwaffe's Enigma code. German tanks advance towards Channel ports.]

Went to Ipswich in car at 9.30 with Sturgeon taking Dad in to go to London. Letter from my darling. Goodness knows when these may stop as it looks as if Italy will come in at any moment. Feel depressed but news a bit better at lunchtime. Ordered another night ark. Dad returned 6pm.

Thursday 23 May

Had an excellent night and felt much better. Letter again from my darling. Southgate busy creosoting my hen house. Wrote to my darling love.

Friday 24 May

No letter today from Bill, but this week has been a gala one for letters. They strengthen me so in these days of sorrow, loneliness and anxiety. Still if they are stopped I must not mind and read and reread all the lovely ones my sweet thoughtful darling has sent me. I should too be thankful he is safe and not in any immediate danger and though we are separated like this and have been for so long, I have a great deal to be thankful for. Lost two chicks today by poison put down for the rats. Sad about this, as they were such a lovely little brood of twelve. Ducks all well, tonight we had first L.S. cockerel weight two and a half pounds, an excellent bird and plump. So now have 10 Light Sussex fortnight old chicks, 22 ducks, 21 Light Sussex chicks 10 weeks old, 13 Light Sussex chicks six weeks old, 28 layers. Therefore 94 head, and Mary's 6, makes exactly 100 head.

News still seems bad. I do so wish we could have a victory for once.

Saturday 25 May [Boulogne falls.]

Letter from my sweetheart that comforted me a lot. Do miss him so, but do not know whether to wish him to come home to danger or to stay where he is where he is safe for present, though if Italy does come in then he won't be safe anywhere. We hear guns going all day on and off. As long as I can keep the fear and misery of this War from the children I feel I shall have accomplished my small bit. Went out early to chicks.

Sunday 26 May

Went to church in the car as it was National Day of Prayer. Took Mother and Dad, Newie, Mary and twins. Came home and was very annoyed to find Bernice was with Ada and the soldiers. Blew her up. News is bad in evening. Margaret rang up asking me whether I would care to send the children down to her.

Monday 27 May [Operation Dynamo - the evacuation of British, French and Belgian troops from the beaches of Dunkirk begins. Calais falls.]

Letter from Mr Blencowe saying they have decided to move Brambletye to Lynton, North Devon and propose to do so shortly. This settled it. I decided to send Mary and twins to Wincanton. Rang Margaret in evening and told her what I had decided and they go on Thursday with Newie and Bernice. Letter from my Darling. Send him an NTL asking his approval over this plan.

Tuesday 28 May [Belgium surrenders.]

Had a wire from Bill insisting on my going as well. This does complicate matters. Felt very tired and worried. News is so bad and it looks as if our troops will be surrounded in N. France and Belgium. In evening heard that traitor Leopold, the Belgian king, had surrendered to Germans! I shall be thankful to get children away as I feel an invasion of England or bombing might start at any moment. Had letter from Mr B asking parents to collect boys on Friday for about a week or 10 days. Decided to take Merlin down to Holnicote, and collect him on Thursday. All furniture arrived from Footman's this afternoon and had it all stacked up in the cottage. Chicks and ducks all well. Trouble over Bernice's coming with the children, but have fixed it with her mother.

Wednesday 29 May

Bill's Mother's birthday so wrote to her. Took Mary to Freeman at 10. Very busy all day making preparations for children to leave. Very tired and sleeping badly. No letter from Bill.

Thursday 30 May

Letter from my Bill that cheered me up a lot. Any day now I feel his letters may stop as Italy seems to be on the brink of war. Went in YY leaving her at station. Good journey to London and across London in taxi. Then crowds at Waterloo but got Mary and the twins all settled comfortably eventually in a carriage to themselves.

Mother had packed them up a lovely lunch and they all left eating and happy! I went to Searcy's and had lunch. Then met Merlin who arrived at 3.00 off the train at London Bridge. Came home on 3.40 for tea at 5.30. Did chicks and ducks.

Friday 31 May

Busy preparing to go away to Holnicote with Merlin on Monday. Rang Mr Lamb and found they can have us. Mother's duck house came. Took Merlin for a bike ride to train bridge.

Saturday 1 June

Sent Bill an NTL to let him know about our plans.

Sunday 2 June

Went to Belstead church across fields with Mer, Mother & Dad. Another glorious day. It is marvellous that they seem to be getting nearly all our BEF troops away from France. After tea Merlin and I biked up to Wherstead where we were told we could get petrol (none to be had in Ipswich) found it was true, so came back and filled up YY. Then a terrible thing happened, Mother out trying to shut up the ducks, picked up Smig who scratched her terribly on her head, ears and neck. I think Smig was frightened by Pepper but he clawed poor Mother's head terribly and I decided it was not safe to leave Smig at Belstead in my absence so rang up Miss Stoney who agreed to have him as a PG cat while I'm away. So off I went in YY across country to Spider Hall. Left Smig and came back.

Monday 3 June [Last night of evacuation from Dunkirk, bringing the total number of men rescued to 220,000 British and 120,000 French and Belgians.] A very hot and tiring day. Merlin and I did chickens and showed Morphew about the chickens and left at 9.30 for station. Dad came and saw us off. Very full train, we went up 1st-class to London, took taxi to Paddington and there the fun began! No porters. Seas of people on platform but managed to get two corner seats in 1st class carriage for self and Merlin. Train absolutely packed with evacuees, BEF men. No food to be had, however a kind woman gave Merlin some chicken rolls and a doughnut. And we eventually got to Taunton one and a half hours late. There we saw train after train of French troops coming through, I talked to them and they said 'Dunkirqe etait un enfer'. Poor devils. Merlin and I eventually got to Minehead at nine then to Holincote and had dinner and then to bed. It was very late before we got to sleep.

Tuesday 4 June

Merlin is none the worse. Had breakfast and then to Minehead for a bathe. Mer very thrilled over this and swimming well. Lovely weather. Visited all the house agents to find out about houses. Bought a paper and a towel for Merlin, then posted letter to Mother. Had NTL from Bill on my arrival here yesterday which cheered me. Wrote to him after lunch. Dinner 7.30 and to bed at 10 after hearing the news. Don't believe Italy will come in after all.

Wednesday 5 June

Another glorious day. Merlin and I set off at 9.30 in a car to Porlock and there we looked at three houses, none I cared for. Then to look at Lynton and Lynemouth and so to Lee Abbey to look at the school. A dreary looking place but in a glorious position just by the sea. We then went up to Exmoor and had our lunch there in the sun on the moor and so to Exford where we saw another terror, Exmead. Very disappointing day from house-hunting point of view, tea in garden. Listen to the news which was bad. Put Merlin to bed and listened again at nine.

Friday 7 June

Had two letters from my darling sent on from Belstead. Also one from Mum, my bank balance etc. A year ago my darling came home on leave. Oh God how I do miss him.

Later. Had to stop here. Took bus to Minehead with Merlin who had his bathe. Then bus to Bridgwater or rather Nestor Stowey to see 'the Old House' belonging to some people called Hart-Davis. Merlin and I had lunch first in the field. It was very, very hot. The H.D's nice and a nice house but no good for us with children. Then we got a taxi and went to see a house advertised in Times called Pardlestone near Holford. This has distinct possibilities, an Esse cooker, electric light, five beds, two baths and modern fittings. Owner, a Miss Barnard, out. Caught bus back after having tea at a farm. Very hot and both Merlin and I felt exhausted. Wire from Bill saying we must move.

Saturday 8 June

Miss Barnard rang up to say lady who had option on her house had not written so feel hopeful. Asked her to send all details and went to Minehead in afternoon where Mer bathed. News bad.

Sunday 9 June

Felt very seedy last night and so faint all night. Fainted before going to bed. My period bad and feel so sad, and worried about what to do. Rang Miss B. and said I'd come to see her tomorrow. Arrange to have car to do so. Like nice couple here, Major and Mrs Wren, he is author of Beaujeste.

Monday 10 June [Italy declares war on Britain and France. USA promises to help the Allies.]

Eventful day. Letter from Bill. In afternoon car to Holford, had tea with Miss Barnard and discussed everything agreeing to take Pardlestone for six months at £100 for period, partly furnished leaving curtains, carpets and certain furniture. That is; an Esse cooker, electric light, Mains water, garage and stables, two paddocks and I have agreed to take on her groom/gardener at £2.2.0 weekly. As I came into the hotel that old brute Mrs Erichson greeted me with the news Italy has come into the War. I felt sick and couldn't sleep all night to think of my darling in danger.

Tuesday 11 June

Posted letter to Bill yesterday, but am afraid it will never get through by airmail. Sent him NTL to tell him I've got the cottage. Had two letters from Bill. Went to Minehead and Mer bathed. Felt sick all day about these bloody Italians but Major Wren cheered me up a lot and said the War with them might be over much sooner than expected. Not so hot. Heavy rain in afternoon and miss my three girls very much and all the animals too. God, how I hate War.

Wednesday 12 June

Wrote to my Darling but heaven alone knows how long it will take. Too chilly for bathing. Rang up Margaret, out, so talked to Newie and Mary.

Thursday 13 June

Finished packing and left to go and stay with Margaret's relations, the old Pellys, at Balsam House, Wincanton. Paid bill, which with the car expenses and tips etc. came to £20. We left by the bus for Minehead and then wandered about after Merlin bathed and I posted letters etc. Went to Yeovil by Blue Line bus. Both felt rather sick! However got there 12.30 and had an awful job to get a taxi and eventually we had to pay £1 to get him to take us over to North Cheriton. Arrived 1.30 very late to find Margaret, and Claude there too, and the children. Claude seems pretty shattered after the Dunkirk episode and slept all afternoon. Lovely to see Mary and the twins again after such a long time. Margaret has quite a nice stone built house with big garden and mullion windows and the garden is charming. Went over after tea to Balsam House and put Merlin to bed after unpacking. I gather I am to stay as a PG and pay £1 for self and same for Merlin over w/end, as they are so poor. Nice old house, but not comfortable, water cold and feel miserable. Do miss Bill so.

Friday 14 June [Germans enter Paris and advance towards Dijon and Lyons.] Had bad night and feel so worried over the situation that seems very serious in every way. Looks as if the French are going to be beaten up. Claude seems very depressed and hardly speaks at all about the War. Miss Bill very much. He seems so far, far away. Spent the day at Margaret's but came back for dinner. Merlin goes back on Tuesday and I shall take him to Salisbury. Heard French had allowed Germans to occupy Paris.

Saturday 15 June

Spent most of the day at Hardings. Claude goes back to work tomorrow but does not know where or what job. Newie doesn't much care about being here as she is much in the nursery and has all meals there. Feel acutely depressed and worried. Letter from Bill sent on from Belstead.

Sunday 16 June

News drastically bad about France and we all feel she will probably give in shortly unless the Petain government can make a stand. Decided not to waste another hour and go off home tomorrow. Newie must see Mer to Salisbury on Tuesday. The Stanley Clarkes came over to see me from Sturminster and it was fun to see them again. They stayed about an hour. Then Margaret took Claude to the station and me back to Hardings, supper and bed. Feel worried and no sleep.

Monday 17 June

Up very early to catch 8.45 from Templecombe. Old Mr Pelly took me to the station in the car and is a dear old man. Very uncomfortable journey. Saw Miss Webb to see if she had any maids on my way across London. 3.40 home, train empty as all along the East Coast is now defence and more or less prohibited area. Took a taxi out to Belstead and arrived for late tea. Mother and Dad delighted to see me and have me with them. Told them all the news and heard at 6.00 that France has asked for an Armistice and as we feared she has given up. Situation seems very grave.

Tuesday 18 June [De Gaulle makes broadcast from London establishing a 'Free France' to continue the fight.]

Frightfully busy trying to get a van or railway container to move me down to Pardlestone on 24th. So far there appears to be nothing at all but I think Wyard are the most likely. Busy too writing letters and getting straight, starting to pack and sort my things. Cleaned out and saw to chickens.

Cesca is frantically busy for the next three days packing to leave Belstead and her parents.

Saturday 22 June [Armistice with Germany divides France into occupied and unoccupied zones.]

Really too busy to write diary and nothing to say except nightly air raids which are I think, hateful. I left this morning having got 10 gallons from Mrs Gosling to get me down. Nice day cool and grey skies and reminds me of those happy heavenly motoring days going north with Bill. How bloody this war is. No Bill, no children, no home, no pleasures in life which make life worth having but I must not grumble. The country is lovely as I drove through it today and worth saving from these Huns no matter what the cost. I got along very well till I got lost at Dedham and the rain came down in sheets. I stopped in Reading, bought some cigarettes and posted letters and eventually arrived at Cheam at 4pm to find a huge party in progress! Parents Day, boys and parents everywhere and no one knowing anything. Ursula very nice but full of misery and if I believed all she said you might as well die and expect England invaded bombed, gassed and finally destroyed. Miss my darling so. Went to bed and slept marvellously, certainly best night I've had this week.

Sunday 23 June

Started in YY in a downpour at 10.30 after saying goodbye to Harold and Ursula. Map-read my way across to Andover and then on, on, on, westwards and arrived at Margaret's for lunch. Claude not there so we had lunch together. Found Newie looking seedy and in fact all children looking pale. I do not think N. Cheriton really suits any of them as it's so very much down in a hole. Left at 3.00 and drove on to Kilve. I stopped for tea on the way and was also stopped by a man in a car who said I'd not stopped at a 'major road ahead' sign. He threatened to arrest me and produced a card saying he was a special constable. Sickening man. I arrived at Pardlestone about 5.30 and found Miss Barnard and Miss Bullock packing up to go but house still left full of things. My heart sank as I saw what a lot of dirt and filth there was everywhere. Felt very depressed. Went down to Miss Clowes who lives at Overland's, just below in a pink house. She was most welcoming and gave me a delicious supper and was so kind and has a sweet house and most comfy little bedroom. Miss my darling Bill and the children so much.

Monday 24 June

Today I take possession of the house. Mrs Harran the daily cook came, also Mrs Maund, the groom's wife, and Maund and I set them to work to clean and get up carpets and get a move on. It has been left too filthy for words. Man called Thorne came and is to distemper sitting room and passage etc. Electricians also came and are getting on with it. And had lunch with Miss Clowes who is most kind. Went to Williton in afternoon to grocers there.

Tuesday 25 June

Left all the cleaners hard at work and Thorne distempering. Then off in YY to Bridgwater, left her at garage and took 10.20 to London. Went to Miss Webb about servants and down to Ipswich on 3.40. Took taxi out and then saw Mum and Dad and immediately after really started to work hard to get transport for the furniture. Find this frightfully difficult. Chicks all well and laying well. To bed early very tired indeed. News seems grave and possibility of invasion at any moment which scares me as I feel must get down there and settled before storm breaks.

Wednesday 26 June

The wretched Lidbetter let me down and now says he can't take furniture until tomorrow. All the same a very busy day so tired.

Thursday 27 June

The most ghastly day! I got up at 5.00 am as Lidbetter said he'd come by 5.30am, of course he never turned up till 7.00, so I need not have done so. Very busy and so tired by end of day, which saw me by 10 pm back at Miss Clowes. Lidbetter came himself and certainly his men work excellently. Had night of raids last night too! So slept most of way down to Pardleston or rather Bridgwater. As Lidbetter was so late I did not get away from Belstead till 11.00. Caught 11.30 to London with suitcases and Smig in a basket. Then went to Harrods to do some shopping as had two hours to kill. 4.15 down to Bridgwater with dinner at the Clarence there, got the car and arrived at 10.00pm tumbled into bed dead tired, miss my Bill so.

Friday 28 June

Smig is a darling and so good. Went up early to the house and found great improvement. Mrs Harman, Maund and Mrs Maund had really worked wonders. Furniture and the chickens arrived safely at 12.00 Sally here too.

Cesca spends the next two days cleaning and preparing the house for the children.

Monday 1 July

Children and Newie arrived at Bridgwater at 11.20. Thrilled to see them again, took car to fetch them and shopped. Managed to get all luggage on the car. Lunched with Miss Clowes who took photos of them. Children and Newie delighted with the little house which is a blessing. Rang up Mother. Have really not had time to write to Bill or even think these days I've been so busy but only sent him wires, the poor darling. How I miss him and love him. Bomb dropped last night.

Wednesday 3 July

Went to Williton with children and Newie. Unpacked glass and china.

Thursday 4 July

Twins learning to ride with Maund on Sally. Wire from Bill. Losing count of time these days. Miss him terribly.

Friday 5 July

Hear German aeroplanes over constantly at night. Very busy still getting straight.

Sunday 7 July

Lovely hot day and went with children to church at Kilve. I am only writing things down briefly now and am too busy to keep this diary. Write all my doings, my heart, my all to my darling and can't write it again. I feel too tired with disturbed nights.

Wednesday 10 July [Germans attack Channel convoys and launch raid on Swansea docks and arms factory in Wales.]

Thursday 11 July

Cold and wet, had a fire. Children seem to be so happy here. So am I. Worried that Miss Barnard will do nothing about signing agreement. It's infuriating. Heard from Mrs Anderson that kitten arrives tomorrow.

Friday 12 July

In afternoon went to Bridgwater. Collected Twigg at GWR at Bridgewater and brought her home. The sweetest baby Siamese with the most lovely eyes. Children thrilled with her. Smig jealous.

Saturday 13 July

Busy dealing with kitten and house etc. having a daily cook gives me more to do. But she really is a very good cook and a nice woman so I put up with it. Bernice seems well settled also as house parlourmaid and Doris isn't bad but hates the country so is leaving as soon as Newie has had her holiday.

Sunday 14 July

All went to church at Kilve where Mr Bush preaches excellently. Went to see Miss Clowes in evening and listened to the news. Discovered yesterday letters now go by Air Mail to Bill so shall send them that way in future.

Monday 15 July St Swithin's Day

Dad's 81st birthday, sent him a wire and wished I could have seen him but the situation does not justify my being away from my home and children these days. Letter from Mer and one in Embassy bag from my darling. I miss him so much that life is hard to bear, but I can do no more than carry on with the children and hope for his safe return.

The week goes by, the children and Cesca enjoying Pardleston and Mary especially loving the pony and
trap journeys to Williton.

Monday 18 July

Went to tea with Mr Luttrell at Courthouse, East Quantoxhead and he showed me all over the house which is most interesting. Flemish work. He is a charming old man and uncle of Bill Luttrell.

Tuesday 19 July

In the move I have lost my ration books. Went to Williton in the pony trap with Mary and Maund and got new ones.

Wednesday 24 July

Man came from Bridgwater to pack up all china and glass that I shall not now need here. Went to dinner with Miss Clowes who had a nice couple there dining who were staying with her. Listened to news. The RAF are doing the most superb work. Poor old Army is being seen off and its day is done.

Thursday 25 July

Went to Bridgwater by car and left YY at garage there. Caught 10.30 to London arriving at 2.30 and rang up Hughes about 2 Walton Place as I am so worried about question of paying rent or not. Cluttons say they will sue me if I don't pay. Dined with John and Mary Wilson and John was very kind and helpful over all this. I stayed night at South Kensington Hotel where Isobel and Ian Smith are. I had tea with her and then shopped at Peter Jones and Harvey Nichols. Then went to see Jim and Gabriel who have Claude Pelly living with them. How I miss my darling. It's no good getting out of the rut of things. It only shakes one up more than one can believe and to see couples happily together like John and Mary, Jim and Gabriel is hard to bear. To bed in my room with my thoughts far away with Bill.

Friday 26 July [Bombing raids over London start in September.]

Feel a bit nervous all the time in London in case this German expected bombing starts and I'm prevented from getting back to my babies. Paid bill at Hotel, and said goodbye to John and Isobel. I was with Hughes from 9.30 till 11.30 and not much further forward. Goodness knows what's going to happen. Met Mother at ESU club and told her all about it. Thought she looked tired and older. She now has that Miss Davies as companion and pays her £50. It's awful the waste that goes on at Belstead. We lunched at Gunters. Then to Harvey Nichols where she bought me a very pretty peach satin blouse for my birthday. Caught 4.15 back to Bridgwater. YY brought me safely home and I found Newie and children, Sally, cats and chickens all alright. To bed very tired indeed.

Monday 29 July

Children's holidays started. I've bought myself a cheap camera for five shillings and so now can take photos to send to my darling. Paid Doris and Mrs Harran.

Tuesday 30 July

My darling Mer home for holidays. Took Clare who was to have a treat to Taunton in YY and shopped. Met Mer at 1.28 looking as always, rather a diminutive small boy and incredibly scruffy and dirty. We all had a nice picnic lunch of cold chicken by the side of a stream in a field and I thought of the many lovely picnics my darling and I have had together. In Egypt, in Scotland, in Suffolk and I longed for him. As I am writing up this diary, time seems of no account only my love and his for me that is everlasting and eternally fresh and lovely.

Thursday 1 August

I feel it is dull for children these holidays. In spite of asking children to stay they cannot come and there is nothing for them to do. Went to Williton with trap taking Mer this time. He thought it fun and we all enjoyed it.

Saturday 3 August

Went to tea with Mr Luttrell taking Newie and children with me. They loved it, bathed and ran wild and ate peaches and cream etc etc. Took a lot of photos and do hope they are successful.

Monday 5 August

Miss my darling and sent him a cable. Letters are coming through from him now and then. It is such a heavenly joy when they come. Went to Bridgwater with Newie to take her to station. Children and I shopped. Back for lunch and they all played quite happily in garden in evening.

Tuesday 6 August

Mary riding. We took over possession of the cottage in evening as the Pollards have gone up to their own cottage at the top of the hill.

Wednesday 7 August

Maids moved over to the cottage. Cabled to Bill as had one from him. Margaret and Jane Pelly came to stay arriving after lunch. We all went after tea and had a bathe at Kilve.

Thursday 8 August

Mr Luttrell and Catherine L came to tea. It was a lovely day and I think they enjoyed it and I gave them quite a good wartime tea! It is nice having Margaret and Jane here though the latter is very spoilt. Mr Luttrell is dear old man.

Friday 9 August

Mary much better. I forgot to say yesterday that she went out riding on Ann Pollard's horse Speckles and this wretched beast fell down with her. She hurt her shoulder and was very bruised and shaken but appeared all right. Then at lunch she collapsed and cried. I put her to bed and she was very sick and continued to be sick all night and all following day. Wrote to my darling and had a letter from him. Miss Clowes and Miss Woodard dined.

Saturday 10 August.

Margaret and I get on excellently together. I only wish she was not so far away and we could see more of each other. Wrote to Grannie Lunn and offered her my cottage which I expect she'll take while she looks for something to take herself.

Monday 12 August

Margaret and Jane left after lunch. They went off with 20lbs of plums for her jam making. I must say I do not find this rationing difficult only as regards providing children with sufficient fats! We all went down to Kilve for a bathe in morning. Busy in evening with the chickens which I seem to have much neglected lately. Wrote to my darling and sent him lots of photos.

Tuesday 13 August

Germans seem to be sending over masses and masses of aeroplanes and losing a good many in the process. John Peel must be in the thick of it at Tangmere, He has the D.F.C. and I hope won't get killed. Later, telegram came from Bill, which was lovely and he seems at last to be getting letters from me. Busy day making jam and bottling fruit. Heard from Mother that she is coming down for my birthday which is lovely.

Wednesday 14 August [In July the Luftwaffe started bombing Swansea docks.]

More air raids. Weather glorious. Wrote to my darling. Mary Clowes came up to hear the news after dinner.

Thursday 15 August

Another lovely day. Wrote to Mother and Dad and sent them photographs of the children. More air raids including a bad one during the night. I had Mary and twins in my bed and a very disturbed night as a result.

Friday 16 August

Felt very tired after bad night. Took Mary and twins to Bridgwater shopping in the car. Mer went for a ride down to Yandles farm with Maund as I bought a poultry house there yesterday. Decided he could get it up the lane all right.

Saturday 17 August

Thirteen months now since I've seen my own darling love. Oh! How long. Feel very sad. I am very worried I can't let the little cottage. Wish I could as it would be a help. Went to the village to fetch the joint from Hood Arms.

Monday 19 August

An awful night of bombs and bombing! Woken up time after time. C and C came into my bed and Mer woke but Mary slept right through it. Went to Williton with material for Miss Banner to make curtains. Made 9lbs plum jam.

Tuesday 20 August

Paid Mrs Herman, also Bernice and Doris. Former says she wants to leave when I can arrange it. Mother is coming on Friday for weekend.

Wednesday 21 August

Feel frightfully tired. Been up nearly all night with air raids, Twins scared of falling bombs etc. worried and tired. Went to Williton in the trap. Home for lunch. Very wild and windy. Thorne brought my bookcase up for me.

Thursday 22 August

Had a lovely night last night. No air raids or misery of any sort. Felt much better and went with Mer to Mr Glandfields to see his poultry and goats etc. Bought two Rhode Island Red pullets for Mary at 6/- each and lots of appliances and a house for myself.

Friday 23 August

Went to Bridgwater in afternoon taking Mer and Mary with me. Left twins to have tea with Doris. Very wild windy day, shopped and took laundry to station and met Mother who arrived looking very well and laden with parcels, presents etc. at 5.30, the train being half an hour late. Lovely to see her. This morning six Pekin ducks arrived from Appleyard at Ixworth which she is giving me as a birthday present. I think she likes the little house and children thrilled to see her again.

Saturday 24 August

Mother did the flowers for me and lots of odd jobs. We went to tea with the Luttrells at East Quantoxhead and Mother was taken all over the house which I think she enjoyed. Lovely day. Peaches for tea.

Sunday 25 August

Went to church at Kilve. Nice service and church very full. Took Mother for walk through the woods to Holford Coombe. Wrote to my darling, miss him so and tomorrow is my 36th birthday. Oh! Dear how sad it is to be away from my own love.

Monday 26 August

My birthday. NTL from my darling and a letter from him too which was simply lovely. I had some lovely presents. Bill gave me two books. Whites' Selbourne and Shakespeare's sonnets. Children all gave me presents. Newie sent me a cookery book. Dad £20. We had a very happy day except for the ache in my heart for my darling. Mrs Thelluson and Anne arrived in the evening to take the cottage for four weeks and moved in. I have leased them plate and linen for an additional five shillings weekly. We had a lovely dinner party in the evening and I wore evening dress and we had tomato soup, roast chicken, (a W.S. Cockerel), and fruit salad and cream for dinner and the children joined us.

Wednesday 28 August

Another lovely day. Mary went riding with Anne Thelluson. Walked with Mum and twins down to the sea. Bernice out, didn't come in until nearly 11. Blew her up. She looked wild and hair all over the place. Very hot night and sad and couldn't sleep.

Thursday 29 August

Newie came back from her holiday. Went to see Grandfield's chickens which he is selling off. He has two rather sweet goats to sell. Wants £1 each for them. Newie came back very cheerful and happy from her holiday and looking very well. Had a raid tonight, gunfire and German aeroplanes over.

Friday 30 August

Dear Mum left today and I took her in the car to Bridgwater. Stopped for some cheese. Train left 11.00 instead of 10.30. Mer came with me and had his hair cut.

Saturday 31 August

My darling has sent me three letters so it has been a heavenly day for me reading them over and over. Sent him a cable.

Sunday 1 September

Went over to hear news at the cottage and had coffee with Mrs T. and Anne. Newie came over too as our wireless has gone wrong.

Monday 2 September

Dandy's birthday today. I wrote to her yesterday. Bernice and Doris both left by 8 o'clock bus to return to Suffolk. Audrey Stockholm from Nether Stowey came in afternoon. Not a bad girl, but very rough and very little experience. Still in this part of the world it's lucky to have anyone at all.

Wednesday 4 September

Audrey out in afternoon. Mrs Herman came. I went to Bridgwater to meet K. Clarke only to find no sign of her and on my return home to be rung up by the Williton station master to say she was there at Williton, so off I had to go again and then make a big detour owing to a bomb in a garden near Williton. Met the girl who seemed more dead than alive and says she has not slept for nights owing to the air raids. London is having a truly ghastly time.

[Start of Blitz on London and other major British cities.]

Sunday 8 September

Today has been a National Day of Prayer. All went to church. Blackberried in afternoon.

Wednesday 11 September

Merlin very thrilled with bicycle Mother has sent him for his Xmas present. Went for a ride with him.

Thursday 12 September

Went to Minehead with Mer on 2.30 bus from Kilve. Shopped, called to see Miss B's lawyers who have not heard a word from her. Came home by bus and just home before it rained. Newie and the girls rather grumpy that they had not come too, but as Mary was riding and the twins had their own arrangements, I did not think of taking them.

Saturday 14 September

The days go by slowly but surely. No news of my darling and I feel very sad to think our youth (what's left of it) is slipping and sliding by all the time we are apart. I love him so and it's awful to think it's 14 months since I have seen him. Paid Maund.

Sunday 15 September

Went to church at Kilve and had very nice service. Lavatory tank burst and Maund had to come in and repair it.

Monday 16 September

Mum and Dad's 49th wedding day. I had sent Mum on Friday some sheepskin slippers from the Pardlestone weavers. Sent them also a greeting telegram and some cheese. Went to Taunton again this afternoon with Mrs T and Ann and took Ann to cinema with Mary and Mer to see Charley's Aunt at which Mer nearly died of laughing.

Thursday 19 September

Merlin's last day at home. Very busy packing up for him and getting his tuck all ready. This children's maid Kathleen is quite hopelessly stupid and useless. Gave her notice to leave at end of her month. All children sat up for dinner.

Friday 20 September

Sad day having to take darling Mer back to school, but we had saved up enough petrol to take the car so really it was quite an outing for us. We left 11.30 and in pouring rain. To Minehead, where we filled up with petrol. We had lunch on the top of Porlock Hill going up which I really thought YY would blow up, but I gave her a good rest and she cooled down and on we went to Lynton. There we had another hill, but eventually arrived at Brambletye and was shown all over the school. I regret to say I do not like the Blencowes any more. Saw Mer's dormitory and then left him. Poor darling he looked more miserable than he had ever done. Mary and I drove away very quickly, then stopped and I had a cigarette. Down in Porlock we filled up the car. Then we went to tea with the Wrens at dear Holincote. Major W. Gave Mary one of his books and Mary was delighted. Home at 6.30.

Saturday 21 September

Mary and Ann Thelluson went off to the Grandfields to fetch the goats. This was a great thrill for both girls. We have named them Hurricane and Spitfire. In the evening went out with Mrs T to Doddington to see the rounded up hill ponies. Doddington is a lovely old manor house about 2 miles from Nether Stowey.

Sunday 22 September

All went to church. Since Monday have been very busy looking after Miss Clowes chickens. They are really most lovely birds and I quite wish they were mine. Poor London and Kent and Sussex seem to be having a terrible time being bombed daily. I think I have a parlourmaid who answered my advertisement and I have also heard from Mrs Hackett who wants to come back so am feeling more cheerful about it all.

Monday 23 September

Thellusons were supposed to have left today but they have stayed on for another night. Went on my bike to see Horace Wire about the mating of the goats.

Tuesday 24 September

Lovely day and Thellusons left the cottage at about 11.00. Mrs Maund busy cleaning it all up, in preparation for Grannie Lunn and George, who arrived in a large limousine. The car was covered with luggage and baggage of every description and Grannie L. covered with rugs and the dog Spot. They all unearthed themselves from the car and were charmed with the cottage and delighted with it all. Had dinner with us which Mrs H. cooked very nicely.

Wednesday 25 September

Lovely weather. Bill's Mother seems to be very happy. She and George came to lunch. Mary, twins and I went to tea with Mr Luttrell at East Quantoxhead.

In evening I took Mrs L. and George down to drinks with the Laytons as they are house hunting and I thought they might help her and George find something suitable.

Thursday 26 September

A lovely day. Mrs L. had a car and we went off to look for houses. Saw two at Stogumber and had lunch at Dragon House, Washford. Then went to Combe House. Came in to dinner having got rooms at Combe House and so somewhere to go to when they leave here.

Friday 27 September

Newie, Mary and I went in YY to Townsend Farm Sale at East Quantoxhead this afternoon. Enjoyed the sale, but did not buy any of the poultry. Bought two old varnished coloured prints and a set of fire irons which were cheap at 2/6. Saw the Summerhayes and all the local farmers there.

Saturday 28 September

Mrs Lunn and George were out for the day. She was in an awful state as she had heard from Dandy. The old lady wanted her and she must be fetched at once. Really these old people like Dandy are the devil. Wrote to my darling. Twins and Mary went to tea with Grannie Lunn at the cottage.

Sunday 29 September

All walked to church at Holford. Terrible old vicar who made us all laugh. Bill's mother and George came to lunch and she talked and talked afterwards till I really thought she'd never stop. George went to sleep.

Monday 30 September

Have decided to have Mrs H. back on Oct. 21st and have told Mrs Herman so. Am now communicating with the house parlour maid Violet Marnot who is in Hampstead and Joyce Banks, a children's maid who lives at Woodbridge. Felt very annoyed with Mrs L. as she and George say they have now decided to take the cottage on top of hill and can get it for 3 guineas a week.

Tuesday 1 October

Took Mrs L. and George to Taunton in YY. Lovely day. Had a big lot of shopping to do and had tea by myself, came home at 5.30.

Wednesday 2 October

Mrs L and George chased off in Knight's car for the day house hunting. They came in to tea in the evening. Then went in the car to Combe House and I gave up the cottage. Mrs Maund came in to clean it up.

Friday 4 October

Goats are flourishing but are very dreary beasts. Mary is highly delighted as she has a pupil, little Sean Hampton from village to give riding lessons to and earns 2/6 an hour! Mary Clowes returned this evening, so I shall not have her birds to do now.

Sunday 6 October

Enjoyed a quiet morning writing and reading. In afternoon put away all summer blankets and got out winter ones.

Monday 7 October

Kathleen Clarke left to return to London. Absolutely daft girl. More than thrilled to get three letters from Bill. Went down to help Mary C. with her chickens. Audrey came for the morning to do house parlour maid work and Mrs Maund came to clean out the maids' room which was absolutely filthy. Sent Maund in trap to meet Violet. I went to Bridgwater to meet Mrs Hackett. Mrs H. never turned up on 5.00 and it was 9.30 by the time she eventually got here from Williton. Hope children's maid will come on Wednesday.

Tuesday 8 October

Paid Mrs Herman who is most disagreeable over Mrs Hackett's arrival. Bought a book yesterday for Bill called Cottage Pie. Grannie Lunn rang up and George to say they are taking a house at Nether Stowey for the winter.

Wednesday 9 October

Went to Bridgwater taking Mary C. and Mrs H with me. Went to the market and bought some nice dressed chickens for table, also 2 pigeons and a lot of groceries, cakes etc. Met 4.50 train, but no girl on it, so came back with Mrs H and went off to bed at 9.30. Was woken 11.30 by Joyce ringing to say she had just arrived at Bridgewater. Told her to get a room and come out on 7.00 am bus.

Thursday 10 October

Went down in the car to meet Joyce. Found her there and she seems a very nice girl. Mrs L rang to say they have settled on the house at Nether Stowey.

Friday 11 October

Cleaned out coop and had a lot of poultry cleaning up to do. I am now trap-nesting the pullets. Wrote to my darling as it was marvellous to get three more letters from him today. Mrs Pollard came into tea and we settled most amicably about the cottage. I am to have the bedrooms and use of bathroom for the maids, and she has a downstairs room for ironing etc.

Saturday 12 October.

Lovely day. Mary Clowes took Mopsy and me to the dentist at Minehead where we made an appointment. We had lunch at Bobby's Restaurant which was rather fun. I shopped and got 2 ties for Bill. Came home to find Grannie L. and George had come over to tea from Combe House. She seemed depressed and did not look well.

Sunday 13 October

Twinnies have colds so Mary and I went to church at Kilve. Mrs Summerhayes took us down in her car. Mary and I then lunched with Mary Clowes. Roast lamb, peaches and cream. Mary is such a dear sweet companion.

Monday 14 October

Mrs Hackett came up to tea. Mary had her pupil. I had busy day with poultry. Twins' colds are better. Mother sent us lovely big box of plums.

Tuesday 15 October

Good servants really are a comfort and Violet and Joyce are an excellent couple and when Mrs Hackett is here permanently I think I shall be very comfy. Wrote to my Bill and Mother. Rang up Mrs L. who leaves Coombe House tomorrow.

Wednesday 16 October

Very wet day. No papers came so raids must be bad again in London. Barbara Gauvain had a baby son on 11th. Have written to her and so have the twins. Still pouring.

Thursday 17 October

A simply lovely morning. Walked down to the village with the twins and met Mr Summerhayes. Newie went to Williton in afternoon.

Friday 18 October

St Luke's summer in truth; lovely warm autumn days and nights. How I miss and long for my darling. Still I feel sustained by his love for me and I think hourly of him. In afternoon took children to tea at Nether Stowey with Grannie L. and George. They have quite a sweet little house there called Greenbank and only pay 2 guineas a week. A modern villa, but very comfortable and of course a huge spread of tea.

Saturday 19 October

Set 27 with twelve eggs today, number 12 with eleven yesterday. Lovely day again and much cheered by having letters from my darling. Maund killed the fox this evening and brought the mangy old brute in to show us. He had killed two of Gibson's pullets today.

Monday 21 October

Wrote to my darling. Had a very busy morning cooking the lunch. Enjoyed a lovely afternoon picking medlars in the orchard. Mrs Hackett arrived. Major Wren sent me copy of his new book. Lovely autumn day.

Tuesday 22 October

Went to Taunton at 10.30 in YY. Managed to get to St Andries garage before filling up and then put in three gallons. Shopped all morning with Mary and Newie. Lunched at Castle Hotel, very expensive and not good. In afternoon Mary had her hair cut. Twins had been to lunch with Mary Clowes and enjoyed themselves. Fed poultry and to bed early.

Wednesday 23 October

Very chilly, raw day, misty and awfully dark. Felt depressed and a bit chilly. Walked to village shop with twins and got some nice beech leaves, but they are not as good as usual as we have had no frosts. Met Dr Gibson who said our black out was very incomplete. In afternoon set no 39 on sitting of thirteen L.S. eggs due to hatch in Nov.

Thursday 24 October

Mrs Pollard rang up to say that Miss B. wanted to take some of the things from the cottage on Friday. Cold day. Busy in morning but had a lovely idle afternoon and went to sleep in my chair.

Friday 25 October

Lovely morning, letter from Gabriel. Later came a cable from Bill which was lovely and most cheering as there seems to be a possibility that his return may not be as remote as I thought. Miss Bullock came at 1.30 and fetched away all the beds and a lot of furniture from the cottage. I biked to village to get a Williton local paper.

Saturday 26 October

Busy doing chickens, before leaving at 11.00 in Knight's taxi for Lynton. Stopped in Williton to get roof felting. Then all on to see Major Wren at Holnicote and thank him for his book. Arrived at Lynton at 1.00. Mer looking very well and old Blencowe most pleasant. I took Mer, Richard Heathcoat and twins, Newie and Mary to lunch in woods about half mile from Brambletye. Had cold chicken, egg and tongue sandwiches, choc buns, coffee, choc biscuits, cream buns and doughnuts and plenty of sweets. The art is good but music I'm afraid is very poor. Shopped in Minehead and got back for late tea at six. Mary Clowes came in to hear news.

Monday 28 October

No news or letters from Bill, felt sad and depressed. Took Mary by bus to dentist at Minehead. Had lunch at the beach. Mary had nothing done to her teeth but I ought to have a wisdom tooth out which is a bore. Home on 3.30 bus and back here for tea.

Friday 1 November

The car is laid up till the end of the year. Very, very thrilled to get a glorious letter from my darling and the children a lovely book from him. It's marvellous to get a letter and really puts new life into me again. Went in the trap to Williton and shopped. Worried about the twin's room which has that peculiar musty smell. Pollard's man came who said it was dry rot. Feel worried about this. Don't like twins to sleep in there at all.

Sunday 3 November

Another awful day. Wrote to my darling a long, long letter in answer to his which came yesterday. He has made a lovely book for the children called 'Told on the Highest Mountain'.

Tuesday 5 November

Nice morning. Went off at 11.00 in the car from N. Stowey for Crowcombe taking Newie, Mary and twins and a picnic lunch. Had a most enjoyable day in spite of showers and spent £3.10.0. for a chest of drawers, a very nice dressing table and some china.

Wednesday 6 November

Had a field day with the chickens! As there is so much rain in the little orchard feel the pullets must not remain there so moved them to the far pen and put ducks in orchard. All this necessitated Joe and Maund's help. Finished by lunchtime, very thrilled as eggs under no. 12 are chipping.

Friday 8 November

Orchid has eleven chicks out of eleven eggs! Highly satisfactory. Mary took me to Bridgwater this afternoon for shopping and I enjoyed the change.

Saturday 9 November

Had two lovely special letters from Bill which was marvellous. Wrote to him at once and of course feel quite a different girl. Paid Maund and Joyce and raised her wages to £45 as she is most satisfactory. Nine out twelve eggs hatched out under Violet. Transferred them all to the garden in coops.

Monday 11 November

A most amazing day! This afternoon Mr Southwood arrived by order of the Sheriffs of the county with a Bailiff and seized all Miss Barnard's possessions on the spot and installed this awful ruffian of a man in the cottage. Apparently she owes Chapmans of Taunton £150 plus the costs of action against her and all the expenses of this Mr Southwood etc. all going on and unless she finds the money in a very short space of time all will be sold. I feel very worried.

Tuesday 12 November

Went to Minehead with twins and Mary and Newie. Took twins to the dentist and they each had one little hole in same tooth. I went to see Newbury and Thorne, Miss Barnard's solicitor and they suggested I should employ my own solicitor and recommended a Mr Pardoe at Bridgwater. Rang up Mr Pardoe and arranged to see him tomorrow.

Wednesday 13 November

Still this man is here, and still Miss Barnard has not found the money! Mr Southwood came to see me at lunchtime and I went off to see Pardoe in Mary Clowes' car after lunch and saw him at 3.30. Find him bright, business like and unlikely to stand any nonsense. Told him the whole story and came home feeling much relieved. He said he would sue her for damages if the things are taken but that won't help me as it will be most uncomfortable without carpets etc. Mary brought me home.

Thursday 14 November

Heavenly respite from worry having four letters from my darling by special air mail which only took five or six days to come. He does not seem to think yet that is much hope of his return. Had an NTL to saying I was to stay where I am. I rang up Pardoe again. Mr Southwood said he thought the matter would be settled. My third lot of chicks hatched, got ten again but one very weak.

Friday 15 November

Went to Taunton with Mary Clowes, shopped and enjoyed my day. Coming home by Bridgwater called on Southwood and rang up home to hear Miss B had settled and the man had left. Told Pardoe what had happened. He is now going to contact Miss B's solicitors and see what is happening and if she will either sell or let the property. Claude rang up in the evening to say he is joining Bill next week. He wants me to meet him and Margaret on Monday in Taunton and take letters out to him. Wrote hectically all the evening.

Saturday 16 November

Had cottage cleaned out and feel much relieved the old man has gone. Mary Clowes came to dinner.

Monday 18 November

Off to Taunton in pouring rain in Arthur Knight's taxi. Enjoy the day awfully. Took Joyce in with me, met Claude and Margaret at the County where we had lunch. Poor Margaret very depressed, and sad over Claude's departure, especially as she is going to have another baby. Gave Claude letters for Bill and then went shopping before coming home arriving back at teatime. Heard from Mr Scott I have sold the goats for £3.10.0. And a breeding pen of L. Sussex for £2.17.6. Also 6 L.S, hens to Miss Clowes for £3.15.0.

Tuesday 19 November

Very busy morning first getting the goats off, second getting off L. S. Breeding pen and all by 9 o'clock when Chilcott came up for them with his lorry.

Thursday 21 November

Paid Mrs Hackett £5. Maund cutting down branches of a tree that is growing into the wall. Have heard nothing from Miss Barnard. Walked to village with Mary Clowes who is negotiating to buy a house at Dawlish.

Friday 22 November

Lovely day after a wild and rainy night. Busy with chickens. Heard Mary had bought the house at Dawlish.

Monday 25 November

A lovely day, busy morning doing the poultry. Patricia came over for the day. She arrived at 12.15. Miss Potter bought 2 dozen eggs at 4/- a dozen. Enjoyed seeing Pat very much. She looks well and we went for a walk and enjoyed ourselves. Walked down to the bus to see her off in the evening.

Wednesday 27 November

Letter from Merlin, also one from Bill. Lovely day for me. So much enjoyed myself as Mary Clowes took me to Dawlish for the day. We left at 9.40 arrived at Dawlish about 12.30. Had lunch at the house Mary has bought, 5, Haldon Terrace Afterwards measured rooms, saw the decorators and home for late tea. Came across field to shut up chickens and pleased to get in to children and Newie, all well.

Friday 29 November

Mary hunting with Maund at East Quantoxhead, saw Miss B there looking very cheerful. Newie and the twins went on foot and all were out till lunchtime.

Saturday 30 November

A lovely day but cold frosty, and slight covering of snow. Fed the chickens and was very busy before starting at 10.30 for Lynton to see Merlin. This was great fun and we all went off in Knight's car. Mary, Newie and also took Violet and complete picnic lunch. Merlin looking well. Great fun to see him again. Saw Mr Blencowe who was very pleasant. We cooked ourselves eggs on our little old nursery spirit stove which was great fun and had cold chicken and hot coffee. Twins quite happy left at home and to their own devices.

Sunday 1 December

Mary and I walked to church. Newie and twins went in Mary Clowes' car. Nice service. Started Christmas letters and had a busy afternoon. Wrote to my Darling. Not having had any letters for so long makes it hard to bear sometimes.

Wednesday 4 December

I had a letter from Richard yesterday saying that they want Bill at Air Ministry and are hoping to make an exchange and get him back sooner or later. So I cabled Bill about this. Patricia came over to lunch and stayed till 6.15 when I walked down to the bus with her. Wrote to Bill and did a few Christmas letters.

Sunday 8 December

Mother's birthday. Rang her up after lunch, found she was well and sounded very cheerful. Wrote letters most of the day. Opened her Christmas parcels. Read papers and did accounts and in the evening moved pullets to big henhouse and hens to run in field house.

Monday 9 December

Nearly finished Christmas letters, cards and calendars. Rang Pardoe, no news about the house. No news of Bill, war seems to have really started in Egypt now and I am so anxious about my darling. Wrote to Mother and sent her a cheese.

Tuesday 10 December

Another awful day, gale and hail, thunder and lightning. Luttrells all came to tea. Very nice wartime tea, egg and celery sandwiches, buns and gingerbread, medlar jelly and honey. He is a dear old man.

Wednesday 11 December

Went to Bridgwater on 12.30 bus. Tearing gale and bitterly cold. Went to get sweets for the children and a good many Christmas presents. Came home laden with parcels.

Thursday 12 December

Mrs Heckett out for day. I went down to Hood Arms and bought bottle of sherry, also to the P.O. with final instalments of letters and cards. Worried over letter from Pardoe and decided to see him tomorrow with Miss Clowes in her car.

Friday 13 December

Had early lunch and went by car with Mary C. to Bridgwater where I interviewed Pardoe about the house and Miss Barnard. I must say he really is a wizard at concocting a letter to her solicitors.

Saturday 14 December

Newie's birthday which was a great thrill for the children. We had parcels and at tea, a cake, candles and crackers. A great thrill for me was two telegrams from Bill. He says he hopes to be home by 12 February. News of Western Desert fighting is most thrilling in every way and our successes are terrific. Heard from Merlin he was in bed. Rang up and found he had flu and was in sick quarters.

Monday 15 December

Mary sick and in bed, looking very seedy poor child. Decided to fetch Merlin on Thursday by car as heard he was much better. Lovely letter from Bill, flowers from Mum and lots of Christmas letters and some cards. Mrs Hackett very rude and offhand. Letter from Patricia who wants to come for Christmas.

Tuesday 17 December

A lovely day, very cold and frosty. Newie ill all night being sick. Gave her castor oil in the evening and then she was up all night! Lots of Christmas letters and cards and a cable from my darling. Send him one for Christmas. Patricia rang up and is definitely coming on Friday to stay.

Thursday 19 December

Set off at 9.00 with twins to fetch Mer home for the Christmas holidays. Lovely morning and I enjoyed the drive immensely. Got there after much trouble with Knight's car to get up the hill! But succeeded and found my little Merlin patiently waiting for me! Not looking very well and very dark under the eyes, but he will I hope soon pick up. Got back for lunch.

Friday 20 December

Mr Blencoe suggested I should have Mer's throat swabbed to check for glandular fever as there was fear of this at the school. So rang up Dr Archer and asked him to come. Busy morning dealing with Christmas ordering, letters etc. Mrs Heckett most disagreeable. Had Knight at 2.30 to go to Bridgwater and set off there with Merlin for him to do his shopping and me mine. Had a most lovely cable from Bill saying he hoped to be back before long perhaps in a month's time. Felt terribly thrilled and excited about this which seems too wonderful. Fetched Patricia at the George and her luggage and then called at Greenbank to see Dandy. Latter I think appears to me to be quite mental. Pat very nice and pleased to be coming to us for Christmas. She has Mary's little room, and Merlin is with me, Mary with the twins in big children's room.

Saturday 21 December

It's lovely to get a letter today from my darling. This Christmas is going to be just awful. Pat very good and helpful and busying herself with the children and my parcels.

Sunday 22 December

Mary Clowes is away at Dawlish. Miss her very much. Pat doing up more and more parcels and the whole house seems to be filled with them. Miss being at Belstead.

Monday 23 December

Merlin not very well, Dr Archer came and swabbed his throat. Still bitterly cold. Letter from Bill written only 10 days ago, was a special Christmas Air Mail one.

Tuesday 24 December

Still cold. Merlin up for the small Christmas Tree party which we had. I went into Williton in the morning in the trap with Maund. Mary came with me and after our shopping we had a cup of very hot coffee in the Egremont Hotel. Home for lunch. The children had decorated the Christmas Tree and made it look lovely with all the lights on. Dr and Mrs Gibson and the three Miss Gibsons, Mary Clowes, came to tea. And later Mrs Pollard came down and Ann Pollard. It was quite a jolly party and I think all enjoyed it. I felt very tired afterwards and the cook, Mrs H is so disagreeable. I felt too, so utterly sad my darling had not been with me. I simply cannot bear yet, another separation. Went to bed after filling all the stockings and doing all the last pre-Christmas jobs.

Wednesday 25 December: Christmas Day

A lovely, warm Christmas day. The bitter cold gone, and is so nice to be warmer again. Woken at 7.00 by Mary wanting to start opening parcels, the children all had lovely presents and so did I. £20 from Dad, a lovely Pyrex glass casserole and a pair of bellows from Mum. My darling has sent me the sweetest most lovely little amethyst coloured clock, but unfortunately it has been damaged in the aeroplane and glass been broken which is very sad. A cable came from him yesterday and this morning by the postman came a letter sent on by Richard. I felt very near to crying a lot today. I sent Newie to Holy Communion with Mary Clowes at nine and myself took the four children at 11.15. We had a lovely turkey, Mother sent a plum pudding; dessert and coffee. In evening Newie, Pat and I had a simple dinner, all children having gone off to bed. How I miss my darling.

Thursday 26 December: Boxing Day

Children busy writing letters. Mrs Hackett & Violet both savage and dissatisfied. Too much Christmas obviously. Postman came as usual & no shops closed this year.

Friday 27 December

Went to Bridgewater with Miss Clowes. Changed one of Mary's books at Smiths. Did shopping and came home at teatime. Violet gave notice. I think Mrs Hackett has endeavoured to upset her as much as possible.

Sunday 29 December

Mrs Hackett left yesterday and I now have a young girl Dorothy Burnham who has been a kitchen maid with me. Rang up Mrs Thelluson and invited her and Ann to tea. Hope she may be a help to Pat.

Monday 30 December

My new little girl is so far getting on quite well, and it is much more peaceful now Mrs H has gone. Took Pat to tea at Luttrell's and to see the house in the afternoon. In the morning I had a super thrill as the car from Bridgwater Motor Co. was brought out and I tried it out and have bought it, a 10hp Morris. And though a tiddler it will be great joy to get about in.

Tuesday 31 December

The last day of a truly ghastly and hateful year, and one I hope I shall never have to live through again away from my darling, away from Suffolk and my parents. The only joy being my dear children & my little home & the comfort of doing as I like and also the permanent joy of the country, my chickens & animals. One has much to be thankful for, but much misery as well and nothing can take from me the eternal ache in my heart that this separation entails. How I long to be with my darling and how I miss him. Patricia, Newie and I solemnly sat up and listened to the wireless and saw the New Year in. Brought Merlin down and made him go outside before midnight and come in as the clock struck with coal, salt and bread! And so to bed, and the end of the year 1940.

1941
Kilve Somerset and Tostock Suffolk

Cesca and her children remain in Somerset until the end of October. Cesca dashes to Suffolk as her Mother is very ill resulting in an operation in hospital early January. The new little car proves very tiresome to start and to drive. Mary has the best Birthday present possible. The search for a house continues in spite of the War, culminating in the purchase of Tostock Old Rectory in August. Cesca is ill for a month in September with possible Glandular Fever. November is taken up with packing up and organising the move from Pardlestone back to Suffolk.

For the first time for seven years Cesca's parents will not be living with her under the same roof but will remain at Belstead.

Wednesday 1 January New Year's Day
A lovely cold frosty day with just a slight sprinkling of snow. Very busy and especially in morning as Grannie Lunn and George came to lunch. They came over by bus. We had delicious leg of lamb, plum pudding and rice pudding, cheese and desert. In afternoon went to New Year's party at Mary Clowes, which we and especially the children thoroughly enjoyed. Felt very sleepy in evening after being up late last night.

Thursday 2 January
Bitterly cold, snow falling and frost. Went down to the village with Merlin in afternoon to post and Hood Arms. Had a bad raid in evening, planes going over all the time.

Friday 3 January
Patricia left in morning from Williton. I took her in with Knight and left her at station. Very busy all day. Mary Clowes came up in evening and talked.

Saturday 4 January
Newie has a bad eye and shall send for Doctor if it goes on. Maund cleaning out poultry houses. My car arrived, five days ago, most

exciting but I find it difficult getting used to driving it! And starting it.

Sunday 5 January

Awful job again to start the car. Old Summerhayes pushing it up and down the stable yard. Very cold indeed. Did not go out except to feed chickens.

Monday 6 January

Warmer today and snow melting. Busy filling in ration books. In afternoon fed chicks. I was reading to Mary and Merlin at 6.45 when telephone went and a strange voice said Dr Bisshopp wishes to speak to Mrs Pearson-Rogers. Goodness I thought. Would I come up to Belstead at once as Mother was very ill in hospital and at that moment undergoing a severe abdominal operation. Of course I would and started to dash around packing.

Tuesday 7 January

Up at 6.00. Violet brought me some tea and bread and butter. Off at 7.15 with Knight to Bridgwater train 8.12. Arrived in London 2.40, desperately slow and no food. Got some tea at waiting room. Down to Ipswich on 3.40 and arrived 5.40. Dad and Sturgeon at station. Found Mother's operation not as serious as at first anticipated ie cancer and stoppage of the bowel. Instead it was severe strangulated hernia. Saw dear Mum looking very ill [78 years old] but in a nice room, very comfy and nice nurses and Sister. Stayed 5 minutes, back to Belstead. A white Belstead, but house so dark and dismal. I'm in oak room with a lovely fire and am so tired I shall be asleep at once tonight. So relieved Mum is not as ill as first thought.

Wednesday 8 January

Wrote to Bill and Newie, then went to hospital to see Mum. Stayed 10 minutes. Saw the Sister. She looked better today. Dad saw the doctor. After lunch read papers, rested and walked to post with letter for children. Saw Southgate and Morphew also Mrs Enefer and Enefer.

Thursday 9 January

Mother very much better. Stayed one hour in morning, half an hour in afternoon. Saw the doctors. Lovely day. Air raid warnings in evening. Came home by bus at 4.30 and met Bernice who is now married.

Friday 10 January

So relieved Mum really looks better. Decided to return home tomorrow. Wired Newie. Wrote to Ursula and Irene Taylor for Mum. Had a letter from Patricia. Lunched at Limmers and had hair shampooed, set and henna rinse. Spent one hour with Mum in afternoon again. Heard from Ursula that Uncle Alfred is very ill with cancer of stomach and kidneys. Dinner with Dad. Said goodbye to Southgate and Morphew and packed in evening. Hate to say goodbye to beloved Belstead but it's all so sad, forlorn and different that I long for cosy little Pardlestone and children's voices.

Saturday 11 January

Up very early and left Belstead after some tea and bread and butter. Said goodbye to Dad [now 82 years] and feel sad leaving him all alone there in that great house. Sturgeon took me in the car to station. Changed at Chelmsford, London 9.30 and across with 10 minutes to spare before getting 10.35 down to Bridgwater. The journey was very easy, no raids only cold and foggy. Arrived Bridgwater at 2.15 but no taxis so eventually shared one with a man who was going to Stugursey and I took it on from there. On Stugursey-Kilve Road went past Anne Thelluson leading Sally, Mary having been to a pony club rally. Had a tremendous welcome from children and Newie. Rang up in evening to let Dad know I had arrived safely and sent Bill a cable. Poor ducks. Two had been killed by a fox. Sad about this.

Sunday 12 January

Mary Clowes came to lunch, and we had a roast chicken. She is off to Dawlish on Tuesday, I shall miss her very much. Wrote letters and started to get straight.

Monday 13 January

Took car to Bridgwater for repairs. Merlin went with me and we came back on bus in time for lunch. Set maids at work altering round the bedrooms in preparation for when Bill and the new maids come. Heard that Mrs Brown is definitely coming and am hoping she will not be too great a trial.

Tuesday 14 January

Mary went off to Dawlish and we all went down to see her off.

Wednesday 15 January

I am worried over Mary who looks very pale and thin. Bitterly cold. Merlin and I went in the little motor to Minehead, shopped and to a sale at The Cottage, Warden Road where I bought a nice Chippendale chair with Jacobean embroidery for 27/- and a table for 14/-, also a tea set for 7/- and a pair of bellows for 7/-. Came home to tea. Newie had fed chicks for me.

Thursday 16 January

Newie went off for her holiday and Mary and I took her in the little motor to Bridgwater. Snow and ice everywhere. Joyce took the children out in afternoon. Have decided to have Dorothy's friend as children's maid on 27th and Dorothy to do houseparlour maid's work. Mary felt seedy and had a bad headache.

Friday 17 January

Merlin should have returned to Brambletye today, but decided to keep him at home. Mother continues to progress but I do wish I was nearer and worry so very much over the old people. Mary has temperature so keeping her in bed, believe she has same infection that Merlin had.

Saturday 18 January

Very cold and wet. Mary in bed all day. Dad rang up to say Mother was getting on all right. Children should have sat up for dinner but they were very naughty so I had to punish them. Merlin especially will lead twins into mischief.

Monday 20 January

Spent the day with the children. Sold my 6 white Sussex pullets for 15 shillings each to Miss Stapleton. Enjoyed being with children so much, but if only my darling would come home. How I miss him.

Tuesday 21 January

A wet cold day. Mother getting on well and hopes to be back at Belstead by the end of the month. Poured with rain in afternoon. Had to go down and meet Newie who returned looking very seedy at 4.30 on Bridgwater bus from Exeter.

Wednesday 22 January

Took Merlin and Clare to Minehead to the dentist. It was first time that Clare had lunch at a restaurant and she was suitably impressed.

Thursday 23 January

The car not going well and won't start so took it into Bridgwater with Merlin and came home on bus for lunch. Mary better and up for lunch, but she still looks seedy. We had a terrible discovery of water under the schoolroom today when Pollard's men came to do the floor. No wonder we are ill and it's so cold and damp. Felt very worried indeed and sent to cable to Bill to ask what I should do, as I had a letter from Mum wanting us to go back to Belstead.

Friday 24 January

Busy altering rooms for children to upstairs. Dr Archer does not think we should use school room any more as it is so terribly damp.

Saturday 25 January

Busy packing up all Merlin's clothes. No news from Bill but news from Libya is absolutely grand and it's a lovely glowing feeling to think a lot is due to my Bill.

Monday 27 January

Violet and Joyce left in afternoon. The weather became too bad for me to take Merlin back, thick mist came down on the hill. So he is with us for one more day. I am anxious to know what Bill thinks we ought to do. Feel very worried.

Tuesday 28 January

Better weather. Merlin and I set off in the little car and did our shopping in Minehead for some last minute things. We had a picnic lunch about half mile from Lee Abbey. Then I took him back and saw the Blencowes. I do wish he was at Cheam. I hurried home, there was thick sea fog and mist over most of Exmoor and I had to go very steadily in places. Bought some kitchen mats and some fibre ones for back door before collecting Mrs Brown at Williton. Poor Mrs Brown is deafer than ever. Rang up to find out how Mother was. Feel sad without Merlin and house very empty.

Wednesday 29 January

A busy day dealing with Mrs Brown who is exceptionally deaf. Had a letter from Bill, a special sent January 4th, but very slow. He said he hoped Cross, his relief would come out by middle of January and that he would then get away.

Thursday 30 January

Had reply from Bill to my cable saying we are to stay put and not go to Belstead or anywhere else and that he hopes to be arriving about February 27. A present for Mary! Cabled to him that I would remain where I was. The sweep came and swept new schoolroom chimney, upstairs.

Friday 31 January

Went to Bridgwater in afternoon to get the girls hair cut and to tea at Grannie Lunn's on way home. Saw Dandy with Grannie Lunn who gave us a very nice tea. Thick mist again.

Saturday 1 February

Heard from Mum that she returns to Belstead on Monday and has a London hospital nurse coming to look after her. A lovely spring-like day. Paid Maund. New girls doing quite well, Mrs Brown very well and it's a treat to get some nice cooking.

Monday 3 February

Sent off egg orders. Had a very rude letter from Mrs Thelluson which I had great pleasure in replying to in a same vein. Wrote to Mother and wrote too to Uncle Alfred who is not expected to live long. Ursula has asked me to be her executor. In evening rang up to see how Mum was. Found she was getting on splendidly. I am sorry Bill won't permit me to go as I should have liked to. I feel so desperate with this shattering separation going on interminably and get so infuriated with it. At times can't write to him as I feel so furious. Have had all ducks killed.

Tuesday 4 February

Took one duck and a dozen eggs down to bus to send to Mrs Lunn. Snowed in evening. Have not heard from Merlin yet. Worried about this damp house and have found same trouble in kitchen now.

Wednesday 5 February

The most awful day I think I can remember. Snow, sleet, hail and thunder and a north east gale! Had bad neuralgia head ache all day and felt seedy. Newie did chickens for me in afternoon. Had an air mail letter from Bill dated December 4, over 2 months old!

Thursday 6 February

After breakfast of sprats, all children were violently sick and remained in bed for rest of the day, poor darlings. Had letter from Mum who is delighted with her nurse and to be home again. And also a letter from Merlin. Newie sick too. Everyone but me!

Friday 7 February

Children all better except Mary who continues to vomit and cling to her basin and stay in bed. Fed up with sick children. Went off in the car to Bridgwater. Shopped, cashed money, paid tiresome little bills. Wrote to Merlin, Bill and Mother. Plumber came and cleaned out boiler that much needed doing.

Saturday 8 February

Heard absolutely grand news that we have now taken Benghazi. Properly twisting the wops! Felt very seedy. Bad headache all day so rested in afternoon. Very cold and drizzling.

Monday 10 February

A truly lovely spring day. Newie went to Minehead. Mary sick again last evening. Really there is no end to it and was seriously considering having Dr A. when Newie said she had drunk stream water and eaten bamboo leaves. Really, what can you expect? Very cross with both. Mrs Brown cooking very well. News from Libya still jolly good. So was Churchill's speech last night.

Tuesday 11 February

Took car to Bridgwater after early lunch and had my hair washed. Shopped and went to Browns where I had my fitting. Children well, Mary really looking much better.

Wednesday 12 February

My 12th wedding anniversary. Feeling so happy! And my darling sent me lovely white carnations ordered by Mary Clowes from Exeter and lilies to come, also a big book on Old China which I have at Belstead. Mother sent me lovely carnations and freesias and Dad us both £20. Then came a cable from Bill which drove me very nearly out of my senses. It said Bill should be with you about 15th. This really is quite marvellous and thrilling only three days! Could scarcely keep it to myself. Do love him so. Oh! Soon, soon he will be here. Children so sweet. Mary had painted me a sweet little ashtray, and the twins gave me a dear little pot of snowdrops and primroses potted with mosses. Rang up Mum but found she had not been well which worried me.

Thursday 13 February

Woke up feeling so frightfully happy. As my Billy will be with me soon, now any day. And this long, long unutterably miserable heartbreaking separation will be over and melt away. Sometimes the apparent hopeless never ending of it has driven me almost beyond endurance. Very busy making preparations for twins birthday tomorrow. Mrs Brown icing their cake, pale pink and putting silver balls on it. Claire and Cecily 7 years! Chickens laying splendidly.

Friday 14 February

Perhaps Bill will come today. It would be a marvellous surprise and present for the twins. The dear little girls spent from 7.15 to 8.00 in my bed opening their parcels. Lovely presents from Mum and 25/- each from Dad. Can't believe Bill may be here at any time. Told Newie who was almost as excited as I was. Twins spent morning playing with their toys. Had their special lunch, roast spring chicken, roast potatoes and sprouts, rasberry soufflé, cheese and biscuits. And for tea iced cake and scones. It poured all day. Lovely lilies of the valley arrived at lunchtime from Bill.

Saturday 15 February

Today is the day he says he will arrive! Wondered whether we ought to go to Taunton in case he rings up and has to be met. Went to Taunton in car and twins shopped and spent their money at toyshops. It was a lovely day, and we all enjoyed it ending up with lunch at Maynard's restaurant. Found two cables one from Bernard Burrows saying Bill had left and one from Bill saying arrived Malta, proceeding in a day or two so he is really on his way. To bed very thrilled and happy.

Sunday 16 February

Anxious when heard in evening that flying boat Clyde had sunk at Lisbon and wondered if it was Bill's flying boat.

Monday 17 February

Still no news of Bill. Feel convinced that the flying boat must have sunk and been his and wonder if he has lost all his luggage. Papers say all British staff are safe. It is sure to delay him. Wrote to Dad and sent Mother a chicken. In afternoon feeling restless and impatient took twins to Williton. Mary rode over to Nether Stowey.

Tuesday 18 February

Had a letter from Dad, saying Mum had been doing too much and ordered back to bed, but is much better now. Gave children their French lesson. Later saw in Times that a naval seaplane en route from Gibraltar to England had been forced down at Setabul, Portugal and it was not yet known whether the crew had been interned for duration or whether they had got away. In a terrible worry over this and eventually had a personal call through to Richard at Air Ministry who told me it was going the other way, and he would let me know if there was any cause for alarm. But I do wish he would come. Had a very bad night.

Wednesday 19 February

Had a cable from Bill that set my mind at rest. 'Still at Malta will wire progress' so I felt relieved. Wrote to Mum and Richard and posted in Minehead when I took Mary to have a tooth out.

Thursday 20 February.

Letter from John who is in Hatfield Military Hospital, after flu with jaundice. Almost expected to find Bill but no news yet. Oh! Dear if only he would but come. Bad raid on.

Friday 21 February

Had a cable from Bill to say arrived Gibraltar, this sent yesterday then a Wing Commander Fressaye rang. Said he had seen Bill yesterday and he would be with me very soon. Had letter from Mum saying the doctor says she has pleurisy, poor dear. I rang up at once. Dad said she was not well and I ought to come. Oh what am I to do? Bill coming any day, any hour, any minute and I must go now or I may not see her again. Feel desperate. Rang up Nurse Wire and asked exact position. She says I must come so will go tomorrow by 8.12 from Bridgwater.

Saturday 22 February

Left for Williton and travelled on 9.55 to Taunton, changed and had Express from there to London arriving 1.50. Taxi to Liverpool Street and 2.15 down arriving Ipswich 4.30 and rang up Belstead. Felt very upset on journey fearing Mother might die. Relief unspeakable on arrival, finding her much better. A very nice nurse too and I saw Dr Banks who said she had been most gravely ill and he had had no hesitation in saying I must come. Dad worried but very trying especially with the nurses. He has had Pepper put to sleep. This seems a great shame and will upset Mother terribly. Felt very tired but so relieved. Do so hope now Bill won't arrive till I get back.

Sunday 23 February

Mother better, spent nearly all day with her except when I went out to take letters to post. Had to break the news to her about Pepper which very much upset her and she cried and cried. Better in evening. Picked lovely carnations and freesias from Belstead garden. Packed and to bed early. Managed to ring Newie. No news of Bill yet.

Monday 24 February

Left at 7.10 in car with wretched Sturgeon who is leaving on Saturday. I never liked him and feel he really has played a hateful trick on the old people. Train very cold and felt acutely depressed, no breakfast. Changed Colchester. Arrived London 9.45. Caught Riviera Express 10.30 for Taunton. Had good lunch on train and felt better. Rang up to hear if any news of my Billy, none alas. Arrived home for tea. Deadly tired but found letter from Bill from Gibraltar to say he was much delayed by weather and that they fly all night from there arriving Plymouth early in the morning. If only he comes tomorrow how thrilling it will be.

Tuesday 25 February

No news this morning after a night of much bombing. Oh! Dear, my darling, do hurry.

Wednesday 26 February

Went to Bridgwater to have my hair washed. Had lunch at Maynards and had a busy morning shopping. Wild windy day. Wrote to Merlin. Prepared for Mary's birthday tomorrow. Mrs Lunn and George came over in a car in my absence and left two cakes and presents for children. Very tired, feel so anxious about Bill.

Thursday 27 February

Mary's 11th birthday and such a lovely day for us all. A cable came from Gibraltar from Bill asking how we all were. I replied and at 11.00 came telephone call and my darling boy speaking to me having just arrived at Plymouth. Felt so excited and after lunch I started to walk down to meet him as he was coming by taxi from

Plymouth. Arrived soon after 3.00 and there was I waiting for him at the Hood Arms. It was lovely to have him home again and the children of course beside themselves with delight. What a lovely birthday for Mary. She had a lot of presents and was thrilled at having Bill home. So lovely and felt we should never stop talking. He looks very tired and grey, poor darling and had a terrible trip home in the flying boat in awful weather. Am so thankful he is home.

February 28 Friday

Took Bill to Taunton to go to London. Mary came with me and we saw him off with his Dispatches etc. Came home to find Dorothy had left because of her eye. Busy all day trying to get domestic help as Bill on fortnight's leave tomorrow. Heard from Mrs Blencowe that Merlin has whooping cough.

Saturday 1 March

Paid Maund. Went to meet Bill at Taunton 4.30 lovely to have him really on leave at last. It is maddening though about maids. Dinner with Newie and Bill, talked and talked. To bed, very late.

March Sunday 2 [Between September 7 1940 and November 12 1941 bombing raids killed over 15,000 in London and make more than 250,000 homeless**].**

All went to church in the car to Kilve. I sat with Clare and Cecily, Mary with Bill as it was a bit of a squash. Slept after lunch. Quite unusual for me, but feel rather tired with relief at having Billy home again. Went over after tea to see Mrs Lunn, George and Dandy. Both found this very trying, but better over as Bill has only a week's leave and goes to Air Ministry next Sunday. Hate to think of him being in London. Bill posting letters for people from Egypt.

Monday 3 March

Decided to see Margaret tomorrow and Merlin on Thursday. Poor boy having whooping cough now is too bad as now he can't come home to be with Bill.

Tuesday 4 March

Went over to Wincanton and got there for lunch. Margaret very big [pregnant] poor dear. Back for late tea with the children.

Wednesday 5 March

Bill rode with Mary on old Joe which he enjoys very much. Elisabeth and Catherine Luttrell came to tea. So lovely Bill being with us again, heard yesterday he is to be here for another week.

Thursday 6 March

Went off at 10 to Minehead. Shopped and took picnic lunch and on to Brambletye. Lovely to see Merlin but poor boy coughing a lot. We had a lovely lunch in the woods, afterwards Merlin drove the car. This pleased him immensely and left him with some sweets and barley sugars. Bill not impressed with the Blencowe's but thinks Merlin is splendid.

Friday 7 March

Bitterly cold, John Peel came down arriving lunchtime. I went in car to Minehead to see a maid and engaged her but don't think she will be much good. Fun to see John again and he is staying at the Hood Arms but having meals with us. Mary Clowes rang up to say she has found me a temporary house parlourmaid.

Saturday 8 March

Really having Bill and John here it is quite like old Belstead days. Wrote to Mum to tell her we are coming down to Belstead next weekend. Bill, John, Mary and the Gibson girls all went riding in the morning. Back for lunch. I returned to meet house parlourmaid, D Weeks. In afternoon went to tea with Luttrells at Court House. Picked up other maid from bus on way home. Children so sweet and happy, especially Mary who loves all her riding. Grace left.

Sunday 9 March

All went to church at Kilve. Heard in evening that Mrs Gibson had died quite suddenly yesterday. Awful for those for girls to be left like that with no mother. Bill went out with twins. John and I slept by the fire in afternoon.

Tuesday 11 March

Set broody on 14 eggs yesterday. Heard from Mary Clowes that she is coming to stay on Thursday for the night. Danish house parlourmaid came for interview and engaged her as this D. Weeks is quite hopeless.

Thursday 13 March

Bill went to Bridgwater and took Newie in. Mary Clowes arrived at teatime. Nice to see her again and she and Bill got on very well. She is going to Bristol tomorrow.

Friday 14 March

D Weeks left in afternoon and K Hendricksen came. Expected children's maid but she did not turn up.

Saturday 15 March

Up early and a rush to get the train at Taunton, to feed hens, to get packed up before leaving at 9.30! However did it! And Bill and I had a very comfy journey up to London, first class and a good lunch. Paid Maund before leaving. Got to London very punctually and went to Pat's Club where we saw her and then to Clarges Street to inspect some perfectly awful flats which were quite hopeless. Caught 3.40 down and got to Belstead at 5.15. Very surprised Sturgeon there to meet us, he evidently has been asked to stay on. Mother up but looking very frail and thin, poor dear. It was lovely to be with her again.

Sunday 16 March

Bill complaining about single beds and being so cold, poor darling. Bill slept after lunch and Mother rested. Bill went off to London on 4.50 to club.

Monday 17 March

My day house hunting. First went with Dad to Ferns where I got Bill a nice gun case which is having his initials inscribed. Nearly missed train to Bury as Sturgeon got stuck down a narrow street. Arrived 11.30 and by taxi to Rutters asking them to make arrangements to view some houses. Meanwhile went to see Alpheton a most depressing and awful place. Then had lunch in

Bury and set off to see Hessett House most depressing and falling to pieces, then Tostock, old Rectory which I liked very much. Georgian and really quite possible, but is so ugly outside and rather dreary grounds. Then to Ixworth House. Hopeless and the Old House, Great Barton, (nice but too small), and home on 4 o'clock arriving back for tea. Told family all about it.

Tuesday 18 March

My darling Bill's birthday. Up to London after collecting Bill's gun case. Went to club and then shopped at Harrods. Met Bill for lunch. Find him rather depressed and withered over his new job. [Bill did not take kindly to desk work at the Air Ministry]. Do hope he will settle down to it, and like it better. He went back and I then started a long dreary flat hunt. Wrote letters at club then had a bath and changed. Bill arrived and we went to Dorchester and dined and danced which was great fun. Came back to bed to find air raid on and guns and bangs.

Wednesday 19 March

Bill went off to office at 8.45. I packed and went to Paddington and down on 10.30 arrived Taunton 1.30 got car and home by 3.15. Lovely to be back and find all children well. New maid, Karen has been hard at work cleaning and house looks very nice.

Saturday 22 March

George Lunn rang up to say he had some poultry food for me so went off to fetch it.

Sunday 23 March

Set another broody hen on 15 eggs. Went to church at Kilve in car. Very cold and wet. Rheumatism so bad. Felt ill and in pain all day.

Wednesday 26 March

Left at 9.30 with suitcase for Taunton in car. Garaged car and went up on 10.50. Met Bill at the Berkeley and found him having lunch with Mrs Ionides. Wished I had not had lunch on the train. Went down to Belstead on 3.50 and Bill came later arriving at 9.45. Mother is looking much better.

Thursday 27 March

Bill got the car from Mum and we went to see Tostock Old Rectory which Bill really liked. I was so surprised. Had lunch at the Angel and came home and went for a walk. Bill returned to London on the 8.00 train.

Friday 28 March

Headache all day. Arrived at teatime at Taunton where I had tea as could not get lunch. Bought some fish. All well at home.

Monday 31 March

Baby chicks hatching and by end of day had 13 out of 14 eggs. So pleased. Mary and I went to meet Bill in the Earwig who arrived at Taunton at 4.30. Very cold. So happy to be together again and talked and talked. Sometimes can't believe he really is home again.

Tuesday 1 April

Children having a wild and cheerful morning making Bill and me April fool's! Set off at 10.15 to meet Merlin at Taunton in the car. Of course he was very late but thrilled to the core to see Bill. Gave him a cup of hot chocolate and home for lunch. Nice to have Merlin home. His report is quite good.

Wednesday 2 April

Merlin and I took Bill to Williton and saw him off on 10 o'clock train. New maid Bertha Green seems pretty hopeless in every way. Baby chicks all growing amazingly well. In afternoon went to Bridgwater to see Pardoe who suggests I should pay Miss Barnard.

Saturday 5 April

Bill rang and told me Tostock Old Rectory had been withdrawn from market. Felt very sad about this.

Monday 7 April

Left for London First class on 9.50 from Williton. Had some tea at an ABC, then saw Hughes at his office and was stuck with him for ages. Then joined Bill at RAC Club and went to see Naughty Ninety One which was poor. Went to dinner at Shepheard in Shepheard's Market. Enjoyed being with Bill so much. Had nice room at the Club and a very good night.

Tuesday 8 April

Up early for breakfast with Bill and walked to the office with him Then to Mary and John's where I collected a lot of things for the children. Peter Jones for shopping, and Harrods. Had a quick lunch at Ecole du Petit Cordon Bleu and then to Club, said goodbye to Bill and home on 1.30. Very full train. Had a bad headache. Worried about Mary who has a temperature of 101 with glands and throat.

Wednesday 9 April

Sent for Dr Archer who came and said Mary is all right, but must gargle a lot. We had an exciting day with Bertha who said she was leaving but eventually did not do so.

Good Friday 11 April

Mary better, went to church with Merlin and twins after taking Newie to the station. Went for a walk with children in afternoon.

Saturday 12 April

Bill was to have rung me up this morning but did not do so. Don't know why. Chicks hatching. Have only 8 out in this batch. In evening took car over to Nether Stowey for petrol. Very tired.

Sunday 13 April Easter Day

A very queer sad sort of Easter with Bill away, and children to look after without Newie. Went to church with children and in afternoon Mary gave a jumping display on Winkle which she did very well. She is really wonderfully good. Felt very seedy all day.

Monday 14 April

Felt better after having two aspirin's and a good dose last night. Went for picnic in afternoon with Mary, Merlin, twins and joined up with Mary Clowes. Home after a good walk. Put children to bed, all Clowes party came to dinner in the evening. Mrs B cooked a very good dinner. Grapefruit, chicken in casserole and plum meringue.

Tuesday 15 April

Very excited about Bill coming tomorrow. Newie returned in evening but not looking much better for her change. Took Mrs

Brown to Nether Stowey to see the doctor in the evening and had to wait an hour there.

Wednesday 16 April

Saw in Times that Captain Pore Trench, owner of Tostock was dead, (ex House master at Eton). Now I wonder whether it will come back on the market. Busy all morning with chicks and etc. Went to Taunton immediately after lunch, shopped and met Bill at 4.30. Bill very tired.

Thursday 17 April

A lovely day and Bill gardened. Went to village with Bill and in afternoon went for a lovely long walk over the hill.

Friday 18 April

Bill left at Williton on 9.58 train, I felt sad and have a bad sore throat and cough. Wet day. Newie in bed, ill again. In evening Grannie Lunn came to see me.

Saturday 19 April

Mary rude at breakfast said she only wanted to go to Hunter trials and not to tea with Luttrells. However I think she may be doing too much riding. All went to tea at the Luttrells. Pleased to get home to nice fire.

Tuesday 22 April

Children very thrilled went off to Rally at Woodlands. Mary and Merlin riding Sally and Winkle. Twins and Newie in trap. I had to go to Bridgwater and unfortunately missed bus home and had a miserable time trying to get a lift. Eventually got to Holford in Philip's bus and walk from there over the fields. Very hot day and felt very tired when I got in.

Thursday 24 April Merlin's 10th birthday

A lovely day and we all had a very happy one. Merlin very thrilled with his presents.

Saturday 26 April

Merlin and Mary off all day at a Rally to Stogursey and then down to the sea where they made tea.

Monday 28 April

Mary and Merlin and I went off at 9.30 in Knight's taxi to Williton where we had one and a half hours wait for train delayed by a bomb on the line. Got to Exeter 12.15 where we shopped, had lunch at Bobbies. M and M highly delighted with the band at the restaurant. I bought two second hand books and we returned to meet Bill at Taunton, then by train to Williton, taxi to Pardlestone and the twins. A lovely day and so lovely to have Bill with us.

Tuesday 29 April

Bill, Merlin and self out bicycling in morning. Very cold and lovely day with Bill.

Wednesday 30 April

Merlin and I went to see Bill off on the train and Merlin was much intrigued by the sight of a coffin being hoisted into the guard's van.

Friday 2 May

Took Merlin to Taunton to catch 5.30. Very wet afternoon, had his hair cut and did some shopping and gave him tea but at station had a very long wait before the train left as it had to wait for London connection. Stayed with Merlin and seven other boys until the Master arrived, then left and drove home.

Monday 5 May

Bertha left this morning to go to Miss Clowes. Went to Williton in car and off to London where met Bill at RAC and left my luggage there. Walked back with him to Air Ministry, then left for Ipswich arriving 5.12 out to Belstead in the car. Found Mother better and a nice nurse looking after her but atmosphere so depressing. Went to bed feeling very cheered up as Bill rang to say he was coming tomorrow to spend one of his days house-hunting with me.

Tuesday 6 May

Bill arrived at 10.00. In afternoon went to see a house at Higham which was quite useless and depressing. Mrs Henderson of Bulmer Tye House rang up and as she did so a bomb dropped, I was scared out of my wits. It fell near London Road demolishing a house. Warnings and sirens sounding a lot.

Wednesday 7 May

Bill and I went to Ipswich in car with Mum and Dad and then shopped. Had coffee and caught bus to Sudbury arriving 1.30. Mum gave us a picnic lunch to eat en route. We took a taxi and went to Clees Hall which Bill liked but I thought quite impossible as so very neglected though structurally sound. Then to Pentlow Hall Cavendish where we met a savage tenant. Quite nice house. Tea in Sudbury and home on bus to Hintlesham, from there we walked home. Bill stayed night returning early in the morning.

Thursday 8 May

Bill and I thought more of Clees Hall after our visit and decided to see if we could get an Esse put in and if we could afford decorators to do work required. Also looked at a house called Nusteads, Polstead which was quite nice. Shall be glad to leave tomorrow as I am so tired of the Belstead atmosphere. Mother very kindly sent me off with big box of apples, fruit and jam.

Friday 9 May

Returned home, meeting Bill in London on way. Comfortable journey and back at 6.00. Lovely to be home again.

Final heavy raid of Blitz is directed at London

Wednesday 14 May

Heard the school has measles and expect Merlin will get it. Since the bad raid in London on 10th impossible to get through to Bill.

Friday 16 May

Went to London on 10.00 train leaving car at Williton. Left luggage at Paddington. Shopped at Peter Jones for children. Casserole dish and some lamp shades. Met Bill at RAC and had tea together then by taxi to Liverpool Street station. Damage really awful in city. Caught train down to Bishops Stortford arriving 6.30. Rang up Mrs Anderson who was very apologetic saying house was now asking

£10,000 and she was afraid too much so didn't even go to see it. Stayed night at The George, a horrible pub.

Saturday 17 May

Poor Bill had to leave early in the morning to get 7.40 train up. I felt very tired and seedy with bad rheumatism in my neck and shoulder. Arrived at Braintree and had lunch before going on to Colchester by bus, then by bus again to Bures. There I got a taxi to Clees Hall and had another look round. This time I was much more impressed and if we get it cheap we'll not do too badly. Back to Colchester, where I got a nice double room for us at the Red Lion. I was very tired and had a sleep and bath. At 9.15 Bill arrived and we had dinner at the Grill Room. This was fun and it was lovely to be together.

Sunday 18 May

Travelled with Bill to London, left him at Whitehall and went on to Paddington. Had a long dreary journey to Bridgwater arriving there at 6.00. Taxi back to Pardlestone and my sweet girls. Heard Merlin has measles.

Friday 23 May

Bill here for weekend and went to meet him at Taunton at 4.30 with Mary. Did some shopping first. Lovely to have him home. Discussed question of houses.

Saturday 24 May

Wet and cold. Bill slept all afternoon and went out for walk after tea. Lovely to have him here, feel so happy.

Monday 26 May

Took Bill to station at Williton.

Thursday 29 May

Grannie Lunn's birthday and she came to tea. Gave her face cream and some eggs and think she enjoyed her day.

Friday May 30 Whit Sun Weekend

Missed Bill very much and am afraid he is lonely and gets depressed in London, poor darling. Decided to go up to London on Monday. [Bill hated working at the Air Ministry].

Sunday 1 June Clothes rationing is introduced.

Heard clothes are to be rationed from tomorrow. Don't think it will worry us at all.

Monday 2 June

Went to London to join Bill and stayed at Dorchester and it was lovely to be with him. Weather warmer.

Tuesday 3 June

In London with Bill.

Wednesday 4 June

Went down to Belstead after a busy day. Felt very tired and had a bad headache. Interviewed maid, R Haggar and engaged her as children's maid to come on Monday.

Thursday 5 June

Left Belstead and went to London. Lunched with Bill at the RAC and then to Bishops Stortford to see house there called Howe Green House which was quite hopeless. Had a long dreary journey back feeling depressed. Bill joined me at Dorchester where we had dinner, danced and went to bed.

Monday 9 June

Busy preparing for R.Haggar who arrived at Williton at 5.30. Clare and Cecily and I went to dentist at Minehead. Very hot day.

Tuesday 10 June

Bill came on leave which was lovely. All excited and went to Taunton to meet him with children.

Wednesday 11 June

We all went for a picnic on the hill, made a fire and had a lovely afternoon. Lovely having Bill with us. Letter from Mrs Blencowe to say Merlin had fallen from roof and cut his head. Rang up and heard he was all right.

Tuesday 17 June

Very hot day went to meet Mother in the car at Minehead. She had come from Exeter. Nice to have her but she looks so very tired.

Wednesday 18 June

Lovely hot day. Mother enjoying herself. Took her and children to Lilstock Bay for picnic by the sea.

Thursday 19 June

Managed to get a taxi from Hobbs of Nether Stowey to take us all over and we had a really lovely day with picnic lunch in the woods. Merlin looking well but thin. Another boy had bashed him on the head so his poor wound had opened again. Lovely drive both ways which we all enjoyed.

Friday 20 June

A frightfully hot day again. Spent the day quietly busy packing to go away.

Saturday 21 June

Extremely hot. Went to London and met Bill at Paddington. Was cross with him and he with me. Soon settled though. Got a car from Shrimpton and went off to Oxfordshire. It really was fantastically hot. We went to see a ghastly house at a place called Ewelme. Awful! Then to stay with Wing Commander and Mrs Fielden for the night at Britwell Salome. They have a nice furnished house called Orchard Close, and a nice shady garden. A queer dinner party. I felt quite the youngest there which was odd.

Sunday 22 June

Heard the Germans had walked into Russia this morning at 5am. [Operation Barbarossa]. Even hotter today. Bill and I in London by noon. We lunched at the Dorchester then tea at Gunters by myself and Bill came back to the Dorchester about 8.00. Dined at Pruniers and back to bed at 11.00.

Monday 23 June

Not quite so hot. Went off on 9.10 train from Paddington to Banbury to see Mrs Foster Coxe's house Souldern Court. I enjoyed seeing her house which is charming but unsuitable for children. Returned after lunch. Met Bill and we dined and danced at the Dorchester which was lovely.

Tuesday 24 June

Returned home on early train, furious on arriving very late as all the rails rose up. Really too awful to be two hours late and so hot. Felt very tired and exhausted.

Saturday 28 June

Bill sent word to say he was coming today for leave instead of Monday. Went off to meet him with Moppet at Taunton. Lovely to have Bill home on leave again.

Monday 30 June

Decided to increase our offer for Clees to £ 3,000. A day of events. Bill made offer on phone after lunch which Boardman and Oliver accepted, then at teatime came a wire from Rutter saying, 'Can offer you Tostock'. My immediate reaction was at all costs to stop offer for Clees as Tostock is so much nicer and more suitable. However when I rang Bill, heard it was too late and offer for Clees had been accepted therefore we must go on with it. Mary Wilson came to stay in evening.

Friday 4 July

Off to London on 10.00 train leaving car at Williton. Lovely day. Stayed night with Bill at Dorchester. Dined there and enjoyed it very much.

Saturday 5 July

Set off by train to Bures and then got a taxi to Clees where I met Mrs Dowell and had a light lunch with her. Saw Deaves, then walked all round the boundaries. Felt very hot and tired. Went to Colchester where I got a bus to Sproughton crossroads and there was met by Sturgeon and Mum and Dad. Told them all about it. Bill rang up in evening.

Sunday 6 July

Went to London in evening and stayed night with Bill at Dorchester. Dined there.

Monday 7 July

A very hot day. Went home, paid Newie and lovely to find all well at home.

Tuesday 8 July

Dined with Mary Clowes. Bill rang up and is busy getting on with arrangements re. Clees, seeing Hughes.

Thursday 10 July

Grannie Lunn came to tea and talked and talked. Rang up Bill.

Saturday 12 July

Went to meet Bill at Taunton. Lovely to have Bill home.

Monday 14 July

Took Bill to station at Williton, also the hens for Newie's sister. Came back to tidy up and get straight. Wrote a lot of letters and did accounts.

Tuesday 15 July

Dad's 82nd birthday. Send him a telegram and a present.

Wednesday 16 July

Busy day making Pot-Pouri and doing chickens.

Saturday 19 July

Bill rang up to say he was going to see Clees this afternoon. Very cold and wet, so had a nice fire in evening

Monday 21 July

Children and I went off for day gathering wortleberries. I went in the evening to get maid, M Haslam from Williton station. Found her but think she is a queer one!

Tuesday 22 July

This maid Haslam is most peculiar and Newie doesn't like her at all. It's too bad.

Wednesday 23 July

Had such a bad headache yesterday I arranged for Dr Archer to come and see me. Haslam more and more peculiar. Went to Bridgwater in the morning, when I came back found the bedroom door locked. In afternoon she became more and more odd. Eventually tearing down the hill screaming. The police found her and said Newie and I must fetch her which we did. I had no sleep but worried all night. Packed for London tomorrow.

Thursday 24 July

Went off with Haslam to London in Dixons taxi, where I left her at Williton station. Have never had a more peculiar creature to deal with. Felt worn out, and with Twiggy also in season it has been no joke. Took Twig to Miss Beckett, Uffington Road, NW10, terrible journey to North London. But a nice kind woman with whom Twig should be all right. Went back to Paddington, collected my suitcases and then to Flat 102, Carrington House, Hertford Street where Bill has been lent a flat. Very nice little flat all pale pink and pale green! And sweet furniture. Bill and I dined at Berkeley.

Friday 25 July

Spent all morning shopping for children at Debenhams. Then joined Bill at lunch at RAC where he had Deave's estimates for Clees Hall amounting to £ 1,112 which just for house itself, we felt was terrific. Discussed it in detail and felt we could not continue. I went back to flat and slept. Then to Hughes where Bill joined me and we decided it couldn't be done. Dined Shepheards.

Saturday 26 July

Bill decided to work today, so I had the morning to myself and shopped. Met Richard for lunch at the RAC and had a very good lunch. Then back to rest at flat after meeting Mother at ESU club. Had tea there with Mother before she went down to Newbury. I went to see Mary and John at 7.00 and to bed early.

Sunday 27 July

Up early and to Paddington. Met Bill and got seats on a very crowded train. Had a poor lunch and arrived at Bridgwater at about 2.45. Got a taxi to Pardlestone. where we found all well with children, Newie, poultry, Smig and ponies. Lovely to be home.

Monday 28 July

Bill took girls and Newie to Minehead. Mary and I waited for her horsebox to take Winkle over to Burnham. Slept after lunch. Bill riding with Mary in the afternoon.

Tuesday 29 July

Bill went off with Mary and Newie in the little car to Burnham. Twins and I did flowers and tidied up the house. Bill went on to fetch Merlin at Bridgwater and then John at Westonzoyland Aerodrome [built in 1925 is one of the country's oldest airfields] as he is staying for a few days. They arrived at lunchtime. John covered with decorations. DSO, DFC and various Polish and Czech orders. Looks so old and tired however, poor dear.

Wednesday 30 July

Grannie Lunn came to lunch. Collected her at bus stop. John slept all afternoon. Lovely to have darling Merlin home too. Took Grannie Lunn to Holford where she is going to see Dandy.

Thursday 31 July

John left to return to work, lovely seeing him again. Went over in little car to see Mary and Newie at Burnham but thought it a terrible place. Had picnic tea on Sandy Beach where sand blew every which way. Home after picking up Merlin's luggage at station.

Friday 1 August

All went for a long walk and in evening Bill and Merlin went out shooting. Lovely day and quite hot.

Saturday 2 August

Went over in YY to Burnham Rally and Gymkhana. Lovely day took big picnic lunch and arrived at 12.00. Mary very excited. And Bill and I loved it. Mary did splendidly in the bending race winning 2nd prize, but not so good in jumping.

Monday 4 August

Sad that Bill's leave is up. Decided we would go ahead with Tostock and accordingly wrote letter to Hempson asking him to survey etc. Bill left at 5.30 and I took him to Taunton and saw him off on a very crowded train. Miss him dreadfully.

Tuesday 5 August

Newie busy packing to go tomorrow for her holiday. The children and I went to tea with Luttrells at East Quantoxshead and children enjoyed a good wack of fruit!

Wednesday 6 August

Took N. to Williton station where she went off in great glee with eggs, honey, and a large basket of fruit and vegetables. Back to the children and we all had a happy day. Wire from Mum to say she was expecting us next week.

Saturday 9 August [Wine consumption limited to 2 litres per person per week.] Wet today, children doing competitions at Burnham Rally. Rang up Bill in evening.

Monday 11 August

Very busy and up early. Showing Mrs Brown how to do the chickens. Then to Bridgwater for final shopping with twins. M and M riding. Packed all afternoon and by evening everything done and ready for the morning.

Tuesday 12 August

Up very early. All children doing their own jobs and helping me each in charge of something. Mary flowers for Bill, Merlin his cricket bat and easel, twins each their dog, Rippin. Dixon came at 9.00 and took M and M and luggage. I waited for post and went on with twins in little car which I left at Pearces. Trains very full and we had to fight for it at Taunton. However children got two first class seats between them and I sat in corridor. We had a very good picnic lunch and then went to Bill's flat where we saw him for half an hour, which was fun and children each had an orange. 3.40 to Ipswich where Dad and Mum met us with Sturgeon and we all drove to Belstead. Mother so good to us all and so helpful. Children thrilled to be back.

Wednesday 13 August

Children were up early and out gathering mushrooms, and seeing all their old haunts and Southgate and Morphew.

August 15 Friday

A pouring wet day. However decided see Rutter at Bury and then on to Tostock. So caught 10.30, saw Rutter who said Mrs Trench would definitely not sell for less than £10,500. After lunching at the Angel went to the old Rectory and saw young Trench. Was even more taken with the house which I think is quite charming. Caught 3.30 to Ipswich and got back to tea.

Saturday 16 August

I went to meet Bill from the 3.40. I thought he looked tired and seedy. Found his temperature was 103. Gave him two aspirins and a good dose and hoped he would be better.

Sunday 17 August

Poor Bill had a terribly restless night and was very seedy in the morning and temperature 104. Rang up Banks who said he had flu and I was not to sleep in his room. Felt worried as he seemed to be so ill. Mother very good and helpful but Dad very trying in every way. Went to Belstead church in morning with children.

Monday 18 August

Bill still very seedy. Went to Ipswich to get him two prescriptions made up.

Tuesday 19 August

Bill better but still high temperature. Feel sure it's not flu. Dr Banks came again.

Wednesday 20 August

Bill insisted on taking more castor oil and certainly was better after it. He is so weak, poor darling.

Thursday 21 August

Took all children to Freeman this afternoon. Found that their teeth had been much neglected. Mary had a front one filled.

Saturday 23 August

A great day as Merlin put it; 'A Tremendous Event in Life'. **We bought Tostock**. At least we hope we have! Went to see Hempson in morning and had a long talk to him. As soon as I returned he rang to say Mrs Trench must know by Monday if we are buying or she could not give possession till the spring. Bill decided to buy at her figure of £10,500 so there we are! Feel very happy!

Sunday 24 August

Went to church at Sproughton and prayed hard. Took Mum and children. Bill better but a bit cross, poor darling. Banks came to see him.

Monday 25 August

Pollard is turning us out of the cottage today, as he has put up rent to 25 shillings a week. So we all feel that going to Tostock will be marvellous. In the evening Bill's Mother rang up to say Dandy [Bill's grandmother] had died that afternoon.

Tuesday 26 August My Birthday

Lovely to spend it with all those I love so much. Bill better. Dad gave me £ 20 and Mum a dining room table and a flower basket. Mary a powder puff, and Merlin, a pink biscuit tin. Twins, a matchbox and a purse. Newie, a pair of secateurs and Aunt Edie £1. We had a lovely morning going over in the Armstrong with Mary and Merlin to Tostock and looking round the outside. We went afterwards to Rutter and then had lunch. We all played croquet in afternoon until it was time for me to take Merlin and twins to Freeman where poor darlings had two teeth out each with Banks giving gas. Made me feel quite ill. Bill is so much better. Sad to be going away from him tomorrow.

Wednesday 27 August

Up early, said goodbye to all at Belstead and left by 9.30. Mum and Bill saw us off. We crossed London and uneventfully travelled down to Taunton where Dixon met us. Nice to be home though Mrs B and Karen seemed to be at daggers drawn. House beautifully clean and tidy. Chickens and ponies and cats all well. Very, very tired.

Friday 29August

Went to Bridgewater with Mary, Merlin and twins and shopped. Rest in afternoon, feeling better but boils have started which must mean I am a bit run down.

Saturday 30 August

Wrote to my darling who rang up last night from Aldeburgh to say 68 shillings and sixpence can be got for Premier Mill company shares which is marvellous. Dandy who died on 25th was buried yesterday at Bristol.

Monday 1 September

Bill returned to London today, poor darling. Do hope he won't do too much. Children and I had a happy day.

Wednesday 3 September

Karen went to dentist and had a wisdom tooth out which hurt her a lot. I fetched her from bus. Poor girl had terribly swollen face.

Thursday 4 September

Great excitement over the West Somerset Pony Gymkhana which is to be held on Saturday and Mary and Merlin are entering Winkle.

Saturday 6 August

Great day, Gymkhana at Cannington. Very wet in morning but cleared after lunch and we all had a really lovely time as Mary excelled herself by winning two 1st, one on Winkle, one on Ann Mason's pony Thrush and 2nd on Winkle in bending and 2nd on Thrush in Handy Hunter class. Newie arrived in evening very full of her marvellous time and looking well. Rang up Bill to tell him all about Mary.

Monday 8 September

Went to Bridgwater to see Mr Pardoe who says I must give three months notice when I leave here i.e. on 29th to leave on December 25th which is a bore. Came back by bus and picked up car at Holford.

Tuesday 9 September

Off to London, felt very tired. Spend long afternoon with Hughes which tired me still more. Then went to Gunters for some tea. Went to Grosvenor House with luggage to find my darling boy who had been patiently waiting for me since 5.00 to take me to a theatre, so although very tired we went to see Diana Wynyard in

'No Time for Comedy' which was well acted and amusing. Returned to Grosvenor House for supper and bed very tired about 12.00.

Wednesday 10 September

Busy morning shopping, joined Bill for lunch at RAC. Then caught 2.25 down to Bury St Edmunds arrived too late to see either Rutter or Mrs Trench's solicitors. Went to Angel and had a poor bedroom. Rang up Mother who is coming over tomorrow. Very tired.

Thursday 11 September

Up early seeing Rutter and Mrs Tuck of Wilson and Co., as Wilson away. Met Mother's train at 11.30 and engaged a car to go over to Tostock. Had lunch at Angel and then to Tostock. Saw Mrs Trench and showed Mother the dining room, little room, hall and drawing room. Went all round road boundaries and saw Stewart, also Mrs Tyrrell. Back to see Mum off. Went to Angel for tea, felt tired.

Friday 12 September

Caught 10.00 train via Ipswich to London having unfortunately missed the fast one up via Cambridge. Arrive London 1.30 and met Bill at the RAC club for quick lunch. Told him everything. Then went to see Hughes for afternoon. Met Bill at Wilton Street where we spent the night.

Saturday 13 September

Felt very tired. After getting Mum a box of sweets and Dad a gold matchbox with matches, packed, caught 10.30. Felt very cold and tired. Home for tea, took aspirin and to bed early.

Sunday 14 September

Had a bad night and did not feel very well. Went to meet Bill at Bridgwater at 2.00. Lovely to see him and took Clare and Merlin with me.

Monday 15 September

Woke up with a very sore throat. Got up however and went out with Bill, Merlin and Clare shooting. Came back and went to bed feeling so seedy.

Tuesday 16 September

Mum and Dad's Golden Wedding Day. Bill left at 9.30, I stayed in bed, throat awful. Dr Archer came to see me at 11.00. Felt very ill.

Cesca is very ill, bedridden from 16 September until 2 October. The diary lapses. She may have had glandular fever brought on by exhaustion, house worries and the damp at Pardlestone. Her Mother came and stayed for five days.

Wednesday 1 October

Bill settled terrible row between Mrs Brown and Karen which threatened to end in Karen going. Secured a daily woman Mrs Wilson to come every day. Up for tea.

Thursday 2 October

Bill went out shooting with Mr Luttrell and got brace partridges, one pheasant and three rabbits.

Friday 3 October

Up for lunch, tea and dinner. Resting in afternoon lovely day.

Sunday 5 October

Up for a little while but feeling awfully limp and seedy.

Monday 6 October

Bill went back to London.

7th, 8th, 9th October.

Trying to get better. Still very deaf, and so weak and limp. Hardly able to walk and no energy.

Friday 10 October

Went to London and Bill met me during his lunch hour and took me to see Dr Layton at Guys Hospital who said there was nothing the matter with my ears. It was only rest and feeding up that I needed. So much cheered up I went by 3.42 Ipswich where I was met by Dad. Still feeling ill and early to bed.

Saturday 11 October

Resting until Tuesday.

Tuesday 14 October

Went in hired car to Tostock to see Mrs Trench, then fetched Bill who came down for two nights.

Wednesday 15 October

Went over to Tostock with Bill by train and saw Rutter and Stewart etc. Bill returned to London.

Friday 17 October

Went to London, met Bill and then off down to Pardleston. Feeling much better. Lovely to be back with children and feel Tostock business is almost settled now.

Wednesday 29 October

Left Pardlestone, after much preparations, in Morris with a load of curtains, covers etc. for Oxford. Did trip easily and enjoyed it in lovely weather. Bill came down and joined me for the night at the Randolph. Dined together and he left next day and I went on to see Ralph and Irene Millais and on to Cambridge (lunch Varsity Arms) and to Angel, Bury St Edmunds arriving there about 4.00. Interviewed maids and early to bed.

Friday 31 October Tostock.

Wire from Newie saying they had had a bomb but all were all right. Felt worried about this. Bill rang up to enquire and found they were very shaken.

[Mary, aged 11, remembers a terrific explosion in the middle of the night. Most of her bedroom ceiling and the lampshade came down on her bed. A policeman banged on the door, had difficulty getting in as the doors had all jammed and the windows had blown out, glass everywhere. He advised them another bomb could explode so they must evacuate to Kilve Court where Mrs Cooke-Hurle lived. Mary, the twins and Newie had to walk down the lane in the dark, with the Siamese cats yowling in their basket. The children were put in a huge fourposter bed, rather cold as the windows had to be left open to stop the glass blowing out. Mary remembers the cats climbing up the curtains and just prevented one going up the chimney. The policeman returned the next day and told them to return home as the bomb in fact was nearer Kilve Court than Pardlestone].

Saturday 1 November

Sale at Tostock. Stewart and self bought a lot of garden stuff also oak seat etc.

Monday 3 November

Went over to Tostock for supposed completion. Mother there and Hughes and Mr Baker

the curtain man and Footman's for carpets. All rushing about in every direction. Very tired but satisfactory. Went up to London afterwards with Hughes to 10 Wilton Street where spent night with Bill.

Tuesday 4 November

Back to Pardlestone.

Wednesday 5 November

Busy all week packing. Cecily ill with nose bleeding, cough and temperature.

Tuesday 11 November

Man packed glass and china which was dispatched.

Cesca travels to London then the next day to Tostock and then returns to Pardelstone via London on Saturday 15 November.

Monday 17 November

Horses went by horsebox. Heard from Howells that they are definitely taking Pardlestone. Really busy from now on with final packings and arranging.

Saturday 22 November

Took Newie and twins to Fleet. Mary to Elizabeth with Bill, self to Tostock.

Monday 24 November

Returned to Pardlestone for final clean up.

Wednesday 26 November

Furniture went by Lidbetter's van. Mrs Brown, self and cats left 3.15 and got as far as Marlborough in YY and spent night at Aylesbury Arms.

Thursday 27 November

Arrived Tostock. Molly hard at work still, carpets down and everything going well. Cats went up chimney. Went to spend the night at Angel.

Friday 28 November

Furniture unloaded.

Saturday 29 November

Bill and I and Mrs Brown slept for the first time at Tostock!

Sunday 30 November

Tyrrell came to see Bill after Tostock Church and bought butter and cream with him.

Monday 1 December

Furniture came from Belstead. Maids arrived. All a most ghastly never ending muddle. Felt half crazy and so tired.

Wednesday 3 December

Children and Newie arrived.

Thursday 4 December

Went to London to fetch Mary who had been ill, an ear infection, met her and nannie. Lunch with Bill.

Tuesday 16 December

Went to London to fetch Merlin home. Lovely to see him again and stayed night with McDonald's in Wilton Street. Rob, the labrador, fetched from Victoria and home on 17th with Merlin and the dog.

Saturday 20 December

Bill started a week's leave which was lovely.

Monday 22 December

Took Cecily to Freeman in YY to have two teeth out.

December 24 Christmas Eve.

Very busy with presents, letters, cards etc.

December 25 Christmas Day

Lovely day for all in spite of no turkey this year! Lovely to have Bill here and all so happy.

December 26 Boxing Day.

Ian Smith's came to stay. Erskine children to lunch and Colonel Coles to tea.

Sunday 28 December

Bill and Ian Smiths went back to London together.

Wednesday 31 December

Last day of the year. So very happy to be in our own home.

Diary 1942
Tostock Old Rectory Bury St Edmunds

Bill is not enjoying his work at the Air Ministry in Whitehall so is relieved to be promoted and given command of No 61, an operational training unit for Spitfire pilots at Rednal. Cesca settles in to her new home and struggles to adjust to the monotony of wartime living in Suffolk including War savings once a week. A string of governesses come and go. Health worries including operations cause concern. Sadness in September involves a fatality on the road. Tostock kitchen garden is producing quantities of vegetables and fruit. Cesca sells these locally listing sales in a Sale of Produce book and also starts breeding Siamese cats for a healthy profit! Bombing raids shatter the peaceful local market towns.

Thursday 1 January New Year's Day
All went over to Ipswich to dentist first lunching at Belstead. Tried unsuccessfully to speak to Bill to wish him a happy New Year but the Club could not find him.

Friday 2 January
Mother and Dad came over to lunch and we had a very nice New Year's Lunch. Roast partridges, Christmas pudding and cream. Dad said he liked the house very much and they left with Sturgeon in the car.

Sunday 4 January
Cocktail party at Coles. Deadly. Glad to get home to warm house and Sunday lunch. Went for a long walk after lunch with children and dog [Rob labrador]. Fed chickens and rabbit which Newie gave twins for Christmas.

Monday 5 January
Bill came down and I met him at Stowmarket and he was rather cross with me. I think he looks so thin and ill and his work is a great strain. Feel very worried about him.

Tuesday 6 January
Bill and Merlin and I went shooting. Bill looking much better by the evening.

Thursday 8 January

Went to London to be with Bill and get him settled in to Mrs Gunns at 25, Cliveden Place. Quite a nice room but so cold!

Friday 9 January

Bitterly cold. Busy in London. Bill and I met for lunch.

Saturday 10 January

Returned on 8.12 from London joining Mary and Merlin at Freemans in Ipswich. Afterwards had a good lunch at Orient cafe and home on 2.15 bus to Tostock. Very cold. Took dog out.

Sunday 11 January

Went to Tostock church alone. Took dog for a walk. All household have bad colds.

Tuesday 13 January

Awful day, heavy snow.

Thursday 15 January

New girl Joyce Sutton came as between maid, seems pretty slow and stupid.

Friday 16 January

Lovely to be with Bill, who I met at Haughley last night in the snow. Bill out shooting and came in with an old hen pheasant and a bunny. Mrs Ackroyd, Mrs Lilley, Mrs Erskine and Lilley the rector and the children came to tea. A deadly party and I nearly expired! Thank heavens Bill was there to help me out with it all.

Saturday 17 January

Merlin should have gone to have three teeth out, but as he was still coughing I put it off and just took Cecily dropping Bill at Stowmarket on the way. Cecily and I had lunch at Belstead and returned in the car with the convex mirror, the Romney, apples and jam.

Tuesday 20 January

Merlin still coughing so arranged for Dr Pretty to give him gas on Thursday before he goes back to school and hope he will be all right.

Wednesday 21 January

Went over with Mother, having met her at Bury, then by car from Cambridge for Aunt Edie's funeral at Aspenden, Buntingford. Bitterly cold, thick snow and arctic wind. Miss Disney, Richardson, Jenna, her cook and two local people were the only ones there. Back to Cambridge and on home where Mother had tea. In the evening I took her to Elmswell station.

Thursday 22 January

Merlin and I left on 10.20. Bitterly cold. Went to dentist where Dr Pretty gave him gas and Freeman pulled out 2 permanent front molars and a baby double tooth. The dear boy was so good. I felt sick. Mother and Dad turned up and kindly invited us to Belstead where Merlin had a rest and later a good lunch. He slept in train going to London and we then took luggage etc. to Mrs Gunn's. Tea at Searcy's, then met Bill at Coliseum where we saw 1st act of Jack and the Beanstalk. A poor show and Merlin very tired. Got him to bed. House <u>arctic.</u>

Friday 23 January

Sad day, seeing darling Merlin off. Snowing and so cold. He was very good. Met my darling at RAC for lunch which helped a lot too. Shopped. Very cold and rather depressing in London. Met Bill and we went to drinks with Group Captain Fressange at RAF club then on to dinner at Gargoyle club. Not much fun. I wished I'd been alone with Bill.

Saturday 24 January

Went down to Ipswich on 10.12 train. Late all along and did not get to Elmswell till 1.30. Stewart met me and we arrived home where children, John and Newie were all having lunch. Nice to be home and to see John again. We both went to fetch my darling at 7.30 at Stowmarket and all had lovely dinner together. John Peel has been promoted to Group Captain. Amazingly young for the job I should think.

Wednesday 28 January

Another ghastly day, snow, ice, hail etc. Had rather bad neuralgia. Went to tea with Mrs Ackroyd and found her less frosty in her own home. Bill rang up in evening and told me Coryton has been made an AVM. (Air Vice Marshall).

Monday 2 February

Letter from Bill who went to Elizabeth's last night. Mrs Brown went off for her holiday and in afternoon I fetched Mrs Skinner the temporary cook from Elmswell.

Tuesday 3 February

Weather really appalling. Snow everywhere, feet deep. Newie rang up to ask how she was to get back, I said I had no idea and eventually she turned up at 7.00 by taxi from Bury St Edmunds, very cold and tired, poor thing. Weather awful, snowing hard.

Wednesday 4 February

Lessons again. I left at 9.00 for London. Went via Stowmarket and Ipswich and met Bill at RAC for lunch. Shopped in afternoon and then went back to Mrs Gunn's with many parcels before going on to tea with Lady Hope. She has a very nice flat in Courtfield Gardens, but so dreary a locality. Bill and I had dinner together and then to bed in a very cold bedroom.

Thursday 5 February

Shopped and heard from Hughes, completion once again is not taking place owing to Mother's Australian Securities being unsaleable. Very disappointed over this. Met Bill for lunch. In evening dined at Queens restaurant Sloane Square. Good dinner.

Saturday 7 February

War savings at Mr Ringrose's. [British savings movement instrumental during WWII in raising funds to support the War effort] Very cold day.

Wednesday 11 February

Mother came over in afternoon bringing Clare a rabbit for her eighth birthday. Brought me flowers and stayed to tea. Took her to station in evening. Still quite arctic.

Thursday 12 February Our 13th Wedding Day

My darling sent me a most lovely old sapphire and diamond brooch beautifully set, also my usual flowers from Fortnum & Mason. I set off for London by bus 12.30 and met him in evening and we went together to 'Quiet Weekend,' which was frightfully funny. Dinner at Queens which was very good.

Friday 13 February

Returned with Bill on 5.10 first class to Stowmarket where Stewart met us with the car. Still very cold. Lovely to be in nice warm house.

Saturday 14 February

My twin girls' 8th birthday. Getting such big girls too. Had a large tea with iced chocolate cakes. Mother came over and Bill was here. Twins had a lot of presents including two rabbits, a bicycle for Cecily and money. Went to War Savings in afternoon.

Monday 16 February

Lessons again. Still bitterly cold. Went to meet Mrs Brown later but she never turned up. Later sent a wire to say she had missed her train. Rita met her at bus and they came home in the dark.

Wednesday 18 February

Another heavy fall of snow and bitterly cold.

Thursday 19 February

Went to London to be with Bill. Shopped and had lunch together at RAC. Mrs Gunn's house frightfully cold. Went to tea with Lady Hope. Dinner at Queen's restaurant.

Friday 20 February

Came home in afternoon and Stewart met me at Stowmarket. Frightfully cold.

Tuesday 24 February

Mrs Clare Walker and Mrs Ridley brought their children to tea. Still very cold. Children enjoyed it very much. Mrs Walker improves on acquaintance.

Wednesday 25 February

Miss Cornwall, elocution mistress came and gave children their 1st elocution lesson. Needless to say they did not like it.

Friday 27 February

Mrs Brown very difficult. Her holiday does not appear to have done her any good what so ever. My Moppet's 12th birthday. Can't believe she is 12 but she is and getting so big. I gave her a lot of little things. Bill gave her books and tennis racket. Nice day but very cold. Mother and Dad came over to lunch. In the evening I took them to Bury station and fetched Rachel Erskine on 5.20. She, Mary and Newie had supper together before Newie went to Mrs Ackroyd's Invasion Meeting at Village Hall. Bill, John and Mary Wilson arrived at about 8.00. We had supper of cold salmon, boiled chicken and cheese. John and Mary said they thought house charming. Lovely happy day. Mary very happy.

Saturday 28 February

Very busy day, Bill and John out shooting in morning. In afternoon Bill's entertainment as a start to Warship Week was given in school. It was an RAF Cinema show given by an RAF film unit and was highly successful. Ringrose and I saw very little of it as we were very busy with people buying War Savings Certificates all afternoon and by end of day had paid in over £100. The evening was spoilt by the Army exercises which meant 40 men were installed in our playroom and a lot of officers in drawing room.

Sunday 1 March

Rachel Erskine left in afternoon. Mary likes her so much. Troops everywhere all day and night.

Tuesday 3 March

John and Mary left in afternoon, also all the troops.

Wednesday 4 March

As I have neglected my diary I am only going to put down just what happened from now on all until I catch up again. I have been so busy it was impossible to keep it up.

Thursday 5 March

Went to London, very cold. Twig's kittens were imminent. Rang up Newie in evening, kittens born 4.00! Great thrill.

Friday 6 March

Home. Lovely kittens. One male, 3 females. [Cesca started a profitable business breeding Siamese cats and had her own prefix from The Governing Council of The Cat Fancy. One guinea for prefix Tostock in perpetuity dated 9 September 1942].

Wednesday 11 March

Bill on two days leave.

Thursday 12 March

Lovely day with Bill and children.

Friday 13 March

Bill returned to London.

Tuesday 17 March

Went to London for Bill's birthday tomorrow. Called on Lady Hope and left her some eggs.

Wednesday 18 March

My darling's birthday. Dined and danced at the Mirabelle.

Friday 20 March

Newie went off for weekend to Mrs Burrows and I found everything left in a ghastly mess and muddle.

Monday 23 March

Sweep swept 3 chimneys. So much enjoyed being with my girls.

Tuesday 24 March

Newie got back at teatime. Very cross. And I too. In evening she gave notice owing she said to her health. Accepted it and gave her piece of my mind over neglect of children's clothes etc.

Monday 30 March

Went to London on 9.35 to meet Bill at office. Then on to lunch with Flight Lieutenant Rawlinson at Carlton Grill. Very dull but good food. Shopped all afternoon. Bill and I dined together in evening.

Tuesday 31 March

Bill and I met for lunch at F & M. We both went to meet Merlin. Bill was promoted to Group Captain last week which was a great thrill for us both. And we went and bought him a lovely gold hat at Hill House. Home with Merlin.

Saturday 4 April

Mum and Dad came for weekend as have no servants in the house. War savings as usual. Put forward all clocks one hour.

Sunday 5 April

All went to church. Mum and Dad and I stayed for Holy Communion. Mrs Sheldrick, a ghastly old woman came to tea in afternoon and stayed and stayed.

Monday 6 April

Mum and Dad left, Mary and I took them in the car to Belstead and we went on to Woodbridge Horse Show which was extremely dull this year, only two pony classes. It took Mary and me four hours to get home too!

Thursday 7 April

Ipswich. Interviewed Miss Langdon and met Bill who arrived on a week's leave.

Friday 10 April

Bill resting feeling so tired, poor dear. Lovely to have him but he looks very done in.

Saturday 11 April

Patricia came to stay and arrived at Elmswell 3.50. I went to meet her, leaving War Savings early. John Peel came to stay late in evening. Lovely to see him again but he too looks fearfully tired.

Sunday 12 April

John, Bill and Patricia were asleep most of the day in garden. John left. Twins sold one of their rabbits to Mrs Bromfield for 10 shillings!

Monday 13 April

Bill not feeling very well and so tired. I rang up Doctor and asked him to come and see him.

Tuesday 14 April

Patricia left on 10.12. I took her to station and saw her off. Dr Ware came and said Bill should have rest.

Wednesday 15 April

Bill's friend Harold Cox came and stayed for a night. Glorious hot sunny weather. Bill and I walked through the fields and woods for the morning.

Thursday 16 April

Again a lovely day. Bill and Harold Cox returned to London in evening from Stowmarket. Very sad he has gone and though he looks better I felt he was not really fit.

Monday 20 April

Went to London in afternoon via Ipswich where I bought a rather nice small mahogany table for 5 guineas. And on arriving in London about 7.30 found Bill looking awfully ill, coughing incessantly and with temperature of 103. Put him to bed and myself arranged to sleep downstairs. Rang up Dr Cregan who said he would come in morning. Gave Bill two aspirins and had a bad night worrying.

Tuesday 21 April

Dr Cregan came and said Bill has patch on his lung and is very seedy and has bronchitis. Temperature lower. Went to Cooper's and got him medicine.

Wednesday 22 April

Bill better. Dr Cregan came and said he hoped Bill would be well enough tomorrow to travel down to Tostock. Wired and wrote to Newie re preparations.

Thursday 23 April

Bill and I went down by 1.00 train, poor darling, feeling very seedy all way, but Stewart met us at Stowmarket and I got him home and to bed. And rang up Dr Ware to come and see him tomorrow.

Friday 24 April

Merlin's 11th birthday. Erskines all to tea. Bill better but very cross, poor darling, Dr Ware came.

Saturday 25 April

Went to War Savings in afternoon. Bill looking better and up for a few hours.

Tuesday 28 April

Bill down for lunch. Busy getting Merlin's clothes together for his return to Brambletye.

Wednesday 29 April

Dr Ware came. Bill better.

Thursday 30 April [This raid was the most severe to hit Norwich during the war, 229 citizens killed, 1000 injured and Norwich City station destroyed]

Went to London with Merlin. Trains very late owing to raid at Norwich last night. Arrived at Fortnum & Mason and left Mer with Mary Wilson who took him to see an Art Exhibition. I took luggage on to Grosvenor Hotel and then I joined Mer at F & M where we lunched. Went to see Maid of Mountains at Coliseum which he enjoyed. Had supper in Sloane Square. Put Mer to bed and spent two hours replying to my Nursery World adverts.

Friday 1 May

Breakfast at the Grosvenor then after buying Mer's lunch from Harrods saw him off at the station. Shopped then home on 3.40. Stewart met me. Bill better but has missed me. Found him sitting in front of the house, poor darling all forlorn. Children at tea with Mrs Sheldrick.

Sunday 3 May

Went to church. Bill better but taking M and B [early antibiotics] tablets have made him feel very queer.

Monday 4 May

Dr Ware came to see Bill and wants to get him X-rayed this week.

Wednesday 6 May

Bill still seedy and gets depressed and miserable, poor darling, but is improving.

Thursday 7 May

Dr Ware came and he wants Bill to be operated on in Bury Hospital for antrum [mastoid antrum if blocked can cause a sinus infection] tomorrow as the X-ray shows that this is blocked. I feel worried leaving him as Newie goes tomorrow and we are going to John Peel's Wedding at Therfield near Royston.

Friday 8 May

Went in the car early with Newie and her luggage, the twins and Mary. Newie left us in floods of tears, poor thing, very distressed at leaving the children. She went on to Tunbridge Wells and we went by taxi to Therfield. Found John's wife's house, rather a nice little house but very richly modernised with unsuitable furniture and furnishings. We were very early but it was nice to see John who was so obviously very happy. I was not very thrilled with Barbara and her people, very common and madly rich. Taxi man said he had made his money in Government caterpillar tractors and before the war had been a taxi proprietor and he looks it. But full of money now. Children were rather disappointed with everything and we had to leave early. Found poor Billy very shaken and hated operation.

Saturday 9 May

War savings. Bill seems better and nose less troublesome.

Monday 11 May

Mr Rutter came out to see extent of damage done by Army to our drive as they have now vacated the loose boxes. Then went to meet Miss McCalmont [new governess] who arrived very grand in first class carriage with masses of luggage. She is, I fear too grand for us. Bill did his best to be nice to her but found her very difficult.

Tuesday 12 May

Miss McC. spent most of the time in her bedroom presumably unpacking the vast quantities of luggage. Dr Ware said Bill was much better.

Wednesday 13 May

Lessons started by Miss McC who still spends a vast amount of time in her bedroom and I seem to have as much to do as ever.

Saturday 16 May

Went to Bury in morning in the car to get cakes etc. Lovely day. At lunch today I asked Miss McC. to take charge of children and Ridley children who were coming to tea. She said she could not possibly take charge of any small children. I was somewhat startled but said no more. Bill had to deal with children whilst I was at War Savings.

Sunday 17 May

Lovely day. Went to Church in morning with Bill and children. Miss McC. spent entire day in her room only appearing for meals. I went up before lunch and tackled her. She said it was the worst misfit she had ever had and suggested leaving at half term. I said it would be better for her, me and children if she left sooner as it was bad for children to get used to her, then leave and they then have to get used to someone else's ways. She said she would write to the PNEU who had recommended her as she was under an obligation to them and did not want to let me down. All together bloody. Went for picnic in afternoon, anything to get out of the house with this foul woman about.

Monday 18 May

Asked Miss McC. for her rations, said she had not got them yet. Last week she lost her identity card.

Tuesday 19 May

Busy getting ready for Mary Clowes. Went to meet her at 6.00 and went to Food Office who said they had sent Miss McC's rations some days ago. Awfully nice to see Mary and she and Bill seem to be getting on better this time.

Wednesday 20 May

We were going to Belstead today but it's impossible with this woman and I tackled her this evening after dinner. All so fearfully unpleasant. I said if she was not prepared to do more it was useless her staying as she was not fulfilling the agreement of our contract. She was rude and impossible so I called Bill in who looked and felt white, poor darling. Eventually she said she would go tomorrow but expected a term's notice. I said she had agreed to go at half term so that was out of the question. All frightful.

Thursday 21 May

She left about 12.00. Thankfully she refused to accept the cheque Bill offered her saying she was going to have a row over the whole thing. Anyhow she has gone, thank God. Mary also equally delighted. Children so very sweet and good.

Friday 22 May

Went over to Belstead with Bill and Mary C. leaving children and house to own devices. Had excellent lunch. Went to Ipswich to shop. Bill very cross all the time. Home late tea.

Sunday 24 May

Baby pheasants hatched and also Clare's rabbit had babies. We don't know how many yet. Went to lunch at Gores, leaving Mary in charge of her sisters. Nice lunch. Mary Clowes leaves tomorrow.

Tuesday 26 May

Went to Bury to see governess friend of Miss Cornwall's, a Mrs Ling. Very nice person but uncertain if she can come as she feels Mary is too advanced. Grannie Lunn's birthday.

Wednesday 27 May

So sad. Bill went back to work, poor darling to see what has been happening in his absence. Back to the house after seeing him off and getting straight once more.

Thursday 28 May

Heard of pony trap at Thurston. So children and I went over to see it. Wrote to Bill who also rang up to say he is coming down next week before he leaves Air Ministry which will be soon. He has been passed fit for full flying duties.

Friday 29 May

Heard Mrs Ling is coming as from June 15 so very pleased. Also heard Miss McC. is going to bring an action against us for wrongful dismissal.

Monday 1 June

Mary went off to stay for a few days with Mrs Anderson at Cheveley. Saw her onto train at 9.45 and shopped in Bury. Lovely day. Very, very hot.

Tuesday 2 June

Took twins off to Belstead by train and Mother and Dad met them. I went on to London. Train very late, so had little time to do anything before meeting Bill at Fortnum & Mason for lunch. Lovely to see him and he had heard news that morning that he has been posted to Heston to command an OTN [Operational Training Unit No 61] as from end of this week so is taking few days leave to come home. All fearfully exciting. Went to Harrods together also to Mrs Gunn's, collected things and came down on 3.40. Out to Belstead to see Mum and Dad and have tea and collect twins. Took the Armstrong and motored back to Tostock in lovely evening weather.

Wednesday 3 June

Very hot again. Lovely to have Bill home. Mrs Anderson and Mary home for lunch. Gave Mrs Anderson some gooseberries. Lovely day. Mother did flowers for me.

Thursday 4 June

Took my darling boy off to station and saw him off. Felt sad. Back to Tostock and then took Mother off to Belstead, and then shopped in Ipswich returning home by bus for late lunch. Very hot and had tea in garden.

Saturday 6 June

Did flowers in morning. Bottling gooseberries. Mrs Lilley called to see me and asked me to be secretary of Jam Centre. In afternoon did War Savings.

Sunday 7 June

Went to Norton church in the car with the girls. Had Holy Eucharist. Cecily and Clare most intrigued, latter started to follow me up the aisle to altar but Mary just stopped her in time and afterwards she said she thought clergyman was about to drink up all the wine. Very hot and roses all out and so lovely.

Monday 8 June

Bill leaves Air Ministry for good and flies up to RAF station, his own, at Rednal, near Oswestry Shropshire today. Mrs Sheldrick came to lunch. Poor old lady. Felt very exhausted with her chatter.

Tuesday 9 June

Mrs Brown's birthday. Gave her a dress length and 10 shillings. In evening had a meeting at schools re Jam Centre. Terrible long job, sat there all evening and nothing was decided. I came home exhausted and feel it is more than I can cope with.

Wednesday 10 June

Wrote to Mrs Lilley and told her I cannot take on secretaryship. Heard from Bill who seems to be in a whirl over new job. Mary and twins went to Bury on bus to collect the rabbit Mrs Ridley is selling them.

Thursday 11 June

Olive Steggles left. Feel Mrs Borley is doing her best to upset all these girls. Another meeting tonight for War Savings at Ringrose's house. Mary, twins and I are having a very happy time together. Wrote to Billy.

Friday 12 June

Pouring wet day. In afternoon went to Bury with Mary in car to meet Miss Vennard who travelled from York for interview as governess for next term. Liked her, similar to Newie in type. Short and grey-haired but pleasant and children took to her. She went out with them to see their rabbits and looked through their books.

Saturday 13 June

Cold day. Miss Vennard went with Stewart to get 8.45 from Bury back to York. Twins, Mary and I fed rabbits and dog then caught

8.50 bus to Ipswich and went to dentist after shopping. Mother sent a taxi for us and we all went to Belstead for lunch and tea. Had a bad headache and felt very tired. Came home by bus, very full, and we with strawberries etc. Children sat up for supper and had strawberries and cream.

Sunday 14 June

Felt better today. Wrote to Bill and did flowers. Went to church. Lilleys came to tea and asked me to employ a girl called Winnie Cox who is at Drinkstone and half sharp!

Tuesday 16 June

Mrs Ling arrived on an early bus and immediately took charge of children. A nice fresh sort of girl. Mary who spent yesterday in bed after eating too many strawberries has recovered today!

Wednesday 17 June

Took Mary to Thurston station to go to London with her Grannie to see Russian Ballet. Then I went on to Bury and shopped.

Thursday 18 June

Letters daily from Billy who I gather is very happy and content at the new job but I do wish it was not so far away. Depressing letters from Hughes about Walton Place and prospects of surrender of the lease. Met Mary at Elmswell. She had much enjoyed herself.

Friday 19 June

Winnie Cox the half daft 'girl' aged about 50 from Drinkstone came and started work! Mrs B thinks she will do. Mrs Ling quite a success.

Saturday 20 June

Mrs Borley is leaving and has apparently taken offence at my having Winnie here. Never mind. Paid her and she'll come no more. Mrs Brown and Stewart are pleased, I gather. Mrs Scillitoe is going to do her best to come for longer. Took War Savings as Ringrose in Bury with child at hospital. Lovely evening with children.

Sunday 21 June

Wrote a long letter to Bill. Looking forward to my visit to him this week and to see my little Merlin. Went to Tostock church. Did all flowers. Fed the dog, cats and chickens. Took children for picnic .

Monday 22 June [Rommel had the advantage of detailed intelligence against the Allies. This enabled German and Italian forces to take Tobruk 21 June 1942].

Very hot day. Went to Bury early in car with Stewart to fetch paint etc. paid £8.11.0 for same. Sold cabbages and lettuces for six shillings. Sent parcel of butter to Bill. Came home and packed. News seems to be very bad about Tobruk being taken. Busy all day getting straight, packing etc. before going tomorrow.

Tuesday 23 June

Nice day and very hot. Started off very early. Stewart taking me to Stowmarket station with large hampers of fruit, flowers and vegetables. Arrived and went straight to Hughes office, only to find he had gone to the courts. Waited for over an hour and then left in despair for Paddington. Having got nicely settled in 1st class carriage I suddenly saw him at the window and we had a short talk before I left for Barnstaple arriving at 7.30 after waiting an hour at Taunton. Had a taxi out to Lynton and arrived at about 8.45. A poor dinner. Heard the news then went to bed in a poor miserable room looking onto the street. Noise of troops was awful. Felt very tired.

Wednesday 24 June

Decided I ready could not face another night at Valley of the Rocks Hotel so told hotel I needed a taxi to take Merlin back to school and me onto Barnstable. Rang up Bill to tell him of change of plans. Taxi out to Lee Abbey and saw the Blencowes and Mr Wilson and all Merlin's drawings and paintings. Then Merlin appeared looking so well, clean and tidy. Took him back to Lynton and we had lovely time together, I had brought down some strawberries and peaches, chocolate biscuits and chocolates. We had a poor lunch then sat in garden and talked. Left at 3.00 and I went on to Barnstaple. Caught connection at Taunton for Shrewsbury and arrived there at 11.00. Met by Bill looking so nice in his best uniform and we drove out to Woodhouse West Felton. It is a large Georgian pile standing high in Park, must have been quite delightful before the RAF took over the property. It is a new Aerodrome and covers miles of land as it is all dispersed to avoid being put out of action by enemy attack.

Bill lives at the Mostyn Owen's house and has his own Vauxhall for getting about from one part of Aerodrome to another, and needs it. The troops, 1700 of them all have bicycles. We went to sleep in a very comfy four poster and I slept well.

Thursday 25 June

Bill had to leave early to the aerodrome and left me in bed! I got up and was escorted to the dining room by one of Bill's Scotch batmen, Jock Calderwood! Two large fat nurses having breakfast and later Mrs and Col Mostyn Owen appeared. [Mrs Mostyn Owen rented Najac for the month of August 1975 for £100]. She very tall, thin and looking ill. He short, ex rifle Brigade. After breakfast, she discussed prospects of our taking over the house from them at a nominal rent of 15 guineas weekly. Felt this to be rather a lot. Went for a walk later trying to find Aerodrome and etc. but it goes for miles and I was unable to find much except huts. In afternoon we visited a poor man, who had lost his arm in an accident, at RAF Hospital near Shrewsbury. Bill's car is very nice. Back for tea. Dinner with strawberries and cream, coffee, and to bed at 10 pm.

Friday 26 June

Bill and I had breakfast with M O's and then he saw me off in my taxi for Gobowen station near Oswestry, and from there I travelled home via London and arrived back at Stowmarket at 6.00. Stewart met me.

Sunday 28 June

Took girls to church. Did flowers. Wrote letters. Pruned roses and watered everything, as so dry. Mended sheets.

Monday 29 June

Went to Bury by bus and met Mrs Coles who have no servants, poor things. Shopped. Very hot day. Had a rest in afternoon and to bed early as have hayfever cold which makes me feel very tired.

Wednesday 1 July [The basic civilian petrol ration was abolished restricting vehicle fuel to official users]. Tried to go to Bury with lettuces etc but bus too full so had to come back.

Friday 3 July

Spent the whole morning picking and doing flowers. Highly delighted that Mrs Scillitoe is not after all leaving as her bungalow has fallen through, poor woman. A message from Oswestry to say Bill was coming up by train and not by air as weather poor that end. Took car to meet him at Stowmarket at 9.35. Mary still awake when he came back. We had some salmon and strawberries and cream. Lovely to have him at home.

Saturday 4 July

Lovely day again and still no rain. Bill and I spent lovely happy day with children in garden and fields. So happy. Slept after lunch. Children very good.

Monday 6 July

Took Bill to Stowmarket to see him off. Very full train. Lovely day but sad my Billy has gone. Went to Bury to sell vegetables and get money. Wrote letters and did accounts. Mrs Ling back at work.

Tuesday 7 July

Not feeling well and much irritated by Mrs Brown's unpunctuality. Busy bottling red currants and making raspberry and strawberry jam. Sold 14lb blackcurrants to Mrs Mann for 16/4. Wrote to Bill and a lot of letters.

Wednesday 8 July

Set off at 8.45 with Mary and Clare for Ipswich arriving 10.15. Took eiderdowns to Corder, had Clare's haircut, Mary and Clare's teeth checked. Dad took us out to lunch at Belstead. Mother rather difficult. Returned on 2.30 bus and felt very tired on my return so went to bed. Bad headache.

Friday 10 July

Went to Bury taking Cecily to try her new bicycle and also Florence who had her day off, poor old thing. It started to pour with rain and continued without ceasing all day. I got soaked shopping so did Cecily. Cecily's bike is no good.

Monday 13 July

Letters from Bill. Went to Bury to take in vegetables. Bought another bicycle for Cecily for £4.5.0. Sold the fairy cycles last week for £4 and £2.10.0 so did quite well and put money into War Savings. Mary rode to Beyton in afternoon. Stewart went to Saxmundham to see a pony trap but it was too small, alas.

Tuesday 14 July

Up early. Went to London on 8.35 and straight to Hughes. With him till 2 pm. regarding McCalmont, Walton Place, Tostock and trustee business. Then to Bill's bank for vouchers and to Metier for Income Tax. Then to Arts Club to pick up sugar Mary is giving me. Had a cup of tea at Searcy's and home on 5.10. Back at 7.25 and motored back from Stowmarket. Bill rang up which was sweet of him.

Wednesday 15 July St Swithin's

And not raining by 10 pm. Dad's 84th birthday. Rang him up. Had a row with governess for being late for tea. Find her manners are appalling! Wrote a lot of letters. Bottled an incredible amount of fruit. Did flowers, and accounts and busy from dawn till dusk.

Thursday 16 July

Went to Bury with Stewart in the car and took in lots of vegetables including 5 lbs of broad beans, 6lbs peas, 24 cauliflowers, 6lbs spring onions etc for £2.5.6.

Friday 17 July

Mrs Ling went off at lunchtime. Children and I went by car to Elmswell and then to Ipswich. No sign of Mother there so sent them by taxi out to Belstead. I got 3.15 to London, arrived in pouring rain and an Air Raid. No taxis and eventually when I got one had no time to go to Arts Club, so went to Paddington and took vegetables etc all to Rednal with me. Arrived there at 10.45pm. Bill met me with car and took me back to the house. Lovely to see him and be with him again.

Saturday 18 July

Had my breakfast then a flight lieutenant Coles took me in his car to the mess to show me where I had to arrange flowers. Then a Corporal and gardener helped me cut the flowers and arrange them. Bill fetched me at lunchtime and introduced me to a good few of his staff. I did flowers again in afternoon. Had tea in mess and rested with Bill and changed for the dance which I thought was great fun with a good band. Bill hated it and got crosser and crosser and we had to go early. I thoroughly enjoyed it and do love dancing so.

Sunday 19 July

Got up late, Bill and I had breakfast upstairs. Bill went to camp and I wrote letters. Lunch and afternoon together. Went for a lovely walk by a canal. Flight Lieutenant 'Pop' Rogers came in then we had our dinner together. Lovely to be alone together.

Monday 20 July

Time has gone all too quickly. Had a very trying journey home. Trains packed. Left eggs for Mary at Arts Club. Arrived at Ipswich at 5.30 out to Belstead to fetch Mother and children. Was rather tired and exhausted. Drove them back to the house and Mrs S there help me unpack thank goodness. All well and early to bed. Very hot day.

Tuesday 21 July

Mother did flowers for me. Mrs Ling back for the last week of lessons. Took Mother and Mary over to Ipswich in afternoon in Armstrong. Very hot day. Mary had Dr Pretty give her gas and had two permanent teeth out. The poor child was very sick on way home. Put her to bed. Mother very difficult.

Wednesday 22 July

Took Mother back to Belstead and had lunch there. Then a taxi out from Ipswich took me to bus and I came home arriving back at 4.00 No kittens yet. Expected tomorrow.

Thursday 23 July

Twigg's kittens arrived, 5 lovely ones, punctually to time this afternoon. I had to go to War Savings meeting in Village Hall.

Friday 24 July

Busy getting Twig and her family straight.

Saturday 25 July

Mrs Ling left. Paid her and all wages. War Savings in afternoon. Lovely to have the house to ourselves and the children.

Tuesday 28 July

Went off to London on 9.35 from Stowmarket. Train late. Shopped at Harrods. Took Mary Wilson and Mrs Green both some eggs. Then met Merlin at 1.35 at Waterloo and hustled him off to Harrods for new shoes and he had an ice cream! Lovely to see him again. Amongst our adventures I dropped my hat on the line at Knightsbridge tube and he his gas mask at Ipswich! Back at 7.00 to find Mary milking and twins bicycling madly!

Thursday 30 July

Went for bicycle ride with children. Felt very tired. Have started ghastly meal of High Tea at 6.00 in order to save work.

Friday 31 July

Went to Ipswich by bus with Mary and Merlin. Went to dentist after shopping and took taxi out to Belstead. Had lunch. Mother looking very seedy after her nose bleed attack. Worried about her and wrote to Dr Banks. Bill rang up when I got in. Enjoyed our day. Twins quite all right when we got home. Mrs Scillitoe rushed in to say she could not come any more. Sold part of table service to her also dark bureau and small table. Advertised the Swingy (garden seat). An old Mr Hewitt paid me 10 guineas for it.

Saturday 1 August

Had to do housework today. In afternoon, War Savings. A Captain Lacy Scott came and bought small mahogany wardrobe for £10 so am making some necessary money!

Sunday 2 August

Went to church at Tostock. Gores came to lunch. Alan and Mary arranged to ride together on Tuesday.

Monday 3 August

Went for a long bicycle ride with Merlin and twins to Great Ashfield to see a possible maid. Mary out with Alan. Slept after lunch and did flowers in evening.

Tuesday 4 August

Letter from Bill. Wrote to him. Did house work which takes me till 11.30. Mulley came to do window sashes. Mary, Merlin and twins went to tea with Mrs Sheldrick at 4.00. And I had tea alone for once. Mrs Gore rang up and invited Mary to lunch on Thursday. Edith rang up and all are coming here to tea on Thursday.

Wednesday 5 August

Mary and I went to Bury. Ordered Mary a pair of jodphurs. Went to WI and got honey and a fig cake. Bought fish, home by 12.30. Merlin went out with Stewart after dinner and shot a pigeon much to his delight.

Thursday 6 August

Heard from Mother that she is much better. Busy morning doing housework, cleaning and laundry. Mary out riding with Alan Gore and stayed there to lunch. Erskines all came over to tea on bicycles. Enjoyed having them so much. Wrote to Hughes re Barn.

Friday 7 August

Most exciting day. Expecting Bill all day and finally we were having high tea, a message came to say he was on his way, then another that he was at RAF Honington so off Merlin and I shot full bore to meet him. He arrived at the guardroom driven by a WAAF. Lovely to have him home.

Saturday 8 August

Went for a bike ride to Drinkstone but it poured with rain and we got very wet. Rained for rest of day so had a fire and Bill and I slept by it after lunch.

Sunday 9 August

Splitting headache all morning. Bicycled to Hessett Church which we rather liked. Erskine's to lunch and tea. Bill and I both feeling very tired.

Monday 10 August

Bill, Mary and I set off at 8.30 to get 9.30 train to Ipswich where we left Bill and proceeded to shop. Bill went to London and then onto Rednal on the 6 o'clock train. Mary and I returned to lunch at home.

Tuesday 11 August

Find all the housework very tiring, but Mary is very good and helps me a lot.

Wednesday 12 August

Answered an advertisement in *Bury Free Press* re. a man wanting a Labrador as I really feel it's not possible to keep Rob. Set off to Bury in car piled with vegetables. Went to Proctors to sell them also to WI then children and I all had lunch in Abbey Gardens. After our shopping we went on to tea with Piercy's at Fornham House which was quite pleasant. Quite nice people but dreary house and dreary children. Merlin and Mary played tennis.

Friday 14 August

Mary is sick in the night. Merlin seedy with pain at side of his nose. Kept him in bed. Mother came over and thought I ought to have the doctor, so rang up Dr Ware and he is coming in morning.

Saturday 15 August

Merlin's face much worse and one side of his face swollen up like a balloon. Bathed it. Dr Ware came and says it is a boil inside his nose. Fomenting Mer's face all day with warm flannel. Temperature 103. Mary better and up for tea.

Sunday 16 August

Merlin had bad night. Was up a good deal bathing his face. Feeling very tired. Mary up for lunch. Dr Ware came to see him.

Monday 17 August

Merlin a little better but not much discharge yet from his nose. Bathing it all day. In evening a slight discharge from nose. Dr Ware came again and said we could not do more than we are doing. Nose discharging quite well by evening and Merlin feeling better.

Tuesday 18 August

Mer's nose much better. After lunch in spite of feeling very tired went off in car shopping and to sale at Grove Road where I bought two nice gilt mirrors and two rugs and a nice little bedside table. Home for high tea.

Wednesday 19 August

Dr Ware came and thought Merlin better as discharge now is frequent and temperature much lower, but says he won't be fit to go to Shropshire this week which is very disappointing. Rang up Bill and told him we would come next week (Monday).

Thursday 20 August

Mother came over and brought Merlin some peaches. Stayed for lunch but left soon afterwards to walk to Elmswell station. Quite crazy on a hot day. Rang Bill up and told him we should be coming on Tuesday. Feeling disappointed not to see him sooner.

Monday 24 August

First anniversary of buying this dear house. Went to Bury very early in car and had hair washed and sold vegetables. In the evening busy packing before the great start tomorrow. Ware came and said Merlin was fit to go.

Tuesday 25 August

Lovely day. Up very early. Finished everything before we set off at 8.30 in Rouse's taxi to station. Children all hugely excited and thrilled over visit. Arrived London at 11.30 after very comfortable journey 1st-class. Taxi to Harrods where we left our luggage. Then Merlin had his hair cut. Twins and I went to the zoo department and saw animals. Both twins bought themselves a book. Mary and I got some sweets. Then taxi to Paddington which was packed and we had a very uncomfortable journey as far as Shrewsbury and there got a first-class carriage. Bill met us at Gobowan at 7.50 and we got to Wood House by 8.00. Children had high tea and went off to bed. Lovely to be with Bill. Very tired.

Wednesday 26 August My 38ᵗʰ Birthday

Bill gave me Constance Spry book. Garden notebook. Mary a pink Rockingham vase, Merlin an ashtray and twins a lovely blue prayer book. Mother a bag and Dad £20. Lovely day. Very hot and lovely to be together. But not feeling too well.

Friday 28 August

Feeling much better and getting more rest. Had a good night. Very hot day. Wing Commander and Mrs Cheatle came to lunch. Mrs C expecting baby daily and living in Nursing Home. Don't like her. Headache in evening and a thunderstorm.

Sunday 30 August

Went to Bill's Church Parade with Mary and Merlin. Latter very impressed. In evening Bill took me to cinema. Sophie the old maid is a shocking cook and I felt very hungry except today when we had a lovely joint for lunch.

Monday 31 August

Mary and I went to watch flying this morning. In afternoon she and I went to Shrewsbury to see about cakes and food for cocktail party we are having tomorrow night. I thought it a wretched town and all we could find was some biscuits, paste and two tins of spam and some grapes for Mrs Cheatle whose baby arrived today.

Tuesday 1 September

Much better. Feeling really a different girl. Busy doing flowers. In evening we had a party. All senior officers and wives came in for drinks and then we took them on to the cinema where we saw a very poor film. Quite enjoyed it. Wore black. Children watched from upstairs. Bill said it was a hopeless failure.

Thursday 3 September

Busy packing and then went for a good walk before lunch.

Friday 4 September

Feeling very sad our holiday is over and we are on our way home. Bill went off to work and I did all tipping and caught the 10.14 from Gobowen. Very crowded. Had our lunch in train and arrived half an hour late at Paddington which was a nuisance. No porters, no taxi and we very nearly missed our connection at Liverpool Street. Had to stand all the way down to Ipswich. Got home at 6.30 to find Mrs Brown and Florence on doorstep to greet us also Stewart. Lovely to be back and house looking so beautifully clean.

Monday 7 September

Went off early to Bury with car loaded with Merlin and plums and lettuces which we took to Proctors and got £1.6.6. Merlin and I shopped and got back about 11.00. Busy all day. In evening gardened. Mrs Lilley called. To bed early, very tired.

Tuesday 8 September

Several bumps in the night, also a catfight under the window. Twins were frightened and came into my bed. Wrote to Bill, Margaret and Peggy. Gores called and ate figs. Did house work. In afternoon Merlin and I went for a long walk over the fields. Saw a lot of partridges and found some blackberries, also got some exercise.

Wednesday 9 September

Mary and I went off to Bury on the bus with 20lbs of tomatoes which we sold at W.I. Shopped and had some coffee and cakes. Home on bus. In afternoon met Mrs Jewitt who arrived from Newmarket. Gores came to tea. Lady rang up about a kitten and bought one.

Thursday 10 September

Another lovely day. Children went to tea at Lilleys. I feel quite a lady of leisure now I have a housemaid. Rang up Mother as Mrs Anderson rang suggesting Mary might have Sirius, an Arab stallion. Busy preparing for Pellys.

Friday 11 September

A lovely day. Busy all day with preparations. In evening Margaret Pelly and Jane arrived to stay for long weekend. Today a very sad thing happened. My poor little Twiggy, I found dead on the road to Thurston. A woman called soon after 9.00 and said she had found a dead Siamese on the road. I tore down and found her dead with her brain cracked. Felt very sad. When Merlin and Mary came home from Bury they too were very sad. We had a funeral and buried her under the lime tree.

Saturday 12 September

Talked to Margaret who is much taken with this place and wants to find somewhere near here to move from Wincanton. Went with Mary and Merlin in Rouse's taxi to meet Richard at Stowmarket. This time he was there in the guard's van!

Sunday 13 September

Went to Holy Communion and later took Cecily and Clare to Harvest Thanksgiving. Merlin and Richard for some unknown reason took it into their heads to bicycle to Bury. The old Bromfields and Betty came to tea and made children very wild. All children sat up for dinner. Played cards in evening.

Monday 14 September

A lot of letters and orders for Siamese kittens. Margaret and I went to Bury by bus. Shopped and had coffee, then went to house agents. Decided to go to Mrs Trenche's and see her house at Onehouse, so had Rouse's taxi. But the house was not large enough, so we came home. In evening Bill rang up to say he could not get here till 12.50 as he had missed his train. No petrol in car so somewhat fussed I sent Stewart to Mulley's who gave him a gallon of petrol. Stewart fetched Bill at Stowmarket and he arrived about 1.30. I woke up and we talked.

Tuesday 15 September

Margaret, Jane and Richard left on 8.40 from Elmswell where I took them in the car. Bill only saw them for a few moments before they left. In afternoon Bill and Merlin went out shooting.

Wednesday 16 September

Mrs Brown impossibly difficult. Mrs Morton now refuses to come because of her. Mrs Brown gave me a month's notice and was very rude. Bill went shooting. Lovely day. I went out for short time with them. Edith Erskine came to lunch and we all had shooting lunch in dining room. Stew and cheese and fruit. In afternoon twins and Mary went out too. All stayed to tea and then went home. Got four brace of partridges. Mum and Dad's 51st wedding day. Daphne Mulley arrived.

Thursday 17 September

Nannie came to stay. Merlin and twins bicycled up to meet her at Elmswell. She was enchanted with twins and all of them, also the house etc. Mrs Brown still very difficult and most bad tempered.

Friday 18 September

Another day's shooting. Col Astley Cooper came and Tyrrell and they had quite a good day, four brace partridge, 1 hair, 1 rabbit, 1 snipe, 1 pigeon. Nannie with twins most of the day. Sent off a kitten to Royston to Miss Harvey.

Saturday 19 September

Bill and children took Nannie to station in the car. Bill and Merlin out shooting and Merlin shot his first snipe, much to our delight and his! I went to Bury and sold game and fruit. No more War Savings which is rather a joy. Heard of cook to replace Mrs Brown.

Sunday 20 September

All bicycled in pouring rain to Norton Church where we had Holy Eucharist and came home feeling cross and disagreeable. So sad Billy's leave is nearly over.

Monday 21 September

Early breakfast and Bill went off back to work on 8.35. Stuart took him to station. I went to Bury later in car to sale at Corn Exchange, one of Woltons, where I bought two rugs and some books and enjoyed myself though felt very tired when I got home.

Wednesday 23 September

Mary, Merlin and I went off to Ipswich to Freeman to see him for last time except for Mary's plate. Busy doing Merlin's packing and getting everything ready. Heard from Dorchester they are full up and cannot take us for tomorrow night. So wired Mary Wilson to see if she could fix things for us.

Thursday 24 September

Took Merlin out shooting for the last time. A lovely fresh September morning. All packed we set off in car for Stowmarket leaving girls all alone with Daphne in charge. Left car at Barnard's, had to change at Ipswich and got to London at 5.00 and were met by Mrs Dunn whom we gave one kitten. Then on to Kings Cross where we sent off the other kitten to Scotland. Then taxi to theatre to see 'Rose Marie' which Merlin and I both thoroughly enjoyed. Then went by taxi to Mrs Richards flat at Shrewsbury House where she welcomed us and gave us coffee and sandwiches. Then we both had a hot bath and off to bed.

Friday 25 September

Mrs Richards came to say she had forgotten to tell me that Mary rang up last night. I got through to her at once to see if all was well and found it was someone ringing up in answer to her advert for selling Sally. So much relieved had excellent breakfast. Took Merlin to Harrods to get him another pair of walking shoes, then to Waterloo where I saw him off. Then to cheer myself up went and saw Mrs Wedgwood's stud cat, Wansfell Ajax at Fulham Park Gardens. Felt even more depressed after visiting this pathetically repulsive locality and evil smelling house! So took myself to Searcy's and had a good lunch where I was joined by chance by Fiona. We talked and talked. Finally came home on 3.40. When I got to Ipswich I discovered Miss Vennard [governess] looking rather forlorn and saying she did not feel well as on train up from Taunton, a nigger soldier had sat next to her and smelt most repulsive and made her faint! Children all well and Mary had arranged the flowers for me and made house look very nice.

Saturday 26 September

Immediately after breakfast, A. Davis, manservant I engaged through Miss Miller, arrived at front door looking as wild as a hawk, stone deaf and laughing. Screamed at me, 'I'm Davis, ha ha!' And then the fun began as he was quite and utterly useless in dining room and as far as I can see, equally so in the kitchen where he spent his time spinning plates round. However it was quite funny to see Mrs Brown yelling at him and he taking no notice at all of her! Quite a day, apart from Davis. Miss V. unpacking and fussing over a curtain for her bedroom window in case she is seen!

Sunday 27 September

Miss V. off to Holy Communion twice.

Monday 28 September

Lessons began, not very auspiciously, as she and Mary started by having rows. Oh dear! Florence should have left but keeping her on. Bicycled up to see Olive and to find out if she'd come back. Poured with rain.

Tuesday 29 September

Mary and Miss Vennard at loggerheads! She was very tactless over Mary's riding and Mary bolshy. Mrs Brown most difficult too. Davis madder than ever! What a household. I wonder I remain sane.

Friday 2 October

Mary and I had an early lunch then went to Ipswich on 12.15 bus. As she got out, poor child, she was violently and badly sick. Mr Freeman fitted her plate. To tea at Belstead, garden looking very lovely. Home by bus and walked home in dark with Mary who thought it a great thrill.

Saturday 3 October

Davies left, thank goodness. Paid Stewart and wrote to Bill. Went to Bury with Mrs Tyrell and sold 9 ½ stone of apples and a lot of plums for a total of £3.0.0

Sunday 4 October

Miss V. off to Holy Communion twice again. Mary and twins riding. Mrs Kimmins has first refusal of Sally and is coming to see her on Tuesday.

Monday 5 October

Mrs Brown still very difficult. Freda Everett between-maid arrived and is coming daily. Rang up Bill in evening and am longing to go down to be with him next weekend. Florence left. Paid her and saw her off on bus.

Tuesday 6 October

A very busy day. Mary and I got 9 o'clock bus to Ipswich. Stewart brought us on dozens of letters and I heard from a lot of cooks. Wrote to Bill and had letter from him. Saw Mrs Fisher and her cat, 'Suffolk Shiane', which she has sold to me for £3.13.6. Went to Freeman, he kept us waiting so that we had a frightful scurry for the train and I ran so hard all the tendons in my legs gave and on getting out at Stowmarket I could hardly walk. Met Mrs Kimmins and brought her back in a taxi to Tostock where she saw Sally being ridden by Mary. She decided to buy her subject to a vet inspection. Took her to Elmswell station. After lunch Mary's plate came adrift again. Sent wires to the various cooks, and was busy till bedtime.

Wednesday 7 October

Went to Bury on 9.50 bus and took in 40 Figs which sold at W.I. for a penny halfpenny and twopence each. Got some honey and a chocolate cake for Bill. Interviewed cook, Mrs Allcock who I did not like. She looks bad tempered. In afternoon went to Collins to get a chicken for Mary Wilson and ordered her an Xmas Turkey. Also to see Mrs Everett as Freda had not come. Packed. Washed children's hair and did up hamper and endless jobs till bedtime.

Thursday 8 September

Had bad night, and got up very early. Mary got up too, came down and had breakfast with me. Miss Vennard in bad temper and hate to leave them with her but feel a change will do me good and I am so longing to see Bill. Miss Rouse took me to the station also laundry and the chickens which are to go to Newie's sister. Changed at Ipswich. Arrived in London to see a cook, but she never turned up. Went to Arts Club and left Mary her chickens and eggs and collected sugar from her. Caught 2.10 to Shrewsbury, changed there, met young Richards who gave me tea and arrived Rednal at 7.15 where Billy met me. Lovely to see him. Lovely fire in room and sitting room. 'Pop' came in at 9.30 and talked to us.

Friday 9 October

Wild windy day. Had quiet morning and slept in afternoon. Wing Commander Frost and Squadron Leader Skinner (the M.O.) came into tea. Bill and I had dinner together.

Saturday 10 October

Went for a walk to the camp. Bill met me, brought me home and we had lunch together. After lunch I went to sleep again. Wrote letters. Bill home for tea. Read in evening and changed early, had dinner and went to the Airman's Entertainment which was quite good. Bill, much to his fury, had to get up and speak afterwards and looked very cross.

Sunday 11 October

Up at 8.00 for breakfast with Bill. Read and sewed. Went for a walk and met Bill. In afternoon both slept and went for walk in afternoon. Lovely quiet day together.

Monday 12 October

Bill went off at 8.30 as usual and I packed. Wrote letters and caught 10.14 from Gobowen to London. Very full but got first class corner seat, read and slept. Home on 3.40. Lovely to be with my girls again.

Tuesday 13 October

Lovely day but did not enjoy it as spoiled by going to Ipswich to beastly dentist who said I have to have my hateful wisdom tooth out in a Nursing Home next week. Mary and I shopped and took taxi out to tea at Belstead. Home at 8.00. Mary sat up to dinner. Vennard awfully grumpy. Rang up Bill.

Wednesday 14 October

Sad getting Sally off to Kimmins at Fleet. Made all preparations with Mary. Miss Vennard bloody.

Thursday 15 October

Spend whole morning trying to get Mrs Brown packed up and off. Poor old woman gets more and more mithered over which is sad. Last evening had a talk with Miss Vennard and do hope she will be better, more placid and pleasant as a result.

Friday 16 October

New cook is so far pleasant and efficient. Busy morning.

Saturday 17 October

Busy cleaning out and altering store cupboards all day. Really did too much and felt exceedingly tired. Erskine children to lunch.

Sunday 18 October St Luke's Day

Felt very seedy with migraine and toothache all day long. In bed till lunch. Lilleys came to tea.

Monday 19 October

Lovely warm day, like summer. Went to Woolpit in morning, feeling much better. Bury in afternoon shopping and tea at Mrs Woltons.. Heard Needham Market was badly bombed.

[This raid is well documented. A Junkers 88 came over very low and the bombs damaged lots of houses along the High Street and some people were killed. Luckily the front of the school where the offices were was hit but the children and teachers escaped. Marlesford and Stratford St Andrew were also bombed and machine gunned that day].

Tuesday 20 October

Another lovely day. Jocelyn rang and asked Mary over for weekend. Went to Salvage Barn about bottles, an impossible job for me to tackle. Felt very ill and tired in evening.

Thursday 22 October

Impossible for me to have operation so cancelled it for now. Miss Vennard quite impossible and so difficult.

Friday 23 October

Went down to Tyrrell about butter, also cream and a chicken for next week and Tyrrell about beaters. Did flowers and then felt very tired. Mother came over in afternoon and stayed to tea. Arrived in car with new chauffeur who looks bad to me. Brought me some old chair covers and my old wedding dress. Mary went off at 3.00 for Bury station and from there to Newmarket stay with Jocelyn Anderson for the weekend.

Saturday 24 October
Awful wild wet night and pouring rain. Went to village. Cleaned cats room out. Did fruit. Heard poor old Mulley had had a stroke and not likely to live.

Monday 26 October In morning went to Bury to meet Mary in pouring rain. Found poor child in floods of tears and very upset as Mother said she could not help her buy Sirius so I said I would buy him and rang up Mrs Anderson to tell her so. Then fetched Bill and the cook, Mrs Wise at 6 pm in Miss Rouse's car. Lovely to have him home.

Tuesday 27 October
Lovely day after yesterday's rain. Bill and I and Colonel Coles went shooting and had most enjoyable day. Tyrrell shooting too and Stewart, Bill, Everett and Gardner beating also two boys of Tyrrell's. We got five pheasants, two pigeon, five Partridge, three hares, two rabbits. Had lunch and tea at home.

Thursday 29 October
Bill left after lunch. We had a lovely morning together and went to the marshes and got a snipe, went round the garden. Took Bill to Stowmarket and sold the hares.

Friday 30 October
Olive most trying and had to speak to her in afternoon after which she left. Mary Wilson arrived in evening, lovely to have her to stay. She agrees with me that Miss Vennard is very trying.

Saturday 31 October
Pouring wet day. Mary and I went shopping and later to Tyrrell's to get some eggs. Heard bomber overhead in mist obviously in difficulties and a moment later, a crash. It blew up at Norton near Alde's shop and all occupants were killed. Mrs Gore came to

lunch. We had roast pheasant and plum tart. Badly cooked and served by this woman, Mrs Wise.

Sunday 1 November

Mary Wilson is sweet and doesn't mind what she does. Clears meals and washes up etc. I went with children to church and on my way, fell off my bicycle and hurt myself very much. Nearly fainted. Mary gave me brandy and dealt with my grazed head and made me lie down. She and children went for a walk. In afternoon she left, going to Bury and up to London from there. Felt rotten and went to bed.

Monday 2 November

Stayed in bed all day. Cold and wet and had fire in my room. Still felt wretched. Miss Vennard quarrelling all day with children. Miserable. Rang up Bill.

Tuesday 3 November

Better, less stiff, got up and bundled about. Poured all day long. Miss V. impossible. Felt very cross and miserable.

Thursday 5 November

Cold wet miserable day. Went off by myself by bus to Ipswich. Met Mother who took me to Nursing Home in Woodbridge Road in car. I got into my bed in quite a nice little room. Mother stayed and talked to me, then left to get her tea. The Sister came and gave me an injection to stop me bleeding. At 5.30 I went along to the theatre. Doctors Pretty and Freeman there, all in white coats and the Sister. I felt very frightened, then I had chloroform and remember no more until later when I came round feeling very queer. Everything smelling of chloroform and sick, but tooth gone.

Friday 6 November

Feeling better but still a bit sick and upheaved. Had tea and later breakfast. Mother came to see me and Dad and Dr Pretty. After lunch, got up, packed and had a taxi and came home by train. Went straight to bed. Great welcome from the children.

Saturday 7 November

Stayed in bed all morning. Then got up and sat in drawing room and wrote letters. Rested after lunch. Felt seedy and tired.

Sunday 8 November

Very cold. Did not go out. Great pain in my jaw all day.

Monday 9 November

Had bad night with jaw most painful. With torch and spike dealt with it and found hole all filled up with food etc. After having cleaned it out it was better. Children and I had a lovely day. 'The Venn' went to London for interviews and weather was lovely. Children cleaned tack and I did flowers and we were very happy.

Wednesday 11 November Armistice Day.

Mary and I went to Ipswich by bus to see Freeman. He looked at my jaw, cleaned it out and syringed it and said it was healing nicely.

Sunday 15 November [13 November 8th Army recaptures Tobruk and Allied victory at El Alamein on 2 November]

Went to Tostock Church with children. Then bicycled over to Drinkstone to hear the bells being rung to celebrate our victory in Egypt. Col Astley Cooper came to tea.

Monday 16 November

Mrs Anderson arrived to stay in afternoon. Mary went to meet her and Sirius at station. Great thrill for Mary buying a new horse.

Wednesday 18 November

Busy packing all morning. Doing laundry, seeing Mrs Wise and to getting everything settled up before leaving. I had taxi to Thurston at 1.30. then to London. Arrived 5.15 Paddington and down here to Rednal by 11.45. Bill met me at station. Lovely to be with him.

Thursday 19 November

Had breakfast in bed and Bill and I had lunch at 12.30. Slept in afternoon, in evening went to dine in WAAF officers mess. They gave us a very good dinner of chestnut soup, pheasant and plum pudding. To bed late.

Friday 20 November

Bill came back to lunch. Wrote a lot of letters. Lovely day but cold. Bill back for dinner. Sat and talked afterwards then to bed.

Saturday 21 November

Breakfast in bed and up at 10.30. Do so much enjoy these lazy and unhurried mornings with plenty of time to read, rest and think. A big mail, letters from governesses etc. Bill back for luncheon. In afternoon went down to sick quarters and saw Wing Commander Cheatle and took him some books. Bathed and changed and Pop dined with us before going to Mess where we picked up the CFI and took him with us to Entertainment. This was poor. The lights fused, but it was all quite amusing. Very cold when we came home.

Sunday 22 November

Bitterly cold day. Frost and icy. Bill working as usual. I had a nice hot bath which warmed me up. Wrote letters in front of the fire. Went for a walk after packing. Met Bill and we had lunch together, then sat and talked by the fire till it was time for me to go in Mr Beauclerk's taxi to Gobowen station. Train very late. Did not reach Paddington until 10.30. Had coffee and a sandwich at Great Western Hotel and a nice room there and to bed by 11.30.

Monday 23 November

Had bad night looking at my watch and wondering if I'd wake up in time. Caught 8.12 from London down to Ipswich which was packed with people and very uncomfortable as far as Ipswich. There met Mother and the children. Children had thoroughly enjoyed their weekend. Thrilled to have two rabbits in a basket bought from Lady Ailwyn. Got back to Tostock 11.30. Found the drawing room finished. 'The Venn' savage and Stewart better. Then began a desperately busy day. Letters, laundry, cooking, house work, unpacking, flowers, food, rations and blackout. To bed worn out.

Tuesday 24 November

Nightmare day. No servants. No time and ending in twenty-one W.I. members coming for their meeting at the house and tea for all. They all enjoyed it though. Mrs Levison, new Cook, arrived at 7.30. Thank God!

Wednesday 25 November

Went to Bury in car taking with me Mrs Lilley. Shopped. Mrs L and I had coffee together. Went to W.I. and got some honey. Met Maud Rose, parlourmaid. Thank Heavens have some servants at last. In afternoon Mary riding Sirius.

Friday 26 November

Went to Bury and interviewed M Berry, head housemaid. Engaged her subject to references. Shopped and came home on bus feeling awfully cheerful. Went to Whist Drive in Village Hall and gave away prizes.

Monday 30 November

Mary's horse Sirius, bolted with her.

Friday 4 December

Went up to London on 9.30 from Stowmarket with luggage and 'Ducksie' [Siamese cat] who had come into season, yowling in the basket. Mrs Wedgwood met me at station. Then to the Dorchester with luggage. Met Bill at Fortnum & Mason for luncheon. Then Bill went off to dentist and I to shop at Harrods etc. Back to Dorchester to meet Elizabeth. Gave her her presents. We returned to the Dorchester for dinner and danced.

Saturday 5 December

Bill went back to Rednal on the early train at 10.00. I did some telephoning and then to Harrods for more shopping. Home on 1 o'clock train after collecting Ducksie from Mrs Wedgwood at station. Home and found children all thankful to have me home again. The Vennard is as impossible as ever.

Monday 7 December

Busy day. Went to station with Mrs Levison and fetched Mrs Sullivan, new cook through Miss Webb.

Tuesday 8 December

Mother's Birthday. Rang her up and wished her many happy returns. Heard parlour maid is coming tomorrow.

Wednesday 9 December

Took Maud Rose into Bury in car and shopped. Mary joined me and I took her to see "Mrs Miniver" which we both much enjoyed. Fetched new parlourmaid, Alexandra Smith from station and new housemaid also arrived so I feel grand.

Saturday, 12 December

Went to Ipswich in car to Elmswell then by train with Mary and twins. Lovely warm day. Lunched at Belstead. Dad gave me his Christmas present. We came home by train.

Sunday 13 December

Another lovely warm day. Went to church at Tostock. Received Miss V's account asking for next term's salary.

Monday 14 December

The last day of this ghastly woman. Had sweep in drawing-room and little sitting-room.

Tuesday 15 December

Miss Vennard left at 8.15. We were all more than delighted and sang songs of delight. A lovely start to the holidays.

Wednesday 16 December

Went to London. Train late. Interviewed Mrs Rickaby who I thought worse than the Vennard.

Friday 18 December

Children and I did up Christmas presents and wrote Christmas letters. Had early lunch and went into Bury in car full of holly and the three girls. Left the holly at Scarfe's for 10/-. Shopped then went to Crosses Nurseries and ordered apple trees.

Monday 21 December

Up early and went to London on 9.35 from Stowmarket. Met Mary Wilson's maid who turned up to collect the turkey. Met Merlin at 1.39 at Waterloo. Home on 3.40 which was packed with people.

Wednesday 23 December

Went to Bury in car with Mary and Merlin. Shopped all morning and went to Crosses Nurseries. In afternoon wrote letters and did up parcels.

Thursday 24 December

Decorated the house in morning. In afternoon went to Tyrrell's with Christmas gifts. Also to Mrs Everett, Mrs Pannats, Miss Goldings, Mrs Hayhoe, Mrs Southgate, Mrs Friend and Mrs Lilley's. Very tired indeed. Did all children's stockings and maids' presents. Rang up Bill.

Friday 25 December Christmas Day

Children awake very early. Merlin crept into my room with one of his socks filled with little things for me including some nuts rolled in chocolate they had done themselves! Rang up Mother. All went to church but only a handful of people there. Had a lovely Christmas dinner. Turkey and plum pudding etc and cream.

Saturday 26 December

Bill rang me up at 7.00, lovely to talk to him. Not feeling well and so shaky and shivery. Coles came to lunch in their pony trap. Very cold. To bed early with aspirins.

Sunday 27 December

Feeling a bit better but with a violent cold. In bed till lunchtime. Did not go out at all. Wrote Christmas letters and did a lot of mending.

Monday 28 December

Went to Bury in car with Merlin, Mary and Clare. Cecily preferred to stay behind to ride and was knocked off. Men came for wood chopping but only half day. Bill rang up at teatime to say he was arriving earlier which was lovely.

Tuesday 29 December

Bitterly cold and snow. Alan Gore and Mrs Gore's gardener came to get their tree. Bicycled to Norton in afternoon to get the meat and was very cold. Mary and twins had a fight and Mary lost her temper and hit the twins with a stick. Punished all.

Wednesday 30 December

Woke up feeling sick, queer and headache to find snow about two inches deep and falling. Worried as to whether to go to London to the pantomime or not. Rang up Mother and decided to go. Was sick at Stowmarket and in train going to London. Mother met us at Ipswich. Mary felt sick too and was sick on way home. We had a filthy lunch at Abercorn rooms at Liverpool Street station and then to Coliseum to see 'Mother Goose' which children all enjoyed. I continued to be sick and felt very rotten. Slow journey home and arctic drive back. Arrived home 8.30. Clare was sick in night.

Thursday 31 December

Clare and Mary in bed all morning. Merlin and Cecily out snowballing! Lovely day. Had sleep in afternoon. Felt much better. Two letters from Bill. Rang him up to wish him a happy New Year but he wasn't there. Felt very sad.

1944 and 1945
One volume incomplete
1943 diary is missing.

It is clear that Cesca is finding it increasingly difficult to keep a diary. The monotonous daily routine, fewer servants and long separations have taken their toll.

Her parents' health and Bill's part in the D-Day Invasion aboard HMS Scylla both cause great anxiety. At Tostock produce from the kitchen garden and sale of pedigree Siamese kittens form a vital income stream.

Saturday 1 January
A bitterly cold day. Bill and Merlin went off with their lunch to a shoot at Sir John Agnew's and came home teatime with a brace for the house having had a very good day. I took Ducksie on bicycle to Elmswell station to send her to Mrs Wedgwood's Wansfell Ajax [£1-15-0 stud fee] as since returning from Mrs Sayer's Oriental Silky Boy, she has persisted in calling.

Sunday 2 January
Went to church. No one there. Bill read the lessons. Our last day together very sad. Bill and Mer were painting in afternoon.

January 3 Monday
We all went out shooting in morning, but so cold and wet, nothing to be seen. After lunch Mary and I went with Bill to Stowmarket to see him off. As usual I felt very sad and cried. Mer and Twins went to tea with Lilleys. Went to bed early. Sad. [Bill is commanding RAF Kirkwall in the Orkneys, far away].

Wednesday 5 January
Went to Bury with apples [50 lbs. £1.13.4] for sale to W.I. office, lavender, celery and curly kale. Clare came with me and bought a Black Rex doe. Mary and Merlin went to lunch with the Piercys at Fornham. Fiona and Tony Hickson came to stay. Latter nice looking little boy. Very cold. Waited three quarters of an hour on Elmswell station as train so very late. Bill rang me up.

Friday 7 January

Fiona and Mary and I went to Bury. Had hair washed. Saw Dr Ware about my pains which he says are not rheumatism at all but [this word is impossible to decipher] caused by doing too much and that I must try to do less. Ordered me medicine and pills that I forget to collect. Home for lunch. Went to tea with Periras. It was the girl's 21st birthday and they had a party for her. Cake and lots of presents. Sir John and Lady Agnew there and Lawrences, Astley-Cooper's, Mrs Grigg etc. Mary and I bicycled home in the wet. Merlin and Tony went on bikes to fetch my medicine and to call on Major Montgomery at Rougham, the American Bill and I met at Astley-Cooper's last week, inviting him to tea on Sunday.

Saturday 8 January

Gores came to tea and Alan and the others played 'Up Jenkins'. Billy rang up in evening, do miss him so.

Sunday 9 January

Fiona, Mary, Tony and Mer all went to Tostock church. Empty except for Mrs Alderton. Went for a walk and fed chickens. Major Montgomery came to tea. We were all rather amused as he arrived late and none of us thought he would come, but he brought us an enormous box of chocolates that we all enjoyed. Has promised to ask Merlin over.

Thursday 13 January

Oakes and Erskine's came to tea here. Mrs Oakes came too.

Friday 14 January

Took Merlin to new dentist, Mr Dawson in Northgate Street. Mended one tooth and 2 more front fillings to do at Easter. Nice man.

Saturday 15 January

Terribly foggy day. Clare and I set off for the day to Rabbit Show at Ipswich by train and spent nearly all day in train. But were rewarded by Onyx winning 2nd prize in Novice and 3rd in Open. Got back by teatime to the others and heard later it was worst fog for years.

Sunday 16 January

Another very cold day of fog. Did not go to church. Wrote letters and rang up Bill whom I miss so much.

Monday 17 January

Packed and sent off Merlin's trunk. Mrs Higgins a great help with his things. Mrs Thinn turned up in evening.

Tuesday 18 January

Had a happy day with children. Bicycled to Norton with Mer.

Wednesday 19 January

Went to Bury as usual, shopped, twins had hair cut. Mary in bed, poor child with a bad cold and temperature. Must be flu. Wired Miss Whitehead that she must come back in evening. Merlin also with cold but not as bad as M. Rang up Bill in evening as felt worried about going to London.

Thursday 20 January

As Merlin no worse decided to take him, Mary too seemed better. Set off in car at 9.00 and caught 9.35 from Stowmarket to London. Went to Connaught and had quite a nice room on top floor. Mother joined us for lunch. Went to see 'She Follows Me About' at the Garrick. Dined with the Pecks at United Hunts Club. Fay and Richard both so nice to us both and he walked home with us.

Friday 21 January

Merlin and I both had a good night with no raids and had breakfast upstairs. Then we went to Harrods to buy bedroom slippers, garters and gloves, also a book and to Searcy's for cakes for Merlin's journey. Then to station and saw the dear boy off. Met Mrs Pearson doing the same thing. Shopped at Fortnum & Mason. Lunched with Dunns at RAC and went to Rayne and Debenhams. Then caught my train home 5.10 from Liverpool Street and had the most awful delayed journey. Two and a half hours late at Ipswich then air raid there, so waited another two hours, arrived at Stowmarket 11.00pm to find impossible to get car from Barnard's garage. Eventually succeeded and got home at 12.45. To bed eventually.

Monday 24 January

Mrs Thinn left again. Hate loathe and detest her offhand ways and feel fed up with her. Wrote letters. Busy all the time with twins in bed. Went to Bury in morning to get them fish, lozenges and medicine etc.

Tuesday 25 January

Feeling rotten myself but up early to get fires going, breakfast and blackout done etc. Went to butchers. Busy all day.

Wednesday 26 January

Twins better but still feeling seedy myself and with temperature 100. Went to Bury and took Mary to dentist. Nothing to be done, fortunately. Back for lunch, decided to go to bed early and not get up in morning as I'm not going to London. Mrs Bell gave notice to add to the general gloom. Rang up my Bill, but the line was shocking and he could not hear me.

Thursday 27 January

In bed all day with rotten cough, glands, and feeling done. Bill rang me up early and insisted on my staying in bed.

Friday 28 January

Better but in bed. Twins up. Had their room turned out. Amazingly dirty creatures they are. Bill rang up again.

April

I have not kept this diary for 3 months but never these days have time. However now Easter and the children's holidays are over and Miss Whitehead is back and term starts tomorrow May 1st, perhaps I shall have more time. Bill did not get his leave in April but came to London for conference so had 2 days at home only. Merlin went back on 28th.

Sunday 30 April

Went to church with Miss Whitehead, nine people there excluding Mr L the vicar, and Miss Mash at organ. Children in the choir behaved disgracefully giggling and talking so, on coming out I spoke to the ringleader and told her what a naughty girl she was. Miss Whitehead is very nice and full of go. Sarah too seems a nice child and gets on well with the twins and to their delight rides well. This is a blessing. Came home and laid lunch. Wrote to Bill. Mrs Bell off-hand and says she has too much to do.

May 30th.

Haven't written for ages. Don't know what's the matter with me this year except perhaps like all of us, utter war weariness. Tired of trying to economise, feed the household with variety and niceness, cope with domestics, children's clothes and schooling problems and above all else, endless separation from one's dearest love. Only to see him for an hour or two, a weekend at the longest, what is the good of that after the years of endless separations we have had and as far as I can see still shall have and now he is going on this ghastly Invasion party which may start at any moment.

[Bill was the RAF Air Adviser to Naval Commander Eastern Task Force D Day Invasion on board the Scylla, the flagship of the combined invasion fleet. He was awarded CBE and mentioned twice in despatches. See Top Secret order signed by Air Marshall Coningham, Commander Advanced Allied Expeditionary Air Force dated 23 May 1944.
The Scylla set sail at 16.30 5 June 1944 from Spithead, Rear Admiral Sir Phillip Vian in command watching the massive invasion convoys sail south before joining them off the invasion beaches. On D-Day Vian visited all the British beaches and the Syclla took part in the bombardment of Sword and Gold beach. At the end of the day she anchored at the eastern end of the fleet to help guard against the feared intervention of the E boats. After 18 days serving off Normandy, the Scylla was badly damaged by a mine on the 23 June.
With both engine rooms out of action she had to be towed back to Plymouth and Vian had to transfer his flag to Headquarters ship HMS Hilary].

Bill hoped to come up and see us yesterday but evidently could not as I heard no more. It is very hot. Been busy picking gooseberries topping and tailing and bottling them. We are having dinner early to let Mrs Bell, Miss W and Mary and Sarah go to school to WI meeting to hear talk on music and percussion band. So I shall have twins to put to bed. They are all such dear sweet children. No news of Merlin and do so hope I shall be able to get to see him this last term of his at Brambletye. Took the car with hamper to Elmswell station. Then to Norton to butcher, blacksmith and shoe repairer. Country is looking so utterly lovely these early summer days. Wrote to Bill also Mrs Fyfe, [head mistress of Mrs Fyffes, Hatherop, boarding school]. My jaw still hurts me a good deal and I wish it would heal up. My chicks are getting on well and growing fast.

Sunday 4 June

This time next year perhaps the War will be over and I shall be at Eton with Bill and Merlin. What fun that will be. After writing rather dismally, the lovely thing happened and the telephone rang and Bill was at Roughham. We had seen an aeroplane circle low over the house, but as so many do these days did not pay any attention to it. Lovely to fetch him in the car with Mary. He left early Wednesday morning and I proceeded into Bury to do my shopping. I also helped at W I stall for a bit.

Mrs Wood came to lunch on Friday. I like her. Wrote to Bill, sent him a book. Today, Sunday, not feeling very well with headache and jaw ache. Feel worried too about this Invasion that must start at any minute now. [Operation Overlord, the long planned Allied invasion of Normandy]. Did not go to Tostock church and did not feel up to bicycling to Thurston. Read by the fire instead.

Monday 5 June

Heard the good news that the US 5th Army has taken Rome. Busy morning, shopping, ordering and paying last month's accounts. Heard of two cooks which seems a marvel. Very cold, but headache is better today.

Wednesday 14 June

The Invasion started 6 June and is now going well. Have heard from Elizabeth and Bill on Monday. Was very anxious about him and felt almost sick with it in the nights. Harrowing service in church on Sunday too. The Clare Walkers and Mrs Schreiber came to lunch that day. Have heard of a cook and have had an electric cooker put in. This morning went to Bury in the car. Took flowers into W I and helped at the stall for a short while. Mrs Clare Walker there and Mrs Sayers. Sold a cockerel. Took Lulu to Coe who says she has eczema due to eating horseflesh. Had a desperate afternoon washing her and applying lotion. Wrote to Bill. Mother rang up and says she has not been well and her couple not yet come. In afternoon went with Cecily to the post. Lessons going full swing.

Thursday 15 June

This morning after breakfast, washing-up, making beds, feeding chickens, doing flowers, seeing Bell and Stewart I got down to letters and accounts. Bottled gooseberries and read papers after lunch. Then went to see cottages at Drinkstone and to tea with Gores after. Everything rather annoyed me today. Kristine and young Mrs Prior Palmer doing a hush hush job. So private! Home on my bike. Mrs Ackroyd rang up and asked me to take on collecting for L. L. Fund. Refused. Bloody well won't run round for her doing her dirty jobs. I loathe and detest that woman.

Saturday 15 July

Dad's 85th birthday. Mrs Erskine's, Sarah's mother left after breakfast. Mary and twins and I went by bus to Ipswich where we shopped. Twins tried on their new winter coats. Had coffee at O's cafe and met Bromfield's there and Mother. Then we went out to Belstead in the car. Had good lunch and long talk to Dad and Mother, enjoyed the day but felt very sad that Dad seems to be failing.

Sometime during 1945 Dr Francis Bisshopp returned unwell to Tunbridge Wells. He had refused to move with his wife to Woodbridge instead preferring to stay as a PG with his old servants, Mr and Mrs Hogben of 2 Shaftesbury Road. Hogben had been his chauffeur.
Francis Bisshopp died in his eighty-eighth year, after an operation for prostate cancer in the Kent and Sussex Hospital on 26 December 1946.

His funeral service was held at King Charles the Martyr church on 31 December and he was buried in Hawkenbury cemetery.

The Times and of course the *Courier* reported his death and, following publication of his will noted that his estate was valued at £43,526 (equivalent to around £1.5 million in 2014) The British Medical Journal (February 8 1947) also marked his passing, describing him as "a quiet and reserved man, but he always continued his association with a few of his earlier contemporaries".

August 15

A month since I have written in my diary! Somehow there never seems to be time this year. And I am keeping the accounts which all takes time. Such a lot has happened too. End of term and Merlin home after visit to Eton. Merlin had mumps and all of us been in quarantine but no one else got it and I am the only one still possible. Merlin went to join Bill yesterday and left on night train for Edinburgh where Bill arranged to meet him and motored him up to Inverness where both are staying with Mrs MacPherson and John and Mary Wilson and David.

This diary lapsed for rest of 1944.

January 1945.

January 10

Must really try to keep this diary going this year. One of my new year resolutions! So far broken. Bill received a CBE in New Years Honours List which was a great thrill for us all. He left after 10 days heavenly leave on January 2 to return to Inverness. Do hope he won't be there for long.

March 19

Hopeless to try and keep diary going. So much to do and always so little time. Bill had his 39th birthday here yesterday. He is now in London at Seaford House, Belgrave Square at that Air Ministry department which works for liaison with foreign airforces.[HQ No.13 Group]. I have not been well, but had to go on just the same as Mary came home at half term February 28 and developed measles and has been really very ill with it. She is better and just up but it has been a great anxiety. The twins are also running wild and having no education this term as it was impossible to get a governess. Merlin seems to be doing well at Eton and made great progress in every way. I have bought Everett's cottage down Norton Road and propose doing it up and letting half of it until he dies. I feel very depressed at times, but must cheer up as the War is going on well and we are in many ways fortunate. Today I went to Hayhoe's for order and went round garden and saw to my baby chicks. I have nine little ones hatched on Friday last.

June 13
Went to Bury with 77 lbs gooseberries, Scabious, Roses, and cucumbers. Went to Menns Cafe with 30 lbs cabbages and 10 lbs gooseberries. Met Mrs Ridley. Letter from Merlin who wants a new cricket bat. Had awful chase after Ducksie who rushed off out early after black tomcat calling at top of her voice. Twins and I failed to catch her but she came back later. Black kittens? Watching her. Heard last kitten sent yesterday had arrived safely at Gleneagles. [Sold for 8 guineas]. Letter from Bill today who is at Cranwell. Twins and Mlle had a row over scribbling in lessons. I had to intervene. Wrote letters and bills, did accounts. Went to cottage in evening. Found 17 eggs in hedge. Went to Conservative meeting in schools at 8.45 and heard Lord Erskine and new prospective Conservative candidate Colonel Clifton Brown speak.

June 14
Colder, up early, fed ducks, Bee, cats. Ducksie still the same. Mrs Friend and Mrs Flatman came and cleaned kitchen and my sitting room. Anne Aldridge ill, so Mrs A. away. Wrote to Bill. Cut roses and dead headed. Edith Erskine rang up and invited me to tea on Thursday next. Invited them to lunch Sunday 24th. Invitation from Mrs Martin, Nether Hall, Thurston to Cocktails and Strawberries on Saturday evening. Seems I shall have a busy day that day. Mlle very tiresome.

September 9

I never seem able to keep this diary this year, so much to do and so little time. Bill had his operation at the end of July. This proved most successful and he is now so much better. Mary is very well now and goes back to school on 19th. So does Merlin. The great problem now is the twins and what we are going to do for the Autumn term, either to go to London, or stay here and twins go to Bury to school. Feeling very tired and old with so much to do these days and need a rest and a change very badly. Bill went to London this morning with Mary to keep him company. Mrs Brown is coming back to help me tomorrow for a week. Newie comes to stay on Tuesday and Mum on Thursday.

Later. Did all my accounts, bills etc. this morning wrote letters. Lunch, roast lamb, carrots and potatoes, apple tart and a custard and cream. Coffee. In spite of the end of lend lease, we in the country don't seem starving. Larder has always something in it and that is heaps of milk with Daphne and Tyrrell's supply. Went out after with twins mushrooming and got about 1 lb. My chickens are thriving. Six eggs from the 12 last year's pullets who are now starting moulting. My 26 new pullets growing splendidly and on range in back park and a small brood of 12 in front park, eight useful cockerels for use from the end of October onwards. Then there are six Khaki Campbell ducks and two stock cockerels. 59 head altogether. Bill rang up to say he and Mary had had a good trip up to London and that they had lunched at the Berkeley. Merlin painting. Mickey called for his game bag after yesterday's boys shoot. Fed hens after tea and did some flowers, also removed suckers from front climbing roses. Cooked fried plaice for children's supper.

Wednesday 19 September

Sad. My two darling children left to go back to school. Had very bad night worrying so took one of Bill's special pills on rising. Rang him up. Saw Mary off after getting her sweets and grapes.

Then came home and took Merlin who had been out shooting getting a hare and a hen pheasant.

November 7

Can't think why it is I seem utterly incapable of keeping a diary this year. Perhaps it's because I have all my accounts to keep instead! Anyhow it is lazy of me and so silly not to keep it daily as I have done for years. We have just had half term and long leave with Merlin home and Mary and Bill. Lovely, but rather spoilt by Pam Fitzgerald, the Universal Aunt woman who came for fortnight while I went to have a rest.

Altogether she was rather a failure as she arrived with streaming cold and gave it to me so that I was ill in bed for two days in London and felt rotten for five. But the change did me a lot of good and I now feel very much better and rested. Twins also had a holiday and fortunately enjoy their school and appear to be getting on very well. They have to be there by nine every morning and I fetch them in the evening.

Tuesday 13 November

Very cold. Took children to school. Shopped in Bury and got a cake at Menn's. Home by way of Norton and fetched meat at butchers. Mrs Tate busy getting on with twins party frocks. Wrote to Bill and Mary's godparents as she is to be confirmed on December 4 at Eley Cathedral. Wrote to Mother. Got flowers ready for W. I. tomorrow.

Then went to fetch children. Fed dog and puppies who are growing simply huge. To bed early after making out my Christmas list.

This is the end of 1945. 1946 and 1947 are missing or were not kept. The next and final diary is 1948 and very brief.

Merlin winning Eton Steeplechase

Mary outside Tostock

Mary debutante

Mary and Bill 25 July 1950
Mary's Wedding

John and Mary, Clare and Cecily with Martin Gosling

Tostock 25th July 1950 Bill's inscription reads; The house has been there longest. The two crones in aprons total in years about 130. From L-R. standing. Herbert, Warren, Florence, the dressmaker, Miss Jeckell, Mary, Cecily, Mrs Stewart. Cesca, Bee, Mrs Davidson, Bill, Ted. Sitting. Clare, Merlin, Jill. Two cats somewhere.
The R-R and the racer, J2 Allard.

Merlin and Cecily

Cecily

Cecily and Clare

Lieut. Robert Creasy and Clare's Wedding 1954

1948
(Incomplete)

Bill was appointed Station Commander at RAF Cranwell in 1946 and retires at his own request in February 1948. Fanny, Cesca's Mother is failing and dies at The Chestnuts, Cumberland Street, Woodbridge of cancer of the colon aged 84 years. 1948 is shrouded in sadness, Cesca's energy for diary writing fizzles out as she adjusts to Bill at home running his own farm and her 'babies' fast growing up, marrying and having families of their own. A post World War world without servants awaits. Reginald Hughes, the family solicitor was then 62yrs old and weighed fifteen stone.

Thursday 1 January New Year's Day
Rang up to find out how Mother was. Nurse said she would probably be awake from drugs about 6-7 pm. Decided to go over then. In morning wrote letters. Bill and Merlin out shooting getting four pigeons. Went over to Woodbridge in Morris, Bill drove. We went via Coddenham and Grundisburgh, 26 miles. The other way is 30 miles. Mother in much pain and distress. Spoke my name but did not know Bill. Felt sad. I like the day Nurse Woodley better than MacWinter the New Zealander. Have dinner at 8.00.

Friday 2 January
Mary and I went to Bury and Mary had hair do while I shopped. Home for lunch. Mrs D is excellent cook. Dr Briscoe rang up and says Mother cannot last long. Bill arranging matters, as Nurse says the funeral must take place quickly owing to Mother's illness. Did laundry with Warren. Bill and Merlin out shooting. Very wet, went to post office. Had bad headache, to bed early.

Saturday 3 January
Had a bad night with Bee, (dachshund), very fidgety and a tapeworm worrying her, poor dog. Down to check on her several times. Bill, Twins, Merlin and Mops set off at 9.15 in the Railton [motor car] for Twickenham. England v Wallabies. Nice warm January day. M and M go on to Haslemere to stay with Durham's

for dance and weekend. I had busy morning, wormed Bee successfully, enormous tapeworm. Went to Oldfields for potatoes, and paid newspaper bill. Tidied lobby and also drawing room, my sitting room and the food cupboard. Paid Stewart. Took dog out, did flowers. Bill and children home at 8.00 for dinner.

Sunday 4 January

Rang up Woodbridge in morning. Nurse said Mother had been unconscious for twenty-four hours and was sinking. Mended socks in morning. Stayed in to be near telephone. Lunch with Twins and Bill. M and M rang up to say they would be back at 7.40. Nurse rang up at 3.30 to say Mother had died at 3.15. Went over at once after a quick cup of tea. Saw Mother looking very white and peaceful. Said goodbye, felt sad no longer. Took her jewellery as nurse said it was too much responsibility. Rang up Hughes and then came home after fetching Merlin and Mary.

Monday 5 January

Went over to Woodbridge with Bill immediately after breakfast. Saw undertaker, Dr Briscoe and another doctor, also nurses. Telephoned Ralph [Taylor cousins] Harold and Ursula, Eva, etc. Had lunch at The Bull. Then came home. Harold rang up in evening also Hughes. Sent notices to the *Times* and *East Anglian Daily Times*.

Tuesday 6 January

Had a much better night. Went to Ipswich with Mary to get fish, cakes, and see about representative from E.A.D.T. attending Mother's Funeral. Bill and Mer out shooting after lunch. Mary not feeling very well. Received many letters of sympathy.

Wednesday 7 January

Went in Railton at 10.30 with Bill, Mary, Merlin and Stewart to Ipswich crematorium for Mother's funeral service. Harold and Ursula there. Harold took the service which was nice and quite short, but at the special prayer, 'Oh Lord support us all the day long', I could bear it no longer and cried. Awful somehow. Then to Woodbridge where we found Mr Hughes and Mrs James and Eva.

Went to lunch at The Bull. Quite good. Afterwards the memorial service at St John's which was charmingly done by Harold and Mr Tydeman. We had three hymns; As with Gladness Men of Old and Through all the Changing Scenes of Life. I felt very sad again. Tea at The Chestnuts. Hughes and Eva went back to London and we all returned to Tostock with Harold and Ursula. Rested before dinner and went early to bed.

Thursday 8 January

Harold and Ursula left about 11.00. Many letters of sympathy. Had a busy day getting straight and doing things. So much to do.

Friday 9 January

Went to Bury with Mary to shop, had my hair washed. Met Francis Newell who came to stay in afternoon. Jeremy and Roger Pemberton also came to stay and arrived at teatime. Mary and Merlin and the three boys all went to the Pierce Lacy's dance at Ampton after dinner. Mary looks lovely in her white dress. I am sure Jeremy P. is in love with her. Bill and I took twins to see The Yearling at Odeon cinema. Dreadful film. Came home in pouring rain at 11.00. To bed feeling tired and sad.

Saturday 10 January

Breakfast at 9.00 after which Roger left. Mary and Jeremy went to the meet at Hessett on foot. Merlin, Francis and Bill shooting (Bill at Ampton). Twins hunting. Went over to Woodbridge as soon as they had all gone. Saw Mrs Peasey and installed her as caretaker. Paid the wages. Mrs James had left and taken much with her. Returned home with remainder of jewellery and certain valuables at teatime. Played games with children after dinner.

Sunday 11 January

Went to church at Thurston with Bill. Jeremy left after lunch. Bill took him to the station. Wrote letters and Bill did a lot to help me. Fed chickens.

Monday 12 January

Children went to cinema party with Robinsons. Went to London to the Bank and spent a long afternoon with Hughes.

Tuesday 13 January

Francis left in the morning. Such a nice boy. Went to Norton with Mary in car. Duck shooting in evening.

Wednesday 14 January

Went to Bury and shopped. Duck shooting in evening.

Thursday 15 January

Mary went to dentist in Ipswich, Merlin and twins went to London to see 'Outrageous Fortune'. We went on in the car to Woodbridge. Met Hempson at the house and discussed everything regarding the sale of house and the furniture. Brought home a few things. Met the children in the evening having much enjoyed their day. Felt very tired in the evening and had a headache.

Friday 16 January

Felt so seedy. Stayed in bed. Headache. So very tired. Children to lunch with Kathleen.

Saturday 17 January

In bed. Robert Clifton-Brown came to breakfast and he and Merlin went to London to see International with Christopher. Up for dinner and better. Mer home in evening.

Sunday 18 January

Went to church at Thurston with Bill.

Monday 19 January

Trunks went. Bill went. End of holidays feeling. Twins went to lunch with the Spicers.

Tuesday 20 January

Merlin and I went to Bury to collect wireless and came back on bus after seeing off Bill on 10.40 with Gill. All rather end of holidays. Packing etc.

Wednesday 21 January

A sad day getting children back to school. Merlin, twins and I caught the 11. 35 from Elmswell. Very cold and snow falling. Had quite a good lunch on train. When we got up to London we took the jewellery to Shapland to be valued for Insurance and Probate. Then to Miss Milne's where I left my suitcase then the twins and I went via Harrods to tea at Searcy's. Saw twins off on 4.50 to Kemble then Merlin and I went to News Theatre till we had dinner at Berkeley Buttery. Merlin had nasty boil on his face. I saw him off at 8.30 to Eton then stayed night at Miss Milne's.

Thursday 22 January

Bed felt damp. Saw Mr Whitehead at Bank, also Plant at my Bank. Went to see Hughes and was with him till lunch. Shopped. Got Mary a travelling iron. Came home on 3.40 and arrived at Elmswell at 7.30 where Stewart met me. Home at 8.00 Supper with Mary and told her all I had done and to bed early. Tired.

Friday 23 January

Busy day getting cleaned up and straight after children's departure. Stewart started to paint Bill's dressing room duck egg blue. Mary and I went to Bury for shopping.

Saturday 24 January

Mary and I went over to The Chestnuts at Woodbridge and had a very busy day till quite late, sorting out what we intend to keep and what to sell and labelling all. Lunched at the Crown. Home very tired at 7.00

Sunday 25 January

Went to church at Thurston with Mary. Went to tea with Astley Cooper's, Gerry's last day before he goes back to Greece. Quite a party. Stephen and Elisabeth Agnew, Keith, Vernon and Margaret, and Lorie, Geoffrey and Jeremy. Wrote a lot of letters in reply to sympathy ones. Nearly finished them all now.

Monday 26 January

Mary and I again over to Woodbridge where we finished our sorting about 3.00 pm. Hempson there with Hatfield making an inventory and taking probate. A Mrs Miller there going round the house. Mrs Peasey we paid and Sayers and came home glad to have finished for late tea.

Thursday 29 January

Mary and I went over to Woodbridge in the car. Cole's men there moving furniture and glass. First load all small things and nearly all glass and some china. Mary and I had quick lunch at the Crown. She went to dentist first. We got back just before van arrived and were there to see them unload and get things in right places. Very tired. I shall leave cleaning and sorting to maids over weekend.

Friday 30 January

Mary and I set off in Armstrong at 11.00. I was rather scared of dealing with this new sort of car, but she went beautifully and we arrived at RAF Cranwell with Bee at 3.30, having had a picnic lunch en route. Weather cleared after pouring wet morning. Arrived to find Bill to meet us. Had a rest after tea and went to dance in the Mess. Pritchard, Reggie and young Robinson dined with us first. Grapefruit, chicken, and a rather beastly, lemon sweet produced by the Sergeant. Dance quite amusing. Mary bored.

Saturday 31 January

Went for walk to camp with Bee. Wrote letters and had rest after lunch. Dined with Bill, Mary to Lodge with Dick and cadets and onto a cinema.

Sunday 1 February.

Went to Church Parade wearing Mother's Persian lamb coat and my new velvet hat. Nice service, Bill read lessons and Ainsworth preached well. To lodge for drinks. Went for a walk to the post with Bee in afternoon. Went to cinema with Dick and 4 senior term cadets. Curtis, Robinson, Maurice and Smith. Dinner at Lodge in evening. To bed 11.00

Monday 2 February

Went off to Sleaford with Mary by bus to get dogs meat and fish etc. Wrote letters, went for a walk in afternoon. Bill dining in College so Mary and I went to the cinema together.

Tuesday 3 February

Packed and got straight in morning. Had 'elevenses' with Mrs Freddie. Gwen Tyrrell there. Left after lunch in Armstrong with Bill for Tostock and got back for late tea. Lovely to be back to nice warm cosy home. Feel guilty always about this.

Wednesday 4 February

Went to Bury with Mary. Sold 16 bunches of snowdrops. Home for lunch. Wrote letters in afternoon and read. Bill left on 10.40 back to Cranwell with Gill. Rang him up in the evening.

Thursday 5 February

Went to London with Mary 8.40 from Stowmarket. Had a rush for the train. Arrived in London late and went to Pitman about insurance of car, jewellery and tractor. Then to Whitehead at Bank. Mary to lunch with Jenny Barnard at the Lansdowne. Had lunch by myself at Searcys. Went to S. Bentley to sell black coat. Ordered more writing paper from Stokes. Collected jewellery from Shapland and came home on 3.40.

Friday 6 February

Felt rather tired. Went to Bury with Mary, met Cynthia. Shopped. Very cold. Rowley Everett came to see me. Picked lovely bunch stylosas. Rested in afternoon. Bill rang up. Had rather bad neuralgia.

Saturday 7 February

Went over to Woodbridge early after breakfast with Mary in Morris. Stopped to see Hempson at Ipswich and discussed plans for sale of The Chestnuts and furniture sale. Decided on 7 April a suitable date for former and 21 April for sale of contents. Went to bank, then Footmans re cleaning carpets. Then to pay Mrs Peasey and Sayers. Brought back contents of Mother's desk. Sorted these and her diaries, and burnt them in the afternoon. Did chickens as Stewart out at Rous garage.

Sunday 8 February

Wild and windy day. Did not go to church. Wrote letters in morning and went down at Norton Road to see Rowley Everett about his poultry houses and sheds. Wants £15 for them. Mary picked lovely snowdrops. Molly Royce Tomkin walked over to tea having been to lunch at The Planche. Gossiped and took her back in the car. In the evening marked and mended Linen. Mary and I listened to wireless. Bill rang up.

Monday 9 February

Letter from Bill saying he is coming on from London here tomorrow. Heard from Clare in morning and Cecily after lunch. Mary and I went to Bury by car after breakfast. Took Mother's clothes to cleaners. Got an extra cwt. of poultry food. Saw man at W.A.G.C. about grafting fruit trees with different apple. Met Cynthia. Home for lunch. Wrote to Hughes. Sent 1lb. of butter to Merlin at Eton. Mary did the chickens and thinks she may take it on. In evening listened to Monday Night at 8.00 and sorted, mended and marked tablecloths.

Tuesday 10 February

Lovely day and had central heating off twice yesterday. Had letters from the twins. Very busy morning and afternoon sorting desk, writing accounts and letters. Mary turned out glass cupboard. After lunch went to Oldfields and ordered another half cwt. of potatoes. Then to Hayhoe for money and farm allowance. Took Bee down to Drift Cottages, came home to tea. Went to Stowmarket with Mary in Morris to meet Bill who had been in London at dentist. Dinner and bed 10.00.

Wednesday 11 February

Bad night with Bee fidgety. Packed and left Tostock at 10.00 in Armstrong with Bill and Mary. Left Bee behind. Arrived Cranwell at about 1.30, having picnic lunch on the way. Bill and I took turns to drive and lovely day. Quite like spring. So different to this time last year. Letter from Mrs Fyffe to say school in quarantine for mumps so cannot have me to stay. In evening went to cinema but film so dismal we came out and went to bed.

Thursday 12 February

Lovely day like spring, walked down to post with Mops and took letter from Merlin into Bill. Thrilled he is likely to be in Library with a fag next half and captain of games for his house in autumn. My 19th wedding anniversary which seems most remarkable. Bill sent me the most lovely flowers white carnations and lilies of the valley and gave me a lovely basket with two Thermoses in it. Very happy. After dinner Reggie Lacon and Scott Malden came in and had a drink and stayed till 10.30.

Friday 13 February

Called 6.45 and down to quick breakfast with Bill at 7.15. Went off to Grantham in Marshall's taxi and caught 8.24 and arrived in London at 11.00 after leaving luggage at Paddington. I went down to Harrods and ordered a pair of white mice for Johnny Peel for his birthday. Bill feels this will annoy Barbara! Went to bank, got notebooks for Clare and scent (Great Expectations), for Cecily and lunched at Searcys. Then had my hair given a henna shampoo and massage at Hugo's. Tried twice to ring Hughes. Wrote to Bill. Caught 4.55 train to Kemble. Excellent journey with tea and upstage GWR coaches. Enjoyed it. Met by taxi and Mrs Fyffe's secretary. Motored 15 miles through Cirencester to the Swan at Bibury. Had dinner, Clare rang up. Had indigestion all day.

Saturday 14 February

Had a very happy day. My little girls' 14th birthdays. Woke up feeling much better, all pain gone and wondered where I was. Leapt out of bed to look out and thought how pretty it was. Charming grey stone houses and cottages and a little stream rushing by quite close. After breakfast walked up to post and sent wire to Merlin. Twins arrived in a taxi at 11.00. Lovely to see them. Both looking very well. Clean and tidy too! We opened presents and I am furious the gramophone has not yet come. Had lunch, read and then for a walk. Looked at the church and walked about 2-3 miles. Had tea and I changed and we went to Hatherop [this became girls school in 1947] in a taxi, had dinner with Mrs Fyffe and saw my twins' bedroom. Then there was a cinema and I said goodbye and came back by taxi, enjoyed my day.

Sunday 15 February.

Lovely morning. Bibury is a sweet place. Paid bill after excellent breakfast and left at 9.30 for Kemble where I caught 10.17 to Reading. Changed there for Slough and from there to Windsor, where I met Merlin and we had lunch at Old House Hotel together. Then just had time to go and see his new room at Cotton Hall House where new pictures look very nice. Caught 3.06 to London and then 4.50 to Stowmarket. Stewart fetched me. Found Bee still all right and no puppies. Warren with an appalling cold. Went to bed early, very tired, but much enjoyed my weekend. Rang up Bill and told him I was home.

Monday 16 February

Woken by Bee at 5.30. Took her out and went back to sleep solidly till 8.00. Had breakfast in bed. Much colder. Wrote letters all morning and did accounts. Had two letters from Bill. Went to Hayhoe and went round the garden. After lunch went to Bury in the car. Shopped and paid bills and posted parcels. Went to tea with Margaret and Vernon which was fun and we gossiped. Nice dinner. Bee still herself and no puppies. Bill and Mary rang up.

Tuesday 17 February

Much colder. Spend morning putting away silver, writing letters. Got linen straight and went to the post. In afternoon picked and bunched iris stylosa, violets and white violets ready for W. I. Did chickens. Had chicken killed and ready for Friday. Taped and marked sheets.

Wednesday 18 February

Bee very restless, feel puppies imminent. Dashed into Bury and went to W.I., *East Anglian*, Electric etc. hurried back but no puppies all day. In afternoon picked snowdrops and violets and arrange them. Bill rang up and also Joan Oakes and Cecily later, got twins room ready. Put away more silver. Much colder.

Thursday 19 February

Woken at 7.00 by Bee whelping puppies. The first one born at 8.30 and being over anxious to clean up she killed. After this she had a chocolate male, then red bitch, then black and tan dog and quite as an afterthought a black and tan bitch. I left 1.15 for London. Lunch on train arriving at 2.00 and went to Hughes office for family meeting at 2.30. Ralph, Eva and Sydney there and we did good work till 5.00. Then I saw Hughes till 5.30 about Woodbridge. Stayed night at Basil Street Hotel.

Friday 20 February

Bitterly cold. Woke up wondering where I was. Had breakfast and went to Raynes and very extravagantly bought new bag and two pairs of new shoes costing £17.13.0. Met twins at Paddington. Lovely to see them. Clare came with me and Cecily went with Virginia Pearson. Clare and I lunched with Dottie Harris at Lansdowne Club. Great fun. Caught 3.40 home and had tea on train. Stewart met us. Bill and Mary back at home. Lovely to see them both. Excellent dinner and to bed tired 10.00.

Saturday 21 February

Bitterly cold. Snowing most of day on and off. Bill went to see Dr Ware about blister spots on his arms and fortunately found it was burns from hot water bottle. Went to Hayhoe. Bob and Betty Daniel and a young man called Tony came to twins' birthday party. Mrs Davidson made a lovely birthday cake for them.

Sunday 22 February

Very cold. Wrote letters and did accounts with Bill. Bill, Mary and twins went for walk in snow. I fed chickens. Twins played their new gramophone most of the day!

Monday 23 February

Still very cold. Bill and I left in Armstrong at 9.30 for RAF Cranwell. Weather cleared at Lynn and no snow there. Arrived at 12.30, said goodbye to twinnies who went back to school and Mary to see them off. Clare starting a cold. In afternoon went through all our things and got them ready for the move tomorrow. Had bad indigestion and flatulence. Walked to post. Dined with Monks and went to cinema, 'Farmers Daughter'.

Tuesday 24 February

Up at 8.30 and to our surprise, Cole's men arrived then and not at 10.30. They packed all china and glass and silver and got everything loaded up by 11.30 and started off. Bill and I had lunch in ladies room and then I left for home in Armstrong, I went non-stop except for petrol and arrived home at 4.00. Van came soon after and unloaded. Everything all right. Mary doing Gill and puppies. Lovely to be home.

Wednesday 25 February

Up early and off to Bury with Mary. Shopping all the morning. Home for lunch. Joan Oakes and her cousin Jenny came at 6.30. Joan stayed the night. Dick Norton also came and they all went after dinner to Suffolk Hunt Dance at Athenaeum. I went to bed early.

Thursday 26 February

Lovely day but very cold. In morning took Joan to bus. Mary quite enjoyed the dance, but looks tired. Left her to rest all afternoon while I went to Woodbridge and Ipswich. Went to Footman's, bank, Corders, Hempsons to see about Catalogue of Sale. Then on to Woodbridge, saw Mrs Peasey and Sayers and paid wages. Home across country, rang up Bill, felt very tired after large dose of castor oil.

Friday 27 February

My little girl's 18th birthday.

Cesca's diaries now come to an end.

Clothes rationing ended 15 March 1949 and my mother Mary's wedding 25 July 1950 benefited from this.

John McMullen and Cecily's Wedding
1955

Merlin in Ibiza 1969

Merlin's Bar Ibiza

Merlin and Miranda Blackett's Wedding 1975

Sarah Gosling and Richard Weller-Poley's Wedding 1970

Linda Gosling and Nigel Jamieson's Wedding 1982

Clare with Edward and William

Clare with Bumble

Official Card £1.50

EASTERN COUNTIES' RETRIEVER SOCIETY
Affiliated to the International Gundog League and
Kennel Club

PROGRAMME
of the

SEVENTY-FIFTH FIELD TRIALS

TUESDAY 9TH NOVEMBER and WEDNESDAY 10TH NOVEMBER 1993

By Gracious permission of

Her Majesty The Queen

These Trials will be held at

SANDRINGHAM ESTATE, NORFOLK.

JUDGES

Mr. P. Allen Mr. N. Rowson Mr. J. Gale Mr. P. Hurst
(ex.officio Members of Committee for the Meeting)

PRESIDENT

Mrs. C. McMullen

COMMITTEE

Mrs. D. Ryan	Mrs. B. Belton
Mr. N. Mann	Mr. S. Harvey
Mr. P. Denny	Mr. M. Skipper
Mr. R. Webb	Mrs. C. McMullen
Mrs. F. Taylor	Mr. P. Sinclair

HONORARY SECRETARY
Mrs. C.A. Wentworth-Smith*
The Old Rectory, Swardeston, Norwich, Norfolk, NR14 8DG.
Telephone: Mulbarton 70231

President.

Official Card £1.50

EASTERN COUNTIES' RETRIEVER SOCIETY
Affiliated to the International Gundog League and
Kennel Club

PROGRAMME
of the

SEVENTY-FOURTH FIELD TRIALS

THURSDAY 5th NOVEMBER and FRIDAY 6th NOVEMBER 1992

by kind permission of

The Viscount Coke and Captain D. Keith

These Trials will be held at

HOLKHAM HALL, WELLS, NORFOLK AND

WEST BARSHAM HALL, FAKENHAM, NORFOLK.

Lady Hugh-Smith Mr. J. Clitheroe Mr. W. Meldrum Mr. A. Thornton
(ex.officio Members of Committee for the Meeting)

PRESIDENT

Mrs. C. McMullen

COMMITTEE

Mrs. D. Ryan	Mrs. B. Belton
Doctor L. Bellamy	Mr. S. Harvey
Mr. P. Denny	Mr. M. Skipper
Mr. R. Webb	Mrs. C. McMullen
Mrs. F. Taylor	Mr. P. Sinclair

HONORARY SECRETARY
Mrs. C.A. Wentworth-Smith*
The Old Rectory, Swardeston, Norwich, Norfolk, NR14 8DG.
Telephone: Mulbarton 70231

Two Field Trial programs

Cecily with James and Fergus
and her FTC dogs

Kate W-P and Rupert Leigh-Wood's Wedding
2001

James McMullen and Leslie Kenyon's Wedding

1949-1999
After the Diaries

Cesca and Bill are living with their four children at the Old Rectory,Tostock, described as a Georgian country residence having six bedrooms, three reception rooms and two bathrooms with stabling and garage in nine acres. Also a very productive walled kitchen garden. World War II was behind them, but they bothe were still somewhat war weary. Rationing continued until 1954, although petrol rationing ended in 1950 and confectionery and sugar in 1953. Cheese production remained depressed for decades afterwards.

Bill had retired from the RAF in 1948, at his own request and devoted his himself to his small farm of some 200 acres where he was a keen advocate of organic methods and a follower of Lady Eve Balfour. Bill was a good shot and he and Cesca enjoyed shooting. Bill shot regularly at Euston and at Boxted with the Weller-Poleys, the Agnews and the Muskers and many others. Bill published Guns This Way in 1962. Several editions currently for sale with Amazon and ABE books for between £40/£90. This book concentrated on the shoots of England and Wales and was a sporting bestseller in its day.

Cesca showed a keen interest all her life in antiques and loved nothing more than spending the day at an Auction with sandwiches and a flask of coffee, alert to bid for a bargain. She was well known in Bury St Edmunds and Ipswich by all the local dealers and auctioneers. Phillips, Christies and Bonhams were all part of her life too.

All three daughters were debutantes. A coming out dance for 150 guests was held for Mary 12 September 1947. Mary had spent two happy years at Constance Spry near Windsor, cakes finding their way to Merlin and a boyfriend Hugh Owen at Eton. Cecily and Clare in 1951 for whom a dance was held on 29 June. The caterers were Dunns of Bury St Edmunds and the menu of Sole Domino, Mousse of chicken and salads followed by strawberries, vanilla ice and cream, coffee and iced orangeade for 10/6 per head.

Smig, the Siamese cat reached ten years of age in September 1949 and Cesca was still breeding from two female Siamese Zoe and Tessa. Also from Bee the dachshund and Bill owned several devoted Labradors amongst them Gill and Julie.

Bill's large red leather bound album is full of photographs, cuttings and sketches of events in the fifties. Mary, my mother married my father, John Gosling on Tuesday 25 July 1950 at St Peter's Church, Thurston and the large photograph taken the morning of her wedding with everyone grouped in front of the Rectory remains a wonderful record of the day.

At Eton Merlin was a natural athlete and was successful at any distance. He won the Eton Steeple Chase three times and was an excellent racquets and squash player. If he had not damaged his Achilles tendon he would have been awarded a blue at Cambridge. After completing his education at Kings College Cambridge, reading Modern languages he was commissioned into the Coldstream Guards in November 1950.

He published a novel in1956 at the age of 24, The Way to Paradise, 'showing extraordinary maturity' and sold for 10/6 then. Now on Amazon there is a copy available for £10. He had a successful career in advertising with J. Walter Thompson and with Ogilvy, Benson & Mather before changing direction completely and buying a little bar in Ibiza. He was a rather dashing and witty godfather and taught me how to end up with one marble playing solitaire. I enjoyed his company. However he had a narrow escape from death after being gored by a bull during the Running of the Bulls in Pamplona. This is run through the narrow streets of Pamplona over an 875 metre course in front of fighting bulls and there have been fifteen fatalities since 1922 usually caused by the horns digging into a runner's lungs. Cesca had to dash out to help care for Merlin in the convent where the nuns had apparently saved his life.

Two more weddings followed Mary's, Clare in July 1954 to Lieut. Robert Creasy in the Chapel of King Henry VII Westminster Abbey and the reception held at Admiralty House in Whitehall. The Bishop of Sodor and Mann, Dr Taylor officiated and his son, the Bishop of Winchester officiated at the marriage of Cecily to John McMullen on the 12 January 1955 in St Margaret's Church, Westminster. Cecily chose Richard and Toby Weller-Poley to be her pages. They duly lived up to their wild reputations imbibing quantities of champagne, climbed all over the furniture and Toby climbed up the curtains. They were then sick! The reception was held at Londonderry House whose fee for using the ballroom and changing rooms was £25 with an additional fee of 1/- per guest attending. The wedding cake 12 guineas and Moet et Chandon champagne at 26/6 per bottle including the hire of glasses. Cigarettes could be provided- Virginian at 25/- per 100 or Turkish at 31/- per 100.

Both Bill and Merlin shared a talent of some skill for painting in oils and watercolours. Bill also wrote letters and articles for the Field under the pen name of Henry Boreas.
However the farm and farm accounts took up many hours and looking through the account books from 1952 Bill employed a foreman F. Taylor for £8.0.0 a week and a tractor driver for £3.18.0. a week. Stewart who was handyman and chauffeur and much more besides was paid £5.15.0 a week. Two more labourers,

handymen both by name of Everett were paid £5.13.0 a week. As was Squirrell the other gardener. There were pigs, cows, heifers and a bull on the farm and in April 1953 ten pigs were sold for £51.12.6. Bill writes in the first week of June 1953 'This was a bad week of little work done what with Coronation, rain and the Suffolk Show and Everett sick for two days'. On 10 July he writes 'Violent storms. Pigs flooded out. A bloody day.' In August 31 sacks of oats to the acre is recorded. Chickens appear to bring in a healthy income of £105 from eggs April to September. Potatoes, beet, oats and barley are farmed and it is clear that Bill is himself physically involved in everything. The gross income April 1955-April 1956 is £7063 = £41 an acre. Milk generated the highest income of £2,343 followed by corn £1,950.

The farm as far as I can make out from the accounts seemed to make a loss in the early sixties, but I am not much of a mathematician!

In 1955 Bill and Cesca discovered the wonderful shared pleasures of taking the car, motoring through France and loving everything about the country especially the empty roads and the delicious food. First in the Wolseley, then the baby Austin van followed by the Alvis a beautiful car and in 1971 the RO 80 'which went like a dream'. The NSU RO 80 had a powerful twin rotor 115hp Wankel engine, a brilliant driver's car, and was perfect for long journeys. Bill kept journals entitled 'Journeys Abroad', 'Najac and other Journeys' that are full of sketches, watercolours, photographs and descriptions of their travels in France. He writes that the first time on our own in France in a car "was like a second honeymoon". Before the sixties it was easy even in June to set off with no plan and always find a nice room and Cesca became an expert at discovering new and exquisite places. These journeys to France over the next sixteen years, culminated in the purchase of the little house nestling beneath the ruined chateau in the village of Najac in 1972. It is nineteen miles by car from the market town of

Villefranche de Rouergue. On Sunday 16 September 1972 a local architect, M. Coustilleres, Tourette senior and Tourette junior assembled for a meeting to discuss the plans in heavy dialect for over three hours! 'Young Tourette fell for Cesca. Such aristocratic French and china doll appearance was startling for a peasant'. There is a marvellous sketch of the meeting, Tourette senior on his knees bent over the plans entitled 'Tourette stupefied by the architect's plans'! The two bedroomed house was rented out very successfully from 1975 for a healthy profit as indicated by the Cashbook for Rue du Chateau kept meticulously by Cesca until 1996. M. & Madame Bessous, the next door neighbours, kept a close eye on things and held a key in case of problems.

The little French house was put up for sale in the 1990's for 580,000 FF.

In 1962 the decision was taken by Bill and Cesca to move out of the Old Rectory and into the Lodge. Clare who had married Anthony Villar in October 1961, then bought the Rectory and the farm. And Bill and Cesca then spent £8,000 on updating the Lodge. Cesca had taught herself to cook and they gave many lunch and dinner parties together over the years that followed. She cooked beautifully making her own bread and pastry. Many of the menus, wines and the guests are listed in a volume 1979-1989 the cover decorated by Bill.

In April 1968 Bill's mother Mrs Lunn died aged 89 of pneumonia at her house Woodlands, Millfield Road, Walberswick. She had been widowed for the second time in 1957 when George Lunn died of a cerebral thrombosis and heart failure.
A memorial service was held for Dick Atcherley (Air Marshal Sir Richard L.R. Atcherley, KBE, CB, AFC) Bill's best man and Mary's godfather on Wednesday 20 May 1970 at St Clement Danes, London.

In 1975 Merlin finally relinquished the life of a bachelor and married Miranda Blackett at Kirkpatrick-Fleming Church near Lockerbie on Saturday 7 June 1975. Except there was a muddle over the documents required so they had to dart into a registry office in Glasgow the next day to marry officially. Jack Rupert duly arrived in 1977 inheriting Cesca's titian hair.

Cecily was very successful with her gun dogs winning so many Field Trials Championships with FTCH Kilderkin Plummer and FTCH Kilderkin Renoir that a special cup was made in her memory named the Cecily McMullen Cup. She won the Essex Open and was President of Eastern Counties. Cecily was a class A1 Field Trial judge and was invited by Her Majesty The Queen on numerous occasions to judge her private Field Trials at Sandringham. Hunting with hounds, flat racing and fishing were Clare's passions and she was Master of the Suffolk Hunt for many years. Mary too enjoyed hunting but after badly breaking her elbow called it a day and bred chinchillas instead.

The Grade II listed Belstead House was sold by the Quilters to Suffolk County Council for £15,000 in 1948 after the Bisshopp's lease expired. It was used as a conference centre for educational purposes until 2015 when a developer, Andy Harding of Rural Community Housing Ltd purchased it from the Council for £1.6 million. In February 2017 we drove up to the house and persuaded the caretaker to let us have a look round inside. Andy Harding intends to develop the surrounding land with a 65 bed care home and 150 houses but wants to live in the house himself. He now, in 2019, has outline planning permission. It looked sad and neglected especially the garden. Even the birdbath was upside down.

Sometime during 1982/83 for whatever reasons, very sadly, Bill and Cesca's marriage of over 50 years broke down. Bill left her and married Mrs Frances Lawrence (who was living with her husband

Jack P-R with Moscovy duck

Jack P-R

Fergus McMullen High Sheriff of
Hertfordshire and Kate with Camelia, Rory
and Hugo.

M. and Madame Bessou
caretaker Najac

The little house,
Rue du Chateau Najac

Old Tourette stupefied by the Architect's plans

Charlie Gosling and Sian
Hughes' Wedding 1991

Bill and Cecily

Kate, Cesca, Mary and Linda 1993 Courage Wedding

Old Rectory Tostock

The Lodge

Cesca outside the Lodge

633

Mary painted by Miss Worsfold 1936   Cesca painted by Miss Worsfold 1938

Guy Weller-Poley and Melissa Hall Wedding   Cesca's Party menu book
1979-1989

Cesca near Limoges June 1965

Ben Creasy and Amy Whitehouse Wedding 2013

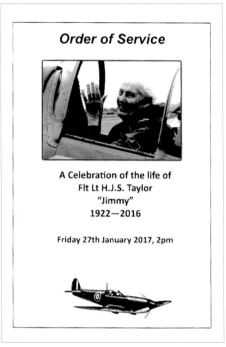

Jimmy Taylor's book
'One Flight Too Many' published 2011
Foreword By HRH Duke of Edinburgh.

Jimmy Taylor's Order of Service 27-1-2017
Held at Cheam School

Jimmy Taylor and 2nd wife Margaret
Chia 2014

Juliet Gosling and Douglas Brown's Wedding
March 2008

and two children, Ruth and Simon in Tostock) in October 1986. They went to live in Norfolk settling in a little house in Wiveton belonging to Desmond McCarthy.

The Eastern Daily Press on 24 February 1994 reported the trial of the trainee Roman Catholic priest Paul Mubanguka who was found guilty of causing the death of former pilot Bill Pearson-Rogers by driving dangerously and was warned by the judge that he faced a substantial jail sentence. He had denied being at fault when he drove from a minor road on to the B1149 Holt road at Felthorpe into the path of a Citroen car being driven by the 86 year old man. Mr Pearson-Rogers had to be cut free from the wreckage and taken to Norwich hospital with multiple injuries, but died two weeks later on August 17 1992. Mubanguka held only a provisional driving licence at the time of the crash and his insurance was invalid. He did not stop at the junction.

On the same page another headline reads:

Wife became second victim of the tragedy.

Former royal pilot Bill Pearson-Rogers was not the only victim of the road crash that killed him. His grief stricken second wife Frances could not bear life without him and killed herself five months later. The Norwich Crown Court jurors who found Paul Mubanguka guilty were told that 52 year-old Mrs Pearson-Rogers had died but the tragic circumstances were not revealed in court. She was found dead in her car in January 1993 having died of carbon monoxide poisoning. Her son Simon Lawrence said she was not the same after the death of her husband. A note found in the car stated: "Bill would have understood this."

In spite of Judge Michael Hyam warning Mubanguka that a substantial custodial sentence was highly probable, he escaped a jail sentence and instead was ordered to do 120 hours community service and banned from driving for three years.

Mary and Bill Norfolk

Bill shooting

Bill

Gp Capt Bill Pearson-Rogers

Pearson-Rogers: airman

GROUP CAPTAIN Bill Pearson-Rogers, who has died aged 86, began his career by flying the Prince of Wales and other VIPs as a pilot in No 24 Communications Squadron in the late 1920s.

This posting confirmed that Pearson-Rogers had matured since passing out from the RAF College Cranwell, where he was described as "apt to be foolhardy and too confident".

The future King Edward VIII would not have known this, as Pearson-Rogers — by then respectably qualified at the Central Flying School as a flying instructor — whisked him around Britain to open airports, launch ships and make speeches.

During the Second World War Pearson-Rogers found himself at sea on D-Day as an RAF liaison officer for the Normandy invasion.

Posted aboard the anti-aircraft cruiser *Scylla*, he was given the task of representing and interpreting the decisions of Adml Sir Philip Vian to the RAF.

This was hardly a taxing role, since the Commander of the Eastern Task Force invariably addressed the RAF vociferously and clearly himself.

Henry William Pearson-Rogers was born in Staffordshire on March 18 1906 and educated at Marlborough; he went to Cranwell as a cadet and was commissioned in 1926. That year he joined No 13, an Army Cooperation squadron flying Bristol fighters. From 1927 to 1929 he was an instructor at No 4 Flying Training School in Egypt.

Pearson-Rogers was returned to his element, though, when in 1930 he joined No 19, a fighter squadron, flying at first Siskins and then Bulldogs.

In 1935, serving with No 65, a Hawker Demon squadron, he was posted briefly to Malta as part of the RAF's urgent Mediterranean reinforcement during the Abyssinian crisis.

When war broke out in 1939 Pearson-Rogers was serving on the Headquarters Staff in the Middle East, but the next year he returned to the Air Ministry, attached to the Chief of Air Staff's Department.

He did not take kindly to desk work, and longed to be back in fighters. To relieve his frustration he used to tear between London and Suffolk on his racing motorbike, a 350cc Manx TT Norton.

In 1942 he was given command of No 61, an operational training unit for Spitfire pilots at Rednal, Shropshire, a post which saw him airborne once more. The next year he was appointed station commander at RAF Kirkwall in the Orkneys.

After a posting to No 13 Group Headquarters, Pearson-Rogers was surprised to find himself in the role of liaison officer on D-Day.

After his retirement in 1948 he farmed near Bury St Edmunds in Suffolk, where he was a keen advocate of organic methods.

A keen shot for much of his life, in 1962 Pearson-Rogers published *Guns This Way*. The book concentrated on the shoots of England and Wales, and was a sporting bestseller in its day.

Pearson-Rogers was mentioned in despatches in 1943 and 1945, and appointed CBE in 1945. He was twice married, and had a son and three daughters by his first wife.

Bill's Obituary 1992

Bill's cremation was held at St Faith's Crematorium, Horsham St Faith, Norwich at noon on Monday 24 August. There were only eight of us present.

Cesca, my darling Grannie, continued to live alone at the Lodge with the support of various companions, sourced by my mother, but not always liked or appreciated. She was always remarkably good company and I visited her as much as possible.

About nine months before her death, Cesca moved into the Elizabeth Flynn Cotswold Home in Burford where she was cared for so well with the bonus of Mary living close by. Having slipped in to a coma, she died peacefully on 21 October 1999.

Cesca's funeral took place on Wednesday 3 November 1999 at the St John Chapel Oxford Crematorium and her ashes were interred at the Parish Church of St Andrew, Tostock.

The service included Love divine, all loves excelling, Mine eyes have seen the glory of the coming of the Lord and this poem, found in her handbag (along with three photographs) and read by Fergus McMullen:

Two pictures of Bill and one of Merlin at Eton
found in Cesca's handbag

GOD'S GARDEN

The Lord God planted a garden
In the first white days of the world;
And set there an angel warden,
In a garment of light enfurled.

So near to the peace of Heaven,
That the hawk might nest with the wren;
For there is the cool of the even,
God walked with the first of men.

And I dream that these garden closes,
With their abode and their sun-flecked sod,
And their lilies and bowers of roses,
Were laid by the hand of God.

The Kiss of the sun for pardon,
The song of the birds for mirth-
One is nearer God's heart in a garden
Than anywhere else on earth.

By Dorothy Frances Gurney
1858-1932

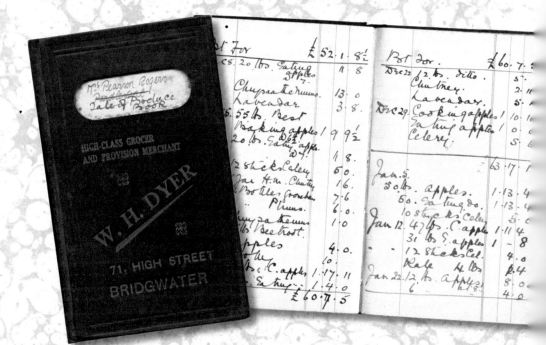